Praise for this book

"Woven like a red thread through Captain Collier's adventures, is his courageously honest recounting of how PTSD affected his life and relationships without being maudlin or overly dramatic. Not all individuals handle it with the strength, awareness and tenacity of Collier. He hopes his writing will help everyone recognize and understand how this illness may wrap itself around the lives of our veterans.
  —Foster Kline, MD, Psychiatrist, co-author with Jim Fay, of the world-renowned "Love and Logic" series of books.

"It's obvious that Captain Bill Collier has spent a lot of time in the cockpit. His flying stories echo with authenticity. Reading about his many different exploits in helicopters will keep you reading till the end."
  —Byron Edgington, author of *PostFlight:* An Old Pilot's Logbook

Bill's life has been a wild ride of extreme life-threatening adventures around the world! I promise you will feel the roller coaster of emotions on Bill's ride into one outlandish situation after another, as he searches for the elusive meaning of life… and finds it.
—Ted Bravos, Captain, United States Marine Coprs, Vietnam veteran and highly experienced world traveler Founder/CEO ITMI Certified Travel Training--The World's Premier School for Tour Guide Training and Tour Director Certification.

"A captivating, well written and fascinating read. The inter-twining of information about the inner workings of the helicopter business with fascinating personal anecdotes keeps the narrative flowing. Informative and entertaining."

—Sylvia Davis, MA, PhD, professor emerita of German and Humanities, Eastern Kentucky University, Richmond, KY

"In this 3rd book of his fascinating trilogy, we find Captain Bill back in civilian life. He gives us a rare look into the day-by-day life of an inveterate helicopter pilot. Be it the Alaskan oil fields, the docks of Saudi Arabia, random construction sites or atop Mount Whitney, follow him to where the flying jobs took him. Enjoy the ride…"

—LtCol Larry Margolies, USAF Retired; F-105 pilot, Vietnam.

"In his third volume of his autobiographical series, Collier rides above every challenge. We see him flying helicopters in locations from Arabia to Alaska and on to California. A remarkable read about a maturing man and an unimaginable life flying improbable machines."

—Captain Thomas Beard, US Coast Guard Helicopter Pilot, Retired.

"If you ever wanted to read a book about flying helicopters from an expert's point of view, then this is the book for you. The author's flying history is riveting. Read this book; you won't be sorry."

—Mark Garrison, author of "GUTS 'n GUNSHIPS" about flying US Army gunships in Vietnam.

The Worldwide Adventures of a Helicopter Pilot
...the rest of the story

Captain Bill Collier

Awarded "Writer of the Year" 2018
by Idaho Writers League

Author of
AIR AMERICA: A CIA Super Pilot Spills the Beans, Flying Helicopters in Laos for AIR AMERICA
First Place, non-fiction
Idaho Writers League, 2016

Copyright 2022 Captain Bill Collier

Front cover:
Captain Bill flying an Evergreen Helicopter Company BELL 205-A-1 while practicing the "short haul" rescue technique for the Orange County Fire Department in Southern California, 1995. Picture taken with author's camera by Fireman Brian Stevens.

Back Cover:
Captain Bill takes his last flight in 2018 in the kiddie playground "trainer" in Port Townsend, Washington airport beside the Spruce Goose Restaurant.

Most of the 100+ photos in this book are from the author's personal archives. Those that aren't are attributed to their source. Many of the photos in the book can be seen in full color at the author's web site, www.captainbillfliesagain.com.

Wandering Star Press
P.O. Box 105
Port Hadlock, WA 98339-9800

ISBN: 978-057837429-1

> "The ultimate responsibility of the pilot
> is to fulfill the dreams of the countless
> millions of earthbound ancestors,
> who could only stare skyward and wish."
>
> Erickson Air Collection web site.

Watching the TV program *60 Minutes* on December 12, 2020, I saw the actor Denzel Washington talk about how he was helped into his acting success by the black actors who proceeded him. He said, "I must pass the baton on to those who follow me."

That is one of my reasons for writing this book, to "pass the baton" on to those who follow me as helicopter pilots. I want to share the highlights, and even some my stupid, dumb blunders, of my wide variety of helicopter flying experiences over thirty-plus years of flying. If just one other helicopter pilot learns something from my writing that assists him or her to help save lives or to avoid a crash, I will be pleased.

This is also a great adventure story.

My bit of original sage advice, garnered from my life experience:
> "Never let your exuberance—
> or your arrogance—
> outfly your experience."

Captain Bill Collier
Port Townsend, Washington

Dedication

Dedicated to the memory of
Lieutenant Colonel James B. Barr,
Fellow Marine Corps aviator,
Vietnam squadron mate,
life-long good friend,
and Best Man at my marriage
to my wonderful wife, Carlita.
November, 2003

R.I.P James
January 4th, 2022

We will fly together again one day.

Contents

DEDICATION VII
PREFACE XIII
INTRODUCTION XVIII

CHAPTER 1 1
   ANCHORAGE, ALASKA 1

CHAPTER 2 3
   TO THE NORTH SLOPE 3

CHAPTER 3 13
   WEST KUPARUK 13

CHAPTER 4 18
   NEAR CRASH AT SAGWON 18

CHAPTER 5 22
   BACK TO THE NORTH SLOPE 22

CHAPTER 6 27
   AMCHITKA 27

CHAPTER 7 35
   THE ATOMIC BLAST 35

CHAPTER 8 43
   FERRY FLIGHT TO VENTURA, CALIFORNIA 43
   FRIENDLY FIRE! 46
   PANIC! 50

CHAPTER 9 51
   I JOIN THE RESERVES 51
   AIR AMERICA, THAILAND AND LAOS 62

CHAPTER 10 63
   RETURN TO REAL LIFE 63

CHAPTER 11 .... **64**

    RESERVES AGAIN 64
    FLIGHT OUT TO THE FARALLON ISLANDS 66

CHAPTER 12 .... **69**

    STOCKTON, CALIFORNIA 69
    FROST CONTROL 72
    MEASURING THE SNOWPACK 82
    FIRST LONG LINE EXPERIENCE 84
    TO MOJAVE 89
    DAYDREAMS, NIGHTMARES 96

CHAPTER 13 .... **99**

    SEQUOIA NATIONAL FOREST 99
    BAMBI BUCKET WORK 101

CHAPTER 14 .... **107**

    ATOP MOUNT WHITNEY 107

CHAPTER 15 .... **111**
CHAPTER 16 .... **114**
CHAPTER 17 .... **125**

    LAST RESERVE MEETING – FIRED! 125

CHAPTER 18 .... **128**

    FLYING FOR BING CROSBY 128

CHAPTER 19 .... **135**

    RETURN TO PEPPERMINT 135
    WE REVISIT PEPPERMINT 139

CHAPTER 20 .... **144**

    SAUDI ARABIA 144
    "DEAD MAN'S CURVE" 155

CHAPTER 21 .... **165**

    SANTA ROSA, CALIFORNIA 165
    WAYCO 165

SANTA ROSA, CALIFORNIA 165
I MEET A LEGEND OF THE HELICOPTER BUSINESS 168

CHAPTER 22 .... **187**
GARLICK HELICOPTER COMPANY 187

CHAPTER 23 .... **192**
CALIFORNIA HELICOPTER COMPANY 192

CHAPTER 24 .... **194**
ALASKA AGAIN 194

CHAPTER 25 .... **199**
A TEMPORARY CAREER CHANGE 199

CHAPTER 26 .... **201**
BACK TO BRISTOL BAY 201

CHAPTER 27 .... **206**
TALKEETNA, ALASKA 206

CHAPTER 28 .... **213**
CRANE HELICOPTER CORP. 213

CHAPTER 29 .... **221**
JEEPERS JAMBOREE 221

CHAPTER 30 .... **233**
FIREFIGHTING NEAR WATSONVILLE 233

CHAPTER 31 .... **236**
CONCRETE HAULING 236
BACK TO SCHOOL 237

CHAPTER 32 .... **238**
MARCHING WITH THE SIKHS IN YUBA CITY 238
SEWAGE SPILL, SONOMA COUNTY 246

CHAPTER 33 .... **248**

Marshall Islands, South Pacific	248
CHAPTER 34	**267**
Flying Metal Meets Mountain Top	267
CHAPTER 35	**271**
Helicopter Logging Insanity	271
The First Crash	274
Second Crash	275
Third Crash	276
CHAPTER 36	**286**
Rocky Mountain Helicopter Company	286
Disaster!	291
CHAPTER 37	**293**
CRANE Again	293
CHAPTER 38	**295**
Evergreen Helicopter Company	295
CHAPTER 39	**309**
San Joaquin Helicopter Company	309
CHAPTER 40	**316**
My Last Engine Failure	316
CHAPTER 41	**320**
Post-Flying	320
CHAPTER 42	**322**
Golden Gate Transit	322
CHAPTER 43	**325**
I Fly An H-43 "Husky" Synchropter	325
COMPANIES/ENTITIES I FLEW FOR	**328**
Breakdown of Aircraft flown and locations.	329
Long Ferry Trips Flown	330

PROFESSIONAL CERTIFICATIONS: 331
BIBLIOGRAPHY 332
OTHER BOOKS BY CAPTAIN BILL COLLIER 335

Preface

June, 1969

I had been out of the Marine Corps for seven months. When I departed active duty in late 1968 at the Marine Corps base at Tustin, California, I could have easily driven across the Los Angeles basin and applied to the LA Sheriff's office for a flying job. They had the same H-34s that I had flown in Vietnam. With my experience, the sheriff very well might have hired me. I could have retired fat and wealthy at age fifty-five. I blame Post Traumatic Stress Disorder (PTSD) for my reluctance to apply. In the Marines, I developed a profound dislike of *uniforms* and *male authority figures*, two of the *many symptoms* of PTSD.

PTSD would color and control most of my actions for the remainder of my life. I felt a threat in every slight or imagined conflict in any job or relationship. The flight side of the "Fight or Flight" reaction always took over. I often flew away a lot, literally (in helicopters), figuratively and emotionally.

I feel fortunate that I went directly to US Navy Flight School as a Marine Aviation Cadet (MARCAD) and never went through Marine Corps boot camp. If I had boot camp's ingrained "killer instinct" might have surfaced at times of anger or frustration during these many years, and I might have acted out in ways that would have me in prison to this day.

As it was, I had an adventure-filled, eventful life. I traveled the world, visited or worked in fifty-five countries and forty-seven of our United States, and flew forty different kinds of helicopters all around the world. I saw and did things that would make Walter Mitty[1] jealous.

PTSD sent me on a quest. I didn't know I was on a quest, I didn't know what I was looking for…until I found it. In this book I present the highlights of my many helicopter flying adventures around the world as a Gypsy helicopter pilot, driven by the unrecognized demons of PTSD, always seeking the next adrenaline rush, the next cheap thrill.

---

[1] **Walter James Mitty** is a fictional character in James Thurber's first short story "The Secret Life of Walter Mitty," first published in *The New Yorker* on March 18, 1939. Mitty is a meek, mild man with a vivid fantasy life. In a few dozen paragraphs, he imagines himself a wartime pilot, an emergency-room surgeon, and a devil-may-care killer. (Wikipedia)

Aviation has often been defined as "hours and hours of boredom interrupted on occasion by a few seconds of sheer terror!"

* * *

Here is the *first of several* events that contributed to my PTSD.

A Night Medevac at Mutter Ridge
September 29, 1966. Dong Ha, South Vietnam

About 10:00 p.m., we were called out on an emergency medical evacuation (medevac) to Mutter Ridge in the northwesternmost corner of South Vietnam. I was flying for a senior first lieutenant. He had flown out to Mutter Ridge many times in the few days prior. He knew where we were going, he knew what to do, and he knew well how to do it.

As we departed Dong Ha in near absolute darkness, we radioed "Landshark Charlie," the disembodied voice in the ethers in charge of artillery in our area. At our request, Landshark shut down the outgoing artillery from our base to the contested area. Once we got near the unit that had the badly wounded Marine, the light from hundreds of tracers, abetted by the occasional flash of a grenade or mortar explosion, illuminated the pick-up zone.

I was a nugget, a brand-new gold-bar second lieutenant, a newbie, a combat virgin along for the ride. I had not yet been into a hot landing zone. I had not yet been out to Mutter Ridge. I had not yet done a high-hover hoist pick-up, and this was my very first night-combat flight in Vietnam. My job was to monitor the instruments while the lieutenant was busy hovering to prevent his overboosting (too much power) or overspeeding (too many rpms) the engine.

The labored breathing of the grunt radio operator and gunshots in the background, told us this landing zone (LZ) was hot. As we spiraled down, I extinguished all external lights to make us invisible to the enemy below. The lieutenant established a high hover above the Marines, and, once we were in a stable hover, the crew chief began unreeling the hoist cable to lower the litter basket.

It was difficult for the lieutenant to maintain a hover in the inky dark over ninety-foot-tall trees. The only ground reference he could relate to was the geometric plane created by dozens of sparkling tracers—red for the Marines', green for the enemy's—zinging back and forth beneath us. Because the terrain was tilted at thirty to forty degrees from level, trying to hover over the sloping ground caused him to repeatedly tilt the helicopter away from the vertical, causing us to drift away from the Marines. If we drifted too far to the north, we might drift into trees on the upslope. We also might drag the basket through the trees, endangering the wounded Marine now in it and perhaps entangling our cable in the treetops. An occasional burst of green tracers passed uncomfortably close to us. Each tracer trail represented three or four bullets.

There was only one solution. The lieutenant asked me, "Bill, do you know where the hover/floodlight switch is?" A millisecond later, I realized, *O'mygod! He is going to have me flip that switch! When those lights come on, we will be the biggest and brightest target in all of Vietnam. We are hovering over who-knows-how-many hundreds or thousands of NVA (North Vietnamese Army) troops. We are going to be shot full of holes and explode into a ball of fire!*

The lieutenant said, "When I tell you, turn on those lights." I placed my fingers on the switch on the overhead panel. *This is it! I am going to die in this war, right here, right now!* But what could I do? Refuse an order? I was a Marine. "Death before dishonor" was our creed. Duty-bound to follow my pilot's orders, even if it meant my immediate, violent, fiery death, and without question, argument, or discussion, I toggled that switch. *Now I die!* I found it interesting that I felt no fear, and accepted the fact that I was now dead.

Under our strong floodlights, every single man on the ground, Marine and enemy combatant alike, must have thought he was the most exposed man on the planet. Each one must have thrown himself into the nearest foxhole or behind the nearest tree for protection. The battle completely ceased for at least ninety seconds while we hovered there, fully lit up like a light standard at a Friday night high school football game. Why dozens of enemy soldiers on the ground didn't simply roll over on their backs and give us full salvos of dozens of bullets, I will never know.

As the crew chief pulled the wounded Marine into the helicopter, the lieutenant told me to switch off the lights. I did with great relief, amazed to be still alive and not a crispy critter in a heap of steaming, smoking rubble on the hillside. We delivered the wounded Marine to the nearby field hospital.

I distinctly remember feeling numb after this. My feelings were numbed, my mind was numbed, and…I believe my very soul was numbed.

Introduction

June 9, 1969
North Alaska

Driving north on highway US 101 towards Ventura, California, I listened to the number one song at the time, "Get Back" by the Beatles. In the sky ahead of me, I spied what looked like a gigantic Bumble Bee. Ascending from the west, it crossed the freeway eastbound, circled back westward, and descended out of sight, only to reappear and repeat the circuit.

As a former Marine Corps helicopter pilot with Vietnam behind me, I recognized the blob as a Korean War vintage H-19. Huge sausage-like floats attached to its bottom in place of landing gear gave it the Bumble Bee appearance. I knew the crate was doing practice-landing circuits called "Touch and Goes."

I saw the AIRPORT traffic sign, took that exit and followed the Bumble Bee to Rotor Aids Helicopter Company. On this balmy June day, I walked through the open door of the business and asked the cute receptionist for the chief pilot. She waved me to the far desk, where sat Pilot Roy Falconer. I introduced myself to the tall, slim, greying gentlemen and asked him, "Are you hiring pilots?"

He replied firmly, "No."

"Oh," I said, "I saw the old H-19 flying around the flight pattern, and I thought you might need an H-19 pilot." He perked up and asked me, "Do you think you can you fly the S-55?" I replied honestly, "I have no H-19 time, but I have about 1,200 hours in the H-34." He asked me three questions, "Can you take a check ride tomorrow? How would you feel about going to Alaska? Do you have any friends who might be interested?"

The next day Steve Eck, Mike Readick, and I successfully flew check flights in the H-19 with Falconer. He hired all three of us to go to Alaska immediately. Because Mike had recently gotten married, he backed out. His beautiful seventeen-year-old sister-in-law, whom I had met at his recent wedding, was the reason for my trip north. I was madly in love with the bright-eyed, beautiful, smart, charming girl, on her way to college…and her daddy was rich. I assumed she would be okay with my absence for the summer.

Four days later, Steve and I travelled by Boeing 707 to Anchorage airport. We were off to the Land of the Midnight Sun, the Klondike, Jack London, Sourdough Gold Miners, Icebergs, Polar bears and the soon-to-be huge oil boom on the North Slope oil fields.

At nearby Merrill Field, we met Era Helicopter Company's CEO and Chief Pilot, Carl Brady. We also met the chief of maintenance, Joe Nightingale. I was impressed that Joe's hangar was immaculate, and all the mechanics wore spotless white coveralls. To put us at ease and make us feel welcomed, Joe told us a story.

"Two helicopter mechanics in a remote Alaska site called into their home base to confer with the chief mechanic. The aircraft they supported wouldn't start, and they disagreed on the reason. The chief mechanic, in far-away Anchorage, asked the two fellows what they thought the problem might be. One spoke for both, "Well, boss, Jim here seems to think that the helicopter won't start because it is upside down. I believe that it won't start because it is underwater."'

I believe this was based on a true event. What probably happened was that after a hard day's work, the pilot had parked the helicopter overnight on a dock and failed to tie it down. A strong wind came up during the night and blew the machine into the lake. Imagine the pilot's surprise the next morning when he came out to go flying.

Thus began my almost three decades as a civilian helicopter pilot. This career would take me to many corners of the world over the next twenty-seven years. On this first of four summers in Alaska, I would spend ninety-three days on the North Slope, then twenty-three days on the extreme west end of the Aleutian Islands chain flying in support of underground atomic test "Operation Milrow."

I would fly for thirty months for Air America (the CIA) in Laos. I would spend two years on Kwajalein Atoll in the South Pacific supporting the STAR WARS missile-testing program, several months in Saudi Arabia off-loading ships, and many years flying for several different companies around California. I fought forest fires, crop-dusted, flew TV news reporters, lifted heavy things to the tops of tall buildings, and much more. I ferried helicopters to

Texas from California, to and from Alaska, and to Tennessee. I would fly 5,500 more hours in forty different kinds of helicopters.

I would face many challenges and dangers. I would come within a royal whisker of death at least a dozen times. I would make a few stupid, dumb errors but survive them. I would lose my sweet first love to AIDS (Aviation Induced Divorce Syndrome) before we could marry but I fell in love several more times over the years.

Even though I had left the Marine Corps, the Marine Corps had not left me. Three values that I learned from the United States Marine Corps stayed with me throughout my flying career. The first was loyalty to my corps or my company. The second was, "Take care of my troops." The third was, "Accomplish the mission or die trying." These three ingrained values would at times get me into big trouble.

These are the highlights of my recollections of those worldwide and worldly adventures in helicopter flying, roughly in chronological order, aided by information from my logbooks, journals, personal photos, news clippings, and…the weakest part…my human memory.

Chapter 1
June 13, 1969
Anchorage, Alaska

I felt fortunate to have this job, as I had less than 1,300 hours of total flight experience. The usual expectation of a commercial helicopter operator was 1,500 hours of flight experience, and employers would not hire anyone with less than that. It's the age-old problem: you cannot get a job without experience, so nobody will hire you and let you acquire that experience. Because I had impressed Falconer with my flying skills during the check ride, he hired me. I would soon reach the magic number of 1,500 hours and become quite employable forever after. The pay was almost twice what I had been earning in the service, all expenses paid.

My mechanic, Jeff, and I lifted off in a sister ship to the H19 I had flown in Ventura, and began our journey to the North Slope. I was excited to be flying a civilian machine into the far reaches of "The Last Frontier." As we passed by majestic Mount McKinley, there was no doubt in my mind why native peoples assigned mystical powers to high mountains. The mountain was magically attractive. I wanted to fly over, reach out and touch it.

We refueled and stayed over in Fairbanks. The next day we refueled at Nenana, then proceeded northward. Approaching Bettles, we crossed the Arctic Circle just a few days before summer solstice. We were now in the land of the midnight sun. We stayed over at the Gateway Lodge in Bettles.

The Worldwide Adventures of a Helicopter Pilot ... the rest of the story

The sun never sets during the summer above the Arctic Circle; it just does "Touch and Goes" on the horizon. Commercial slide courtesy of Arctic Circle Enterprises, Inc., Anchorage, Alaska.

Chapter 2
To The North Slope

The next morning, we flew through the Brooks Mountain Range via Anaktuvic Pass. I was in awe at the physical beauty of the majestic mountains, the snow-covered peaks, and the profusion of colors of the vegetation along the way. I saw a large geologic "slump" where an entire side of a mountain had slid down a mountainside sometime in the far past. Emerging from that pass, we stopped at Anaktuvic Village airport and pumped fuel from a barrel to give us enough to continue northeast to Deadhorse at Prudhoe Bay – The North Slope.

In 1969, the state of Alaska was allowing various oil companies to explore huge tracts of land for which the mineral rights (oil) would then be put up for auction. This was the beginning of the Alaska oil boom, the pipeline, the port of Valdez, the Valdez oil spill, and all those other things that were the down-line offshoots of the big oil boom in Alaska.

At Deadhorse, I reported to Mr. Hunt of the Atlantic Richfield Oil Company. My assignment was to support a three- to four-man team drilling a test well on Reindeer Island, a tiny sand spit about 100-yards wide and less than a quarter-mile long, just offshore in the Beaufort Sea. A huge Sikorsky H-54 Air Crane carried a portable drilling rig out to this island, and a trailer house for the roughnecks to use as a break room and a shelter should the weather turn sour.

My friend Rip Green, flying a giant Sikorsky H-54 Sky Crane, lifts a mobile home out to Reindeer Island. I was impressed at the time that the flat of eggs on the table of the mobile home arrived intact.

Rip Green, flying a ROWAN Sky Crane, lifts a portable oil drill to Reindeer Island. I would do this kind of work a few years later, flying an H-34 supporting smaller rigs near Talkeetna.

I would meet Rip again in the hallway outside the Air America chief pilot's office in Udorn, Thailand, in mid-1971, and never saw him again. He remained on the Air America seniority list for years, so he must have been involved in some other, perhaps clandestine, projects. With a degree in electrical engineering, he was probably involved in the silent helicopters that the CIA put together to tap into the communication lines in North Vietnam in 1972. I had a tiny, peripheral part supporting that secret project, which became unclassified only a few years ago. (See my book, "Air America: A Super Pilot Spills the Beans" for that story.)

In early 2005, I received word that Rip had died. R.I.P, Rip.

* * *

There was no control tower at Deadhorse Airport. We shared a common radio frequency, and everybody talked to everybody else to keep track of traffic. All helicopters avoided the fixed-wing traffic patterns. At first, there was an attempt to have a controller to control air traffic, but he ended up being worse than ineffectual. For instance, I called and requested clearance to cross the airstrip to depart to the south. His reply was, "Helicopter N874, climb straight up to ten thousand feet and hold." He had absolutely no concept of the capabilities of a helicopter and obviously had no idea how to handle air traffic. He soon disappeared. We pilots found that simply broadcasting our intentions on the common frequency was all that we needed to avoid each other and the occasional landing airplane.

The Reindeer Island drill rig operated around the clock. My job was simple. Every twelve hours, at noon and again at midnight, I rotated the roughnecks. I flew three or four men out to the island and the same number back. The island was only about five miles away, and the round trip usually took about eighteen to twenty minutes. I was flying roughly forty minutes a day. About every third or fourth day, I might make a third trip out to deliver a tool or a drum of lubricating oil. Once I rescued an injured worker.

The rest of the time, I was on my own but had to always be available in case of emergencies. I spent a lot of time sleeping, reading, watching movies...lots of movies, talking with the other fellows, and just being bored. I became the camp projectionist for the many reel-to-reel movies we watched, a talent I learned in eighth grade.

The camp was composed of several trailer house units connected with branching off hallways, shaped like a giant letter "E." I shared a room with my mechanic, Jeff. Because of the twenty-four-hour daylight, we lived by the clock. At mid-summer, midnight was no different than noon. If one really paid attention, he could discern that the sun moved around in the sky in a small circle, never setting. To enable sleep, we covered the windows with blankets to darken the room. During the peak of summer, the weather was suitable for short sleeves.

The kitchen and the dining room were at the bottom of the E, nearest the airport's gravel ramp. The outstanding cooks provided excellent and plentiful food. They served four meals a day, seven days a week, to accommodate the round-the-clock workings of the camp. A pastry bar near the serving window always held a plethora of succulent chocolate éclairs, donuts, apple fritters, fruit, and other delights. Coffee, juice, milk, and other drinks were always available. Booze and beer were prohibited, understandably. In this situation, where men are working hard in close quarters, it wouldn't be conducive to getting the jobs done if anyone got drunk and disorderly. We had poker games at first, but then management decided that gambling should not be allowed, so that form of recreation was nixed. Some fellows walked a short distance to the nearby river and fished, catching beautiful foot-long Dolly Varden trout.

The major highlight of each day was to go out to the airplane ramp and wait for the Wein Airways 737 to come in so we could see the stewardesses at the door atop the boarding stairs. That was a big thrill and the only women I saw for ninety-three days.

My mechanic Jeff, fresh out of mechanic's school, was smart and eager to learn. He spent much of his time in the lounge reading the helicopter maintenance manuals, so usually I had our room to myself. One day, a fuel transfer pump in the center fuel cell in my helicopter crapped out, so I asked Jeff to replace it. He ordered a new pump and then began to study the manual on how to replace the dead pump. At first, he thought he would have to drill out the rivets on the belly of the helicopter to remove the sheet metal, then lower the fuel tank to have access to the pump. When he told me this, I showed him the access panels on the cargo floor. All he had to do was unscrew a dozen or so bolts to open a hatch. The fuel cell was easily accessible without drilling the whole belly of the machine apart. He was pleased to see that it was going to be a quick, easy repair instead of hours and hours of tedious drilling out and then replacing all the rivets.

July 7, 1969

In the Vietnam I left in mid-1967, the US troops were starting to withdraw:

"A battalion of the US 9th Infantry Division leaves Saigon in the initial withdrawal of US troops. The 814 soldiers were the first of 25,000 troops that were withdrawn in the first stage of the US disengagement from the war." From History.com.

The North Slope is a wide, flat, treeless plain, covered by tundra, dotted with thousands of small ponds, varying in size but otherwise looking alike. One exception to the flat terrain was a few small hills called pingoes. These, as it turned out, were salt domes, positive indications of oil beneath the surface.

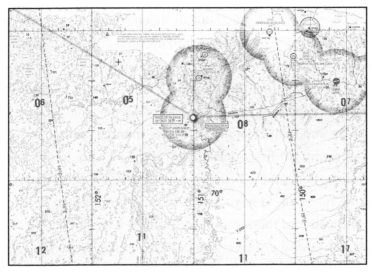

On this recent aviation chart of the North Slope, one can see how many thousands of ponds and lakes dotted the landscape.
(All the aviation-related markings were not on my charts in 1969).

Sparse shrub-like trees that never get more than six to eight inches off the ground grew parallel to the ground due to the fierce winds that blow over this area in the wintertime. I saw lots of tiny lemmings scurrying around under the scrub brush, but I never saw hordes of them following each other into the sea. There were immense flocks of geese and ducks in their summer nesting grounds and vast herds of reindeer.

With the twenty-four hours of daylight, navigating was quite easy. I could often see my destination before I broke ground. Many good landmarks dotted the area; oil drilling rigs, camps, airports, and the seashore made navigation easy. Electronic navigation aids like OMNI and TACAN existed but were not necessary most of the time. Later, in the West Kuparuk basecamp, I used an ADF (Automatic Direction Finder) radio beacon.

One day I flew about twenty miles out onto the pack ice in the Arctic Ocean. Over many years, snow and ice had built up and creating the occasional small ice island about twenty-five feet thick. These islands seemed stable, and the geologist wondered if one could be used as a base to drill into the bottom of the sea to search for oil under the sea floor.

They picked one of the islands and started an experiment. They built a plastic fence around the perimeter of the island and brought out a large, gasoline-powered pump to pump water inside the fence, creating a pool, which then froze solid. The hope was that the extra ice would make the island heavier, grounding it even more firmly onto the bottom of the sea, and to create a flat surface for drilling. My tiny bit in this experiment was to carry a drum of fuel for the pump and some passengers out to the ice island, two trips out and back. Going out and back, my passengers said they saw a polar bear and some walruses; I did not. That day I flew 3.3 hours.

Bell Jet Ranger pilot preparing to lift the big pump to the Ice Island and lifting it.

One day when the crew flew out to inspect the experiment, they found that the island had split and cracked into two tilted halves. End of experiment.

As the summer season faded into fall, we began to get days that were half daylight and half night. The mid-winter time of twenty-four-hour darkness rapidly approached, and the weather began to worsen, bringing lots of fog. At these times, we used the slightest landmark to navigate by in the heavy fog. Sometimes a pair of blue barrels on the tundra was a landmark…or three barrels, one fallen over, or a group of barrels, or one slightly removed from the rest, or barrels of different colors. This system worked fine…most of the time. The way we avoided running into each other was by reporting over the common radio frequency where we were, where we were headed, and at what altitude. We always flew on the right side of the single road, whichever direction we were flying.

One fall day, while out groping around in heavy fog, I heard several helicopter pilots report various landmarks nearby. I knew the traffic was getting too thick for this sort of navigation, and I felt uncomfortable risking my passengers' lives. I chose to land beside one of the small ponds and shut down for a while and wait for the traffic to abate. My passengers and I got out of the H-19 to stretch our legs and have a smoke. (They smoked; I never have.) What I was about to hear surprised and shocked me.

As we sat beside the pond, I heard a helicopter go by. By its distinct "thweet, thweet, thweet" sound, I knew it was a Bell 47 "Whirlybird." About the time it passed out of hearing, a Jet Ranger passed by with its particular higher-pitched, "tsweet, tsweet, tsweet," whistling sound. As that one faded, the sound of a huge Sikorsky Sky Crane replaced it. Its noise signature was a low, rumbling, throbbing, "thuwunga, thuwunga, thuwunga" as it chewed through the sky. Yet another helicopter passed by. For about fifteen minutes, there was a constant cacophony of traffic, but I had visual contact with nary a one of them. After that experience, I decided to limit my flying to when I could see a little better. To my knowledge, there was never a mid-air collision on the North Slope.

Flying along the shoreline west of Deadhorse, returning from Reindeer Island empty, I spied a tree stump lying on the beach. It caught my eye as a spectacular natural work of art. The stump had obviously grown somewhere upriver in a location that had permafrost. Because the tree grew in tundra, all the roots had terminated at the same depth, so the bottoms of all the roots were in the same geometric plane. At its extreme measurement, the whole thing was about seven feet in diameter. The gnarly roots had many knots, twists, and turns all over them. In two places, roots had grown across from one root branch to the other.

Properly prepared and stained, with a glass top, I knew it would make a spectacular coffee table for my sweetie's parent's home, perched on a bluff overlooking the Pacific Ocean just north of Moro Bay, California. This would be a great way to ingratiate myself with her parents. I landed on the beach and wrestled the stump into my H-19.

While at Deadhorse, I made friends with a fellow named Hal Jowers, flying a Hiller 1100. He let me have a few minutes of stick time in it. I scared us both when I first took off because this machine was very delicate on the lateral cyclic (stick) control, and I wobbled dramatically sideways on takeoff. Then I caught a feel for the delicacy of the controls and had no more problems. That is the only Hiller time I have in my logbooks, about .3 hours.

The Worldwide Adventures of a Helicopter Pilot ... the rest of the story

In our conversation, Hal said he previously worked for Air America in Laos. Curious, I pressed him for details. He minimized the experience and gave some obscure reason why he quit. I found out later, when I worked for Air America, that he got fired for having an accident. While landing at the Luang Pra Bang airport in northwest Laos, he managed to drive the rotor blade tips of his H-34 through the nose of a Lao Airline Boeing 307, one of only three four-engine tail draggers ever built. I was told that Lao pilots were not too pleased that he chopped up the nose of their airplane just inches from their toes while they sat in the cockpit executing their pre-start checklist. They wanted to shoot Hal. Maybe he didn't quit or get fired; maybe he simply ran away to escape with his life. I never saw or heard about Hal again.

I also met Lou Love and Ed Miller, two of the few helicopter pilots that I met in all my years of flying who didn't start their chopper piloting careers in the military. Both got all their ratings and flight time as civilians, became instructors, and earned their ways to the big time.

While returning to Anchorage one day from the North Slope, Ed took a circuitous route to avoid some bad weather, but neglected to report his route to anyone. He stopped to refuel from a barrel south of Umiat at Gunsight Gap, named after a prominent geographic feature that resembles a gigantic gun sight. After refueling, he discovered that his battery was dead. He couldn't restart, and his radios were inoperative. After nearly two weeks, a pilot passed nearby, and Ed was able to get the pilot's attention and was rescued. He returned to base somewhat thinner and most hungry. (This was after I had gone home.)

Chapter 3
West Kuparuk
Oil Exploration Support

When the arduous Reindeer Island job finished up, I flew about twenty-five miles west across the tundra to a camp named West Kuparuk to support a seismic survey team. I brought my tree stump. This camp had a decrepit, old black and white TV with fuzzy reception on which I was able to view replays of that historic moment when Neil Armstrong stepped on the moon.

I also celebrated my birthday at this base, precipitating a mid-life crisis at the young age of twenty-six. I believe it was because of PTSD. I had lived through the Vietnam war but lost a lot of friends, and I constantly felt I didn't have very long left to live. I had secretly gotten engaged to my sweetie just before departing California. She was beautiful, charming, bright, sexy, had iridescent blue eyes…and her daddy was rich. What more could I ask for? We corresponded regularly, but I didn't feel I was ready to marry.

I was a confirmed bachelor trapped in a wonderful dilemma. Part of me wanted to marry her, but part of me had no desire to ever marry. I had grown up in a dysfunctional family and saw no advantage to marriage and home life. Why commit to a future that was doomed to fail, when I could continue to play the field?

I learned later that feelings of *expecting a short life* and *difficulty committing* are more serious signs of PTSD. Early 2019, I had my annual physical at our local VA clinic. One of the questions the young lady physician assistant asked me was, "Sir, do you ever have feelings that your life may be foreshortened?" I answered honestly, "Yes, miss, I do. You won't believe this, but I'll soon be seventy-seven, and I still feel every day that I won't live to see twenty-five."

Hauling the survey crews out of West Kuparuk, I often flew five to ten miles away from camp. Due to magnetic deviation caused by our extreme northern location, magnetic compasses could vary by thirty-five degrees, because we were close to the actual magnetic north pole, which is not actually located at the true North Pole, but a few hundred miles south of the true North Pole in northern Canada.

The surveyors' job was to strike straight lines across the tundra within the tracts that were up for bid and leave a marker every quarter mile so that later teams could do seismic studies. I leapfrogged the surveyors along the string of points.

Seismic studies consisted of drilling holes in the ground at each of the survey points a quarter mile apart and then detonating dynamite in each hole sequentially. Sensitive microphones placed along the survey line recorded the underground reverberations of the explosions and transmitted the information to a recorder in a metal cube about six feet on each side called the "Dog House." A Bell 205 was tasked to move that Dog House from place to place for each seismic shot. The tapes were expedited to geological experts at various oil company labs in Houston, Los Angeles, and elsewhere for interpretation. Considered top secret, these multiple squiggles on the computer paper determined what lay below the surface of the earth and whether a particular tract was worth bidding on. Most of the tracts must have been valuable because an enormous amount of oil later flowed from the North Slope.

Sometimes I had a little time on my hands. Once I made it a point to see how many of the giant North Slope mosquitoes I could mash against the instrument panel. My record was 118 in half an hour. At one spot, I was able to sit in my pilot's seat and watch as a herd of thousands of caribou passed by. Caribou are not native to Alaska but were imported from Siberia in the 1800s to try and give the natives industry and food, an experiment which displayed good results. Later, Musk Oxen were imported, too. They also thrive in the remote regions of Alaska. (Read James A. Michener's novel *Alaska* for more details.)

August 15-18, 1969

The Woodstock Music Festival in Belmont, New York. Many of the big names in rock and roll played. The top song at the time was "The Year 2525" by Zager and Evans.
I couldn't have been much farther away.
Where were you?

Later in the summer, it began to get dark much sooner. One afternoon, a heavy fog crawled over the tundra, making it urgent that I retrieve two survey crews. When I reached the first team, it was obvious to me that the "pea soup" fog was going to soon obscure everything. I feared that once I returned to the camp with the first group, I wouldn't be able to find my way back to the second crew.

To complicate matters, my ADF (automatic direction finder) navigation radio had been acting up for the previous few days to the point that if I wanted to home in on the camp's beacon, I had to hold the needle seventy degrees off my nose to find my way back. The problem had been getting a bit worse every day, and I was not sure that adjusting my heading even seventy degrees would be

15

enough. This was okay when I could see the camp from ten miles away. But now, with the fog gobbling up the world, even if I could find the second crew again, I feared I might not find my way back to camp.

My tired old Sikorsky, with its Wright R-1300 HP seven-cylinder radial engine, was most underpowered. There was no way I could lift seven or eight guys off the tundra, even with a good headwind. They also had two or three hundred pounds of seismic cable and surveying equipment. I was low on fuel, which was in our favor.

I picked up the first batch of fellows and flew about a quarter-mile to the second group. How could I take off with all this weight? I decided I must try it. *I must rescue the troops!* I instructed the fellows below to throw out every bit of unnecessary cargo...everything that wasn't attached to the helicopter. I put all the men in seats and made sure everybody was tightly strapped in. Then I used a little something I had learned in Vietnam.

I wound the H-19's engine up to its limits and picked it up to a hover. The over-laden machine would not hold a hover and slowly settled right back down to the ground. I tried again but still could not maintain a hover. I needed to move forward until I reached translational lift, that magical airspeed at which the entire rotor system begins to act like an airplane wing and becomes more efficient. The H-34 I flew in Vietnam had wheels on it; I could roll it off like an airplane. Wheels would not have worked in this situation; the tundra was too soft, and we would have sunk into it and rolled over. Hueys have skids and are easy to slide off the ground, but here, where the tundra was soft and uneven, skids might dig into the tundra with similarly disastrous results.

This old beast had floats...no wheels or skids to catch on anything. The tundra was coated with moisture from the fog. *Perhaps I could slide the H-19 forward on its floats.* I felt responsible for these guys. *I must accomplish the mission or die trying!* If I left them out on the tundra overnight, they could die from exposure or get eaten by polar bears. (Polar bears consider humans to be part of their food chain.)

I dragged the tired old machine once more to a hover, using RPM well past the red line and more manifold pressure than the handbook allowed. Before it could again settle to the tundra, I fed in a bit of forward stick and increased throttle again. I stopped looking at the gages, knowing full well that I was overboosting and over-speeding the old piston engine. At perhaps two feet above the ground, we began to move forward ever so slowly, then a little faster. Then the bottom fell out.

The old beastie plopped back down to the tundra in a sliding, pancaking bounce, spring-boarding us off the tundra. The bouncing boost launched us into the slight nose wind, gaining us the forward speed needed to attain transnational lift. We were flying!

Correcting for the 70 degree aberration on my ADF, I lumbered back to the base camp at West Kuparuk with my heavy load. Inspection of the engine revealed no great harm done. The next day we flew out and retrieved all the equipment left behind the night before. None of the hardware had been eaten by polar bears.

Chapter 4
September 13, 1969
Near Crash At Sagwon

Finally, the day came that my tour on the North Slope was complete. Ninety-three days away from my sweet young fiancé was ninety-three days too many. First stop: Sagwon; then onwards to Anchorage and from there home to her welcoming arms. Navigation was not to be a problem. For the first leg, all I had to do was fly directly south for about forty-five miles until I found the Sagavanirktok River. From there, it would be a simple matter to follow the river southwest to Sagwon. On a clear day, I could see the river bluffs above Sagwon from West Kuparuk. This was not a clear day.

Jeff and I loaded up the H-19, including my tree stump, and blasted off...right into a blizzard. Heavy, sticky, sloppy snow impeded our progress. Still not worried, I thought, *What could go wrong in a thirty-five-minute flight?* As I flew south, the snow built up on the windshield to the point where the wipers could no longer handle it. I landed once and had Jeff scrape the excess snow off my windscreen. I had my carb heat on full forward to prevent carburetor icing. I hoped that once we got to Sagwon, the weather would break, and we could continue southward. My young hormones were urging me on.

I found the river and followed it to Sagwon. That was the end of staying on plan for this day. Sagwon sat nestled into the curve of the river, just below high white cliffs, sheltered from the ravages of the arctic west winds. I made a left one-eighty over the river and approached to land into the wind. An open spot away from other helicopters near the hostel beckoned us.

On the final approach, I increased throttle to slow my rate of descent but saw no lessening of it. I added more power, then I rolled on full throttle but still no change. I realized I was in trouble. Even though I had used full carb heat, that old horse thief, carburetor icing, had stolen my horsepower. I was about to drive smartly into the ground. I could do nothing more but hold on as the H-19 slid out of the sky at a rate not recommended in the handbook. Close to the ground, I pulled in full collective pitch to try and lessen our impact.

We hit the snow-covered ground with at least a five hundred-feet-per-minute rate of descent and about fifteen miles per hour forward speed. The machine hit, bounced, contacted the snow a second time, slid about fifty feet and the left float dug into a snowbank, tripping the machine. The nose pitched down as the tail rose, simultaneously rolling it over to its left side, the rotor blades precariously close to a snowbank. My cyclic stick was full right and aft. A crash was imminent, and there wasn't a hell of a lot I could do about it! I felt if I reduced power, that would contribute to the rolling momentum, and I would complete the roll onto the left side. If I added power, of which I had none left anyway, that would pull my nose forward and aggravate my nosing over. I was screwed either way. Frozen with indecision, I held onto what I had and hoped for the best.

The machine hung there in suspended animation for what seemed forever, balanced on the end of its left float, like a ballerina dancer doing point. My heart hung in my throat like a clock pendulum stopped in mid-swing, not sure whether to tick or to tock. Would we Tick…roll over and crash…or Tock, not crash? If we did roll over, Tick… would we die, or Tock, would we live?

We hung there, balanced between safety and eternity, between life and doom; fate would decide if we would capitulate to the inevitable or stay intact for another go around. After only a few seconds, but what seemed to be an hour, Tock. Gradually and slowly, the helicopter sighed down to a level position onto the snow.

We endured a heavy blizzard for the next three days until better weather allowed us to press on. The next leg was a long one. In addition to full tanks, I had to carry an extra barrel of fuel. With full tanks, the barrel of fuel, a fuel pump, all Jeff's tools, the spare parts on board, and our personal baggage, we were already over max gross weight. The tree stump, which weighed about 100 pounds, had to be sacrificed. I tossed it out, and for all I know, it's still there beside the Sagwon airstrip.

Our next stop was at Anaktuvik Village airport at the north end of the Anaktuvik Pass. We refueled from the drum of fuel we brought along. I took time to walk down into the village and see a bit of how the Aleuts lived. The houses were half-buried into the ground, covered in hides and driftwood with no paint nor any color of any kind. The whole village resembled a war zone. By the most meager of any stateside standards, the whole village reeked of stark poverty. I know the oil boom eventually made a huge difference for the natives.

I visited a native home where the whole native family lived in one small room. They slept in a pile under furs on a raised platform in the corner. I was glad to give $20 for what seemed to be a high-priced souvenir because I thought the native family could use the money. A native face mask made of reindeer hide and dog fur still hangs on my wall, some fifty-two years later.

Anaktuvic Village at the North end of Anaktuvic Pass and The native home in Anaktuvic village where I bought the mask. Caribou hides freeze-drying in the cold weather.

Flying south through the pass, the scenery was some of the most beautiful I have ever seen. Fall temperatures had brought out a veritable painter's box of colors along the way. Flying past Bettles, I saw the mighty Yukon River meandering off to the west towards Nome.

Chapter 5
August 20, 1969
Back To The North Slope

I delivered the H-19 to Anchorage, eager to depart for points south, but Carl Brady asked me to return to the North Slope for a short time. The pilot flying a Jet Ranger near Deadhorse had quit abruptly, and the company needed someone to complete his contract. I wanted to fly the sleek little machine, and I knew my sweetie would understand.

During these few days in Anchorage, I tried to start a little business adventure. A good friend of my soon-to-be ex-future-father-in-law, a Mr. Wheat, of Lilburn, Georgia, had bought the Overland Train at a government auction.

The Overland Train (Wikipedia)

The US Army had commissioned the building of this amazing and unwieldy beast to use in desert warfare. Every wheel of it was independently electrically driven. It carried its own turbine engine generators, and some of the cars were fuel tanks for the generator turbines. Mr. Wheat asked me to shop around Alaska and see if I could market his new toy to the oil explorers. I spent a few dollars making up rough brochures and even bought a whole new salesman's business outfit…sports coat, slacks, white shirt, tie, and brand-new wing-tip shoes…at Penny's department store downtown Anchorage, but it was too late. Most of the exploration on the North Slope was being concluded, and there was no need for the Train. A couple of people I called upon said, yes, they could and would have used it a few months sooner. Videos are available on YouTube of this amazing Overland Train. I don't know what happened to it after that.

The Bell 206 Jet Ranger that I flew on the North Slope, fall 1969.

At this camp, I had better quarters, a new housing trailer all to myself for three weeks. Much better than at West Kuparuk, where I had shared a shipping-container bunkhouse with two survey crews. I had the opportunity to experience what geographers call "ground truth." I had always heard that only a few inches under the tundra, the earth remains frozen solid all year round. I borrowed a surveyor's shovel and dug an eight-inch square hole in the spongy-like tundra. Sure enough, about eighteen inches down, I encountered solidly frozen earth. This was also the only place where I had the experience of actually walking on the tundra, which felt like walking on eighteen inches of squishy sponge.

I learned a few months later that one of my Vietnam comrades had been killed while flying a Jet Ranger around the North Slope about the same time I was there. It seems that his skid slid under a root of one of the small, horizontally growing trees on the tundra, and when he started to take off, he "tripped" and rolled over. R.I.P Paul "Prunes" Murray, one of the very best.

One short mission I had with the Jet Ranger was flying scout for the hovercraft. These strange and extremely noisy machines could hover-fly about a foot off the ground and could hover-fly almost anywhere on the tundra without bogging down or leaving tracks. The engineers tried to rig them up with mighty shakers to vibrate the ground in an attempt to replicate the dynamite explosions for seismic studies. All they succeeded in doing was shaking a hovercraft to bits; yet another unsuccessful experiment. But the big oil companies had big money, the stakes were high, and they needed to expedite everything they could during the short summer to define which tracts held the oil.

On some places on the tundra, there were natural dikes. The hovercraft found they had little trouble crossing these. They would get a running start and slide their rubber skirts up and over these natural obstacles. One driver mis-estimated his high-speed approach. The inflated rubber skirt of the craft dug in, and the machine flipped over. The driver died, and the rig was destroyed.

This hovercraft looks a little tired because its skirt-bumpers are deflated. You can see the seismic shaker on the front of it.

Finishing up on the North Slope with almost sixty hours of Jet Ranger time in my logbook, I again reported to the ERA office in Anchorage, fully prepared to return to my sweetie, who I believed was waiting patiently for my return. Carl Brady intrigued me with a question. "How would you like to go someplace that is further south than Seattle and further west than Hawaii?" I have always had a great mind for geography, but this description puzzled me. After those last few days on the North Slope in the freezing weather and the near-crash in Sagwon due to carburetor icing, he had captured my attention. *South...warmth...no ice, no snow.* Yes, I was interested.

I tried to picture in my mind what place met those geographic coordinates and drew a blank. Where could this place be? It would almost have to be mid-Pacific somewhere. Hawaii? "Where?" I asked.

"Amchitka." He said. I still didn't know.

"The Aleutian Islands," Brady said, "the far western end of the Aleutians. I lied a bit about the 'South of Seattle' bit." How could I pass on seeing this exotic and fascinating area? I agreed to go.

Chapter 6
Amchitka

A little historical perspective here: After international treaties banned atmospheric testing of atomic weapons, nations began testing such weapons underground. The Atomic Energy Commission (AEC) was preparing an underground atomic test on this isolated island near the end of the Aleutian chain for the very reason that it is so isolated from the rest of the world. If you look on a map, Amchitka is 1,400 air miles from Anchorage, part of the Rat Island group, far closer to Russia than it is to the main body of Alaska. The western-most Rat Island group is so far west that the International Date Line bends around it to keep them in the same day as the rest of the USA.

ERA put two mechanics and me on a chartered 727 and jetted us out to this desolate location. I dropped my sweetheart a quick note to let her know that there would be yet another three-week delay before I returned. I knew she would understand and be supportive.

I was off on another adventure.

The Worldwide Adventures of a Helicopter Pilot ... the rest of the story

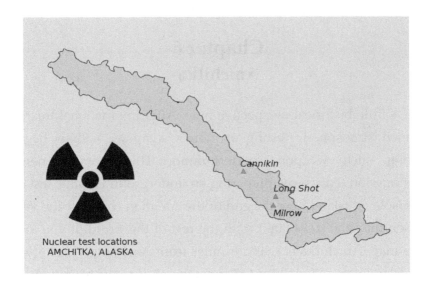

Courtesy of Wikipedia

This is what the Amchitka docks looked like when I arrived. We based our operations out of a small airfield left over from WWII, right where the island pinches together.

Hundreds of old WWII Quonset huts dotted Amchitka.

Amchitka had been an Army Air Corps base with 15,000 troops on it during World War II. The island was about forty miles long and about two miles wide, on average. It was very reminiscent in size and shape of Okinawa, in the Pacific south of Japan, where I spent several weeks during my overseas tour with the Marines Corps. That was just about all that resembled Okinawa. In contrast to Okinawa's heat, humidity, jungle-covered mountains, and numerous population, Amchitka was bleak and barren and cold and foggy and windy and unpopulated. According to wikipedia, the last native Aleuts left the island in 1872. The Russians had semi-enslaved the Aleuts to hunt down and nearly exterminate the sea otters for their fur. Once the otters were all gone, there was no way for the Aleuts to make a living.

There were almost no trees on Amchitka. I say 'almost' because there were two. GIs planted two trees in the leeward side of the officers' club during WWII. Those two trees were still only about two feet tall twenty-four years after the war was over. A small, hand-lettered sign beside them said, "Amchitka Forest." We called it the Amchitka National Forest.

*The Amchitka Forest on either side of the pathway.
The two trees were less than three feet tall.*

The Aleutian Islands are the only place where the Japanese actually did attack and occupy US soil during WWII. For an in-depth account of that battle, read the book *The Aleutian Islands Campaign: The History of Japan's Invasion of Alaska during World War II* by Charles River Editors.

At the Amchitka airport, I discovered two old WWII wrecks. I'm sure airplane collectors have scarfed up those remains by now, sad as they were. Could these be the remains of P-40s?

In 1998, in Palo Alto, California, I met a former Army Air Force pilot who had flown from Amchitka during the war. I wonder if he flew either of these before they became wrecks. He said all he ever did was patrol and never saw an enemy airplane. Perhaps he wrecked one of them?

On the rare clear day, we could see Semisopochnoi, a still-steaming volcanic cone, to the North, and Rat, Segula, Little Sitkind Kiska islands to the West. Attu is close to the Kamchatka Peninsula of Russia.

For the atomic test, the AEC drilled large holes as much as ten feet in diameter into the Island to a depth of 4,000 feet. The bomb, "MILROW" was placed in one of the holes, sealed off and triggered.

For twenty-three days, I hopped teams of AEC biologists all over the island so they could observe and record the existing wildlife on and about the island. They planned to count the pre-and post-blast populations of the native animals to determine if the testing was harmful to the wildlife. We flew all the way around the island, taking pictures of the coastal waters with a Hasselblad Camera using a polarized lens to cut glare from the water. When the film was developed, the biologists counted the sea otters in the photos. From this, they believed they made a reasonable estimate of the pre- and post-shot populations of sea otters. A few of the otters were captured and penned up close to ground zero. I found it amusing that to keep them alive, the captive sea otters were fed fish that had to be flown in fresh daily from Seattle.

On one occasion, I took two biologists to a site a few miles up the east coast of the island. Here they used an electrified dip net to stun and catch some of the native Dolly Varden in a small lake. The scientists put most of those fish in a small pen right there in their home waters. A few of the fish were sacrificed for "pre-test studies," which means they went home with the biologists for that night's dinner. After the blast, the fish were checked again to see what, if any, effects the blast might have had.

The biologists placing captured fish in a cage.

One day, I took a trio of biologists to the most northernmost point of the island. They brought scuba gear and intended to do an underwater survey of whatever wildlife might exist under the frigid waters. When I told them I was a certified scuba diver, they offered to outfit me with gear and let me accompany them into the near-freezing water. I declined the offer.

My souvenir whale bones that I have been packing around for more than fifty years. My size-11 bedroom slipper is on the pallet is for comparison of size. Japanese fish net floats that I found on the Amchitka beach. SPRITE 750ml bottle for comparison of size.

I had many hours wandering around the island, exploring and beach combing during these "take and wait" missions. All I had to do was stay within sight of the helicopter in case the weather turned bad, or someone was injured. While the scientists were stunning the fish, I explored a rocky beach. I found several of the coveted green glass Japanese fishing floats of various sizes, a nice piece of fishing net which I used for decorating purposes later in one of my bachelor pads, and three vertebrae of a blue whale. The largest of the vertebrae weighs forty-two pounds.

The weather on Amchitka was atrocious. I was there for twenty-three days in October, and I saw the sun only two or three times in this, the summer season, and a chilling wind blew constantly. Can you imagine what it had to be like to be stationed in this very isolated, cold, damp, windy, always foggy place, all the while anticipating a Japanese attack? It is no wonder that during

World War II, more GIs were evacuated from Amchitka for battle fatigue than for any other reason.

The father of my fiancé (I still call him my ex-future-father-in-law), John A. was an Army engineer during World War II. Stationed on Amchitka during the war, he helped design and build the port facilities. When I returned to California in the late fall and showed him my slides, he saw structures that he had helped build now deteriorated and falling down. He told me about the battle fatigue stats I mentioned above.

The dilapidated infrastructure left over from World War II.

Chapter 7
The Atomic Blast

As the big day of the underground blast approached, we moved everything about twenty miles north for safety. That meant I did a lot of flying back and forth. One day, I took the scenic route along the coast and I saw huge flat coastal rocks festooned with hundreds of seals and another rock nearby covered with sea lions.

I flew past an amazing geologic formation, what could only have been a volcanic crater with one small cleft opened to the sea. I wanted to land and beachcomb the secret cove.

One day I was flying south, scud running under the always-present fog. The fog kept forcing me lower and lower, nearly down to sea level. I decided, *Enough of this!* I pulled back on the stick and made a quick 180-climbing turn into the fog and planted the helicopter on top of the bluff. Knowing that the North-South dirt road was only a few hundred meters away, I walked over to it and waited a few minutes until a pickup truck came by and took me back to base. The H-19 spent the night on the cliff, and I retrieved it the next morning.

As B-day (B for blast) approached, concerns grew because these islands, like most islands, are the tops of high underwater mountains. Geologists and environmentalists feared that the underground testing might trigger a massive earthquake. The risk that the island might sink into the sea was considered high enough that the AEC decided to evacuate all unnecessary personnel from the island before triggering the device. What to do? How to protect dozens of people? (So far as I know, no thought was given to the possibility that subsequent gigantic tsunami waves might inundate thousands of miles of coastline throughout the Pacific Rim and kill tens of thousands of people.)

The United States Marine Corps to the rescue. The government dispatched the small aircraft carrier, USS *Princeton*, carrying a detachment of H-46 helicopters from Marine Corps Air Facility, Tustin, California, where just eleven months prior, I had separated from active duty. The plan was to have the Marine helicopters evacuate all unnecessary personnel off the island to the USS *Princeton*, then bring them back after the blast…provided there was an island to return to. I felt the odds were very good that I would know some of the pilots. Sure enough, I knew two of them. One was Captain Dan Smithson, whom I knew from flight school and had roomed and flown with in Vietnam. The other was a major whom I had known as a captain in Primary Flight Training Squadron I, Saufley Field, near Pensacola, Florida in the fall of 1964. Bill Cody had been my ground school instructor for T-34C Mentor engine studies at Saufley, before my first solo flight in November of 1964.

USMC to the rescue...the USS Princeton offshore of Amchitka Island. An H-46 at the airport to ferry folks out to the ship.

Photos taken out the back of my ride to the ship. I was pleased to see an old friend on the flight deck, an H-34.

This detachment of Marines flew the dreaded H-46, the main reason I had opted to get out of the service. This aircraft was, in my opinion, a widow maker. Early on in its career, this machine had some "developmental problems." (Read: they had a bad habit of coming apart in the sky, killing everyone on board, and raining a hail of aluminum bits and body parts all over the countryside!) I suspect that, if I had a direct line to God and could know absolute truth, three hundred Marines died in this machine before its many problems were resolved. Just my opinion.

I surely did not want to ride in an H-46 to or from the *Princeton* but had little choice. I donned a survival suit and prayed for the duration of the five-minute flight to the ship. Made it! The first thing we had to do upon arriving aboard the *Princeton* was to go below decks to receive our room assignments. While filling out various forms, I signed a declaration that I would not bring any alcohol aboard the ship. Too late! I had two bottles of my favorite Scotch, Johnnie Walker Black Label, in my hand-carry. What to do? Nothing. I nonchalantly signed the paper and carried the booze to my room. I had carried booze to my room aboard ship when I was in the service; why should this be any different? I wasn't going to surrender my beloved Johnnie Walker to those navy pukes; they would just drink it themselves. Besides, I brought it aboard to share with my Marine Corps buddies.

Every other time I had ever been on Navy ships, I had been in a "Junior Officer's Bunk Room," which meant anywhere from six to twenty men in a large room crowded with four-tier bunk beds. For this visit, I was assigned my own small private stateroom, and I had—unheard of for a junior Marine Corps officer—my very own porthole. I even had a phone. Vietnam roomie Dan Smithson came to my room, and we really tied one on as we listened to the music of The Temptations, including "I Can't Get Close To You." I know we finished one of the bottles because I remember we put a note in the bottle and threw it out the porthole...my porthole. I think we may have done serious damage to the second because the next morning, about 7:30, when the phone rang, I felt pretty bad.

I had been told that I would be on the ship until after the blast, scheduled for noon. I wasn't allowed to bring my civilian H-19 aboard the *Princeton* for insurance and security reasons, so I was supposed to stand down until after the blast. I felt safe from being called out to fly, so being hung over wouldn't be a factor I'd have to deal with.

October 2, 1969
The Atomic Blast

Someone whose pay grade was much higher than mine decided differently. Perhaps I should be ashore, "Just in case." What if the island *did* sink? Who would be in a better position to rescue folks than me in my large helicopter on floats? I suited up once more in a survival suit and flew back to the island. It was not a pleasant five minutes. Feeling as poorly as I was, I was not sure if I would have cared if the H-46 crashed into the frigid arctic waters.

The actual atomic test was quite anti-climactic. All of us "essential" personnel were hunkered down in a large underground bunker at the command post, twenty miles north of ground zero. Closed-circuit TV at ground zero (GZ) scanned the site so we could watch. What we saw was a little trembling of the picture, and then the screen went blank. A few seconds later, we experienced a mild earthquake. The overhead lights swayed a bit, then stopped. That was it?

An hour later, I was hovering at GZ with the scientists aboard, using Geiger Counters to detect if any radiation had broken the surface. It was only later that I realized how astoundingly dangerous that was—what if the radiation burped up to the surface while I hovered there? We could have gotten a lethal dose in a flash.

The only damage I saw as a result of the blast was that some of the buildings at ground zero were badly shaken, and a small lake on the surface had cracked enough to cause it to drain dry. As far as we could tell with post-test surveys, none of the wildlife on the Amchitka suffered in any way. One of the captive sea otters in the holding pen died, but the scientists attributed the loss to natural causes.

Ground Zero before the blast.

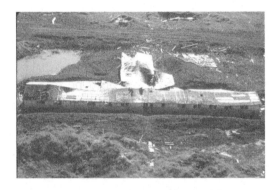

Ground Zero after the blast.

While on Amchitka, I visited our resident paramedic for some minor health complaints. As we talked, he asked what role I played in the atomic test project. When I told him I was the helicopter pilot, he was quite impressed. He asked me, "Just what is it that makes them helicopters work, anyway?" He was a young man with a southern accent, whom I believe was fresh out of the Army and working his first real job. He seemed a bit naïve, so I decided to play him a bit. I replied, "It's the black boxes. All aircraft have black boxes, and that's where the magic happens." Of course, his next question followed, "Well, then, what's in them black boxes?"

I continued, "You know, when I was in the Marines, I often wondered myself what was in the black boxes. One night, when I had squadron duty, I was making my rounds through the maintenance shops. I realized I was there alone. In the electronics shop, I saw a black box sitting on the workbench to be repaired, so I decided to see for myself what was in it. I found a screwdriver, and in no time at all, I had the box opened. You know what I found in there?"

By now, he was spellbound, his eyes wide open in anticipation that he was soon to be privy to a great military secret. I swore him to secrecy by pretending to zip my lips closed. He nodded his head in agreement. I held up my right hand with my thumb and forefinger extended about four inches apart, depicting the size of the secret thing I had discovered, and told him, "I found an itty-bitty witch doctor, sticking teeny-tiny pins into weensy-teensy birds!" He reacted with wide-eyed amazement and the lifting of his eyebrows. Then he realized that he had been had, and we shared a belly laugh.

* * *

After the atomic testing was completed, rumors circulated about the possibility of re-naming Amchitka. Because of the damage done by the atomic testing, the proposed new name was Am-Ka, because the atomic bomb had blown the "chit" out of it.

Finally, it really was time for me to return to California. Once again, adventure beckoned. Brady asked me if I would ferry a Jet Ranger from Anchorage to Ventura. Sure, why not? My sweetie would understand.

Chapter 8
October 13, 1969
Ferry Flight To Ventura, California

Another pilot, Merv Weatherly, and I blasted off in loose formation for California. On our first leg, we flew only as far as Gulkana, our first refueling stop. Full of fuel, Merv's Jet Ranger wouldn't restart. We stayed overnight while the mechanics came from Anchorage and dinked with the engine. The next morning, they still hadn't repaired the 206, so I took off on my own.

A couple of mornings later, I sat in my 206 at Prince George, British Columbia (BC), awaiting the fog to clear so I could depart. I heard Merv call the tower and request clearance to fly by. We joined up again. I learned that at Gulkana, some contamination in his fuel system caused his engine to not start. After the mechanics changed it out, the replacement engine had the very same problem. It, too, had to be replaced.

After Gulkana, I stayed overnight at Watson Lake, Yukon Territory, Prince George, British Columbia, passed through US Customs at Bellingham, Washington Airport, and stayed over in Portland, Oregon, before landing for an overnight visit at my fiancé's parents' ranch on the Pacific Coast.

Merv Weatherly flying south near Prince George, B.C. after I rejoined with him on our ferry trip south together.

When we got into north Oregon, we came to a mountain pass obscured by fog. Merv led us back to a large farmer's field so we could land and wait for the weather to clear. As I approached the farmer's field, I could see a power pole off to my left, at about ten o'clock. In the fog, I couldn't see any wires coming to or from it. I looked off to my right and saw another pole, so I assumed that any wires would be strung from pole to pole. I slowly and gingerly lowered myself down towards the pasture. About twenty feet above the ground, I heard a metallic slap-slap-slapping noise of a wire hitting against the tail of my Jet Ranger. Reflexively, I jumped the 206 up to about eighty feet and executed a hovering 360, looking for the wire I had just hit. I was right about the wire starting at the pole to my ten o'clock, but it ran at a sharp angle to a different pole at my five o'clock. I was most fortunate that the wire didn't engage my tail rotor blades and that it didn't catch on my skids as I jumped abruptly away from it. Either of those events would have brought me down hard.

I had grown accustomed to an occasional close call and rarely had an emotional response to them, but this near-death experience got to me. Shaking, I was glad to take a break until the fog cleared.

Later the next day, after we got through the pass, I separated from Merv again. I was scud running down highway I-5 at Albany, Oregon, when I flew into heavy fog and lost sight of the ground. I slowed way down, went onto my instruments, and started a tight 180 left turn. As I did, I saw the tops of some trees poking up out of the fog. I circled the treetops until my rotor wash blew enough fog away that I could see the cloverleaf intersection that I had just passed. I landed in the center of one of the loops, shut down, and walked across the on-ramp to a gas station and bought myself some coffee to wait for the fog to clear.

When I finally got to the central California coast, I landed on my fiancé's parents' five-hundred-acre ranch right on the coastal bluff, leaving my helicopter in the pasture overnight. The next morning, I took her and her mother for a ride around their property. Sadly, her father was not available. Then I departed for Ventura and returned to her that same evening.

I soon learned that she had not understood my long absences. She had had it and broke it off between us. I was only there for her a few days of our eight-to-nine-month-long "relationship." I understood and felt somewhat relieved. I was free to move about the world. I'm glad I didn't spend a lot of money shipping that tree stump to her parent's home. Remarkably, the number one song of that month was "I Can't Get Close To You" by the Temptations.

* * *

Right after my return to the lower 48 states, I found waiting for me a telegram telling me to call a number in Washington DC "... if I was interested in flying Helicopter in South East Asia." I knew it was Air America, the CIA. I was not interested. I had seen enough death, destruction, carnage, and waste of lives and resources in Vietnam to last several lifetimes. I wanted nothing more to do with the war. I had learned to be a pilot. I loved flying aircraft, and I wanted to be an airline pilot.

But I held on to the telegram...just in case.

* * *

Here is the second major event that aggravated the PTSD that drove me to continually seek the adrenaline rush:

Friendly Fire!
Dong Ha, South Vietnam 25 Sept. 1966, well after dark.

The shrill, irritating ring of the field phone jarred us awake for another perilous night medevac. Much like the previous frightening mission, a seriously wounded Marine needed a ride to the field hospital. We manned our two H-34s, called "Landshark Charlie" to quell the outgoing artillery and flew out towards the hot landing zone.

I was flying copilot for senior Captain Peter Janss. As flight leader, he commanded the flight of four helicopters, our two H-34s and an armed escort of two Huey gunships that trailed behind our two H-34s in loose formation in case we need them to suppress enemy fire while we descended into the hot landing zone. The second H-34, YR-3, with its crew of four and a US Navy corpsman, would descend into the hot landing zone (LZ). We, in the lead helicopter, would not be required to go down into the hot LZ unless No. 2 crashed or was shot down. There was slim chance of that happening because an aggressive, experienced young captain, Phil Ducat, piloted it. I knew his copilot, First Lieutenant Dean Reiter, a friend from Navy flight school. I knew his wife and had partied at their house prior to Vietnam.

As we neared the LZ, we switched radio frequencies to communicate with the grunts. Again, the grunt radio operator breathed heavily over the radio as he exerted himself to avoid the shots we heard in the background. He instructed us to orbit for a while … as they weren't ready for us yet. This was a huge understatement. They were being overrun by enemy troops.

Captain Janss put us into a racetrack pattern at a cozy 4,000 feet, well above the reach of small-arms fire, halfway between the battle and our home base. We monitored the radio, awaiting the call that would reactivate the mission. It seemed things couldn't be safer. I was lulled into complacency by the continuous drone of our loud radial engine as we orbited, "fat, dumb and happy" in the dreary darkness.

Suddenly we flew into violent turbulence which I imagine would be like riding a bicycle off smooth pavement onto the cross ties of a railroad trestle. A split second after the turbulence began, we heard a mighty whooshing, roaring sound like you would hear if you were standing right below that same railroad trestle as a high-speed freight train passed overhead. Before either of us could click the mike and voice the usual," What the fuck, over?" both the noise and turbulence ceased as abruptly as they had begun. They were replaced by an intense, bright glow flooding the cockpit from the left. As I turned my head to see its source, what I saw etched itself indelibly into my memory forever. YR-3 had exploded into an intense, sun-bright fireball right there off our wing, not 200 feet away.

As YR-3 burned, it slowed and lagged behind, plunging from the sky, dripping molten bits as it disintegrated. At 1,000 feet below us, I observed the entire rotor system flicker a farewell as it departed the helicopter and spun off into darkness. Plunging further down into the black abyss, the fireball grew smaller and smaller, became less white hot until it cooled down to yellow, then to a glowing red ember, then winked out, perhaps as it hit the ground. In 10 seconds, the two pilots, two crewmen and the Navy corpsman were incinerated alive!

I triggered the mike and said to Captain Janss, "They shot down our wingman, sir!" Then I had an instant of sheer panic as I realized that if they could shoot down our wingman, they could shoot us down, too. Did the enemy have some new weapon capable of shooting higher than a rifle...a missile perhaps? I didn't want to die a fiery instant death like my squadron mates. I strained against the safety straps that confined me to the cockpit. Had I not been tightly strapped in, I might have tried to jump out of the aircraft.

We scrubbed the rest of the mission and returned to base.

* * *

The cause of this disaster was miscommunication. While we orbited, the Marines were overrun by the enemy, and the battle devolved into hand-to-hand combat. The grunts called artillery right into their own position, an act of absolute desperation on their part. They knew that some of their own would die from the artillery, but if they didn't call for it, they would all die at the hands of the enemy. The emergency artillery request overrode our previous request to Landshark to hold fire. Because we were off frequency, we were not aware of the call. The safe place Captain Janss chose to orbit was directly in the path of the huge 155mm artillery shells. In the lead ship, we had flown right between two salvos of the huge Howitzer rounds. Our wingman was not so lucky.

An incident like this is called, "Friendly fire."

After landing, I went to my tent, but I felt I needed to be alone. I slunk out back by the bunker, unable to talk to anyone about this terrible event I had just witnessed. I looked up into the dark western sky that had just consumed my five comrades and tried to make sense of it all. What happened? Why? Why them? Why them and not me? (Survivor Guilt another symptom of PTSD.) I sunk into a state of emotional numbness and depression. My psyche was in shock. My mind was in shock. My very soul was in shock…again.

I felt doomed. I saw no way to survive this war. I had been in Vietnam only about eight weeks and had come close to a fiery death twice already. I still had 11 months to go to complete my tour. After pondering on life…and death…for a few days, I determined that I would not give up. I would do my job as best I could. I would be vigilant and careful. Maybe, just maybe somehow, I might survive this war. Somehow I did, but not without several more equally hairy events.

* * *

PANIC!

> For decades afterwards, every time I found myself in any situation of stress or confrontation, the choking, mind confusing panic resurfaced. Every disagreement, cross word or confrontation I saw as a threat, danger, real or imagined that I couldn't talk about. I repeatedly ran away from every potential threat.
>
> I never meant this book to be about PTSD, but over 30-plus years, it has evolved into what it is...a helluva adventure story of a young man conflicted, trying to avoid danger of any sort, but repeatedly inviting danger to be his companion.

* * *

In 1969, all the airlines were still furloughing. I had friends in my reserve squadron who were hired and then serially laid off by three major airlines. There were no airline jobs to be had. After several months of being unemployed, I began to think more and more about that telegram. I knew that Air America was the CIA, and hiring on with them meant returning to the war in South East Asia. My best friend Gary had gone with Air America, and we corresponded.

Chapter 9
Late 1969 To June, 1970
I Join the Reserves

I kept in touch with a half-dozen of my former Marine Corps pilot friends who resided in the Bay Area. We were a tight group and visited whenever we could. After returning from Alaska, they kept telling me that I should join the reserve unit at Alameda Naval Air Station (NAS). At first, I was hesitant because I didn't want anything more to do with the Marine Corps. I knew reserves were subject to being called up in times of national emergency, and I did not want to return to Vietnam.

Finally, they convinced me, saying, "It is just a gentleman's flying club. No uniforms, no military duties, and you go to work in your flight suit. If you aren't on the flight schedule, you can go out to breakfast with the guys or back to your room for a nap. It pays pretty well, too." That was hard to resist, and what they said was true. (Naval Air Station Alameda was where, in early 1964, I had been processed into the Marine Corps Aviation Cadet (MARCAD) program, which started me on this incredible 30-plus year journey.)

The monthly weekend drill meetings consisted of attending an All-Pilots Meeting on Saturday morning at 7:30. After that, if on the flight schedule, we would go flying for about two hours. If not on the flight schedule, we'd go out to breakfast, as advertised. Another mandatory meeting at 1:00 determined who would fly the afternoon hops. That second hop counted as another day's work. I got paid for two day's work for flying two short hops. I liked this. I could also volunteer for what we called "AFTPs" (auxiliary flights) during off times. The airlines were still not hiring, and this created enough income to keep me alive during this slow time. I kept thinking about that telegram from DC and continued to correspond with my good friend Gary, who had quit the reserve squadron about the time I joined to go fly with Air America.

Rarely, we would be assigned a real mission to fly in support of a Marine Corps Reserve ground unit on some maneuver or another, but usually, we just flew around and did whatever we wanted. We called it "boring holes in the sky."

We sometimes flew to our homes and aroused our families or friends to come out and wave. I was flying with Captain Larry Gaggero early one Saturday. We buzzed around his house in San Jose, circling about fifteen times at an illegally low altitude until his children came out to wave. His neighbors were not pleased with our low-level nuisance and reported us to the FAA, who in turn called our squadron commanding officer. Gaggero lied, saying that we had only made one circle, and I swore to his fabrication. The Commanding Officer (CO) didn't buy it, and we both were grounded for two months. That lasted about twenty-four hours, as the group commander knew that if the squadron didn't fly enough hours, it would look bad on the monthly report to Wing. We flew again on Sunday, staying well away from Larry's house.

Sometimes we flew down to Monterey, north to Sacramento, or over to Stockton for lunch. Each hop counted as a full day's work. Each return flight counted as another day's work. We weren't allowed to go much further because the H-34s tended to break down, and it was too hard to repair and retrieve a broken-down H-34 much further away than these cities.

Good buddy Alan and I often flew to Mather AFB on the northern outskirts of Sacramento. Our girlfriends would pick us up, and we would have our routine Saturday night out on the town. Sunday morning, our ladies would drive us out to our machines, and we would fly back to Alameda. Great fun!

One Sunday morning, returning to Alameda, the weather was terrible, with low clouds and torrential rain. We had to file and fly in instrument conditions all the way, which included an instrument takeoff into the low-lying clouds. I was a bit apprehensive, as I had let my instrument flying skills deteriorate during my time in Alaska and didn't feel confident doing this, but Alan was the aircraft commander, and I trusted him. We flew about 75 minutes from Mather to Alameda in the soup all the way. We saw the sun once briefly and had one glimpse of the ground during these 75 minutes.

As we neared Alameda, we contacted approach control and began our Ground Controlled Approach (GCA). The radar man guided down through the clouds. He gave us "Missed Approach" instructions that were so convoluted and confusing that I couldn't write them all down on my kneepad fast enough. I was about to call Approach Control and request him to repeat the instructions when Alan instructed, "Just 'Roger' that," confident that we didn't need those missed approach instructions.

I knew that at one point, we crossed low over the Oakland Bay Bridge, but we never saw it. Finally, we broke out of the clouds at about 100 feet above the Alameda airport, landed, and taxied to our parking spot. WHEW! Was I relieved to be on the ground? To the officers' club for lunch.

I was excited to fly a real support mission. I was tasked to fly to Crissy Army Airfield at the north edge of the Presidio bordering San Francisco Bay. At Crissy awaited a cargo of three barrels of diesel fuel in an external load cargo net. The destination of those barrels of fuel was Mile Rock, a tiny landing pad atop a squatty round structure sticking up out of the Pacific Ocean on the south side of the channel, a mile west of the south end of Golden Gate Bridge. This structure was a base for navigation lights to warn ships about the treacherous rocks upon which the beacon sat. Many ships have crashed onto these rocks over the decades since the Spanish first discovered San Francisco Bay in 1776. These lights were powered by a diesel generator down inside the structure, hence the need for fuel.

At Crissy, I hovered while my crew chief connected the cargo net loop to my external load hook. He scrambled back into my machine, and I lifted off, spiraling up to carry the load away. At this time, my wingman, Captain Ken M., was kind enough to remind me that I must not fly over the bridge or the highway with an external load, an FAA rule which I had temporarily forgotten. External loads are famous for accidentally detaching themselves from helicopters and falling to Earth. It might be frowned upon should I drop three drums of fuel onto several lanes of traffic on the Golden Gate Bridge.

I spiraled back down and flew westward underneath the bridge, all the way dangling the net full of drums underneath my H-34. I hadn't made a pinnacle approach since mid 1967 in Vietnam, and I had never carried a heavy external load to the top of a peak. This would be a challenge. I carefully made a textbook approach to the landing pad, staying on a steep path, alert to instantly wave off should I need to. I made sure to stay a bit higher to accommodate for the load hanging twenty feet below me. I gently placed the net full of drums to one side and then landed beside it, on the landing pad, which was barely large enough for me to set my aircraft down. My crewman got out of the machine and removed the drums from the net. It felt good to accomplish this challenging mission.

Author flying past the Golden Gate Bridge in an H-34, 1969.

We returned to Alameda the long way around, flying more than two hours, boring holes in the sky around the Bay Area. I believe we bored enough holes in the sky that we caused the sky to leak, as it rained heavily for the next two days. Over the following years, I would fly under the Golden Gate Bridge many times. I have flown under every bridge in the Bay Area except the Carquinez Bridge connecting Vallejo with Martinez.

One flight we flew over my childhood home in El Verano, a suburb of Sonoma. I saw the picket fence that I started building as a teen, still unfinished and unpainted, awaiting my attention.

* * *

Under President Clinton, the Presidio was closed as an Army base and turned into a business park. The Crissy Army Airfield airstrip has been returned to its original state, a natural estuary of the bay in the middle of a beautiful park.

The Worldwide Adventures of a Helicopter Pilot ... the rest of the story

In 2012, I took a trip under the Golden Gate Bridge in a sailing boat. A good friend and reserve mate, Michael Kennett, died, and I was on the sailboat with his family and friends to bury his cremains at sea. It was strange to be directly under the bridge and see only the roadway, so high and narrow, from beneath and not see the suspension cables holding it up. It made me wonder, "What the heck is keeping this bridge aloft."

Mike Kennett had been a MARCAD like me, only a few weeks ahead of me in flight school. He was Mr. Personality. When he departed the Marine Corps, he had serious intention to be an airline pilot. In those days, if you didn't have a college degree and thousands of hours of multi-engine time, you were considered worthless by the airlines. Kennett refused to buy that. Even though he had minimal fixed-wing time, he had all the proper ratings from Navy flight school. He lived with his parents near San Francisco, the mother home of United Airlines. He found the office of United's chief pilot and made friends with him.

Mike took it as a full-time job to get hired by United. His self-appointed job was sitting, well-groomed in a suit and tie, in the lobby (lobbying!) of the chief pilot's office, making himself available. He stood by for months.

Sure enough, one day, the chief pilot came out to Mike and said, "Mike, can you be in Denver tomorrow? We just had a last-minute cancellation for our next pilot class, and you can have the slot if you want it." Hell, yes, he wanted it. Mike stayed with United for decades and worked his way up to Senior Instructor Pilot.

The most interesting part of Mike's story is that as a young man, he had completed Marine Corps boot camp. A Lance Corporal, he was out in a field somewhere actually digging a ditch when his sergeant said to him, "Kennett, you are a smart kid, and you have two years of college. Why don't you apply for this MARCAD pilot program?" In his flying career, Mike went from digging ditches to being a senior instructor pilot for United. Sadly, Mike got colon cancer and died a few weeks short of what would have been a sweet retirement.

* * *

Another interesting bit about our reserve squadron was that the average enlisted man had much more education than most of the officers. Most of the "snuffies" were in the reserves to avoid the draft; to stay ineligible for the draft they kept going to school. We had several enlisted Marines who had master's degrees, and a couple even had doctorate degrees they had earned while avoiding Vietnam. Many of the officers, like me, had only two years of college or fewer.

Our Commanding Officer, Peter W. Defty, was a true character. He had finished flight school about the time the WW II ended. He was a "flying sergeant," even though he was only a lance corporal, but he never got to fly in combat. Defty stayed in the Marine reserves and eventually made Lieutenant Colonel. When he retired from the reserves about 1970, he got promoted to full bird colonel. At his retirement party, he was pleased that the enlisted personnel of the squadron conspired to promote him to full corporal. He was prouder of that promotion to corporal than he was of becoming a full bird colonel. In real life, Defty was a senior captain with Pan American World Airways.

Sometimes we would fly our H-34s over to Angel Island and make practice mountain landings to the peak atop the highest hill. That changed when a USAF placed a NIKE anti-aircraft missile unit there. The missile launchers took up what had been our practice-landing zone. Drat! Afterward, whenever we flew past Angel Island, we watched as the missiles turned on their swivels to track our movements. The missile operators were probably bored and glad to have something to track. We hoped they knew we were friendlies. Occasionally, we would fly down the coast to peruse a nude beach.

Sometimes our flying around would take us up the Sacramento River to the Carquinez Straight, where we would see dozens of ships left over from World War II parked in nice, neat rows, the "Ghost Fleet." Eventually, most were scrapped. One of the ships was Howard Hughes' *Glomar Explorer*, which had been funded by the CIA in an attempt to salvage the remains of a lost Russian submarine from the deepest waters of the Pacific. We would fly by low and slow and wave to the skeleton crews aboard the ships.

One of the major bennies of the monthly meeting was the officers' club. A different reserve squadron met each weekend of every month, so the officers' club was always a hot spot to party. Young women from all over the Bay Area flocked to the club to drink, dance, and connect with the pilots. We never had to worry about getting too inebriated because our quarters were nearby, and we could always walk home...with a friend if we got lucky.

In 1970, the full-time regular operations officer of our squadron, Captain Ken M., received a phone call from a senior Air Force officer. The Air Force needed two H-34 pilots for some special, secret mission. They gave no details except that the Air Force decided it would be easier and cheaper to hire a couple of Vietnam Marines to fly their H-34s than it would be to train Air Force pilots to fly this model with its piston engine and manual throttle. Captain Ken talked to his good friend, Alan T., about this opportunity to become full-time, active-duty Air Force pilots. Good buddies, they agreed to take the challenge.

They were in the Air Force for only a short while before this mysterious Air Force H-34 project evaporated. Years later, at a reunion in Las Vegas, I asked Alan what he thought the Air Force was up to with the H-34s, but he denies knowing what the mission might have been. My guess, and it is only my guess, is that because the H-34 can carry enough fuel to fly for four hours, the Air Force was going to utilize them for the November 21, 1970 raid on the POW camp at Son Tay, North Vietnam, but something changed, and the H-34s were scrubbed from the mission. One Air Force H-3 was purposely crashed into the POW compound to facilitate an instant insertion of troops and was abandoned there. The raid on Son Tay was a tactical success, however, all the POWs had been removed from the base weeks before the raid took place. (I was working for Air America in Laos at the time of the raid. We Air America pilots were sad to not be part of this mission.)

What was the Air Force going to do with two former Marine Corps helicopter pilots who had zero turbine engine flight experience? Captain Ken was retrained to fly the huge KC-135 tankers that flew out of McClellan Air Force Base near Sacramento and eventually retired from the Air Force Reserve. Alan decided he didn't want to pilot Air Force helicopters, so he used his background as a licensed Airframes and Power Plant mechanic to become a supervisor of aircraft maintenance at Travis AFB. He, too, retired from the USAF. Ken and Alan remain life-long friends and live near each other in Northern California.

Before departing Sacramento, I made the acquaintance of an Air Force captain about my age. Based at Mather AFB just north of our city, David Reed flew twin-engine Convair T-29s full of navigator students on long cross-country flights to practice navigation procedures. One day he asked me, "Bill, we are leaving in two days to fly a group of students for training. We are spending our first night in New Orleans, two nights in Homestead AFB in Florida, and then returning via Las Vegas, then home. Would you like to go along?" Would I? I jumped at the chance.

We had ten navigator students on board. We had a fun time in New Orleans. Details are fuzzy. When we departed New Orleans, we followed a course that would take us almost directly across the Gulf of Mexico to south Florida.

In the back, I slept off my hangover under an unused navigation table. My friend Dave was asleep under an adjoining table. I woke up refreshed and moseyed up to the cockpit. The pilot in command, whom I had only briefly met the day before when we departed Mather, was glad to see me. He needed a bathroom break and he asked me if I would take over. Sure, I said. Later, I glanced into the back and saw that he had replaced me under the worktable that I had just vacated.

After I had adjusted to the command seat of the T-29, I noticed on our chart that we were approaching a radio intersection in the sky. Reaching the intersection, I twisted the little knob on the radio console to change our heading by about 20 degrees to stay on course. Such an intersection transit required a report to Air Traffic Control, so I dialed up the number and made the official report, just like I had done many times in my helicopters.. "Miami Center, Air Force 123 (or similar call sign), Lobster at 46, 10,000, estimating Neptune, 04, Trident next."

After the report, I started talking to the young exchange pilot from Norway in the right seat; I assumed he was another relief pilot brought along for backup. I asked him, "How much flight experience do you have?" This is always the first topic of conversation between pilots. He replied, "Oh, I have about an hour and a half in a Cessna 150. I am one of the navigation students." I was amused that I flew as command pilot in an USAF T-29 for about forty-five minutes. You can bet I wrote that in my logbook as T-29 Pilot in Command time.

In the meantime, I kept corresponding with my best friend, Gary, who had gone with Air America immediately in response to that telegram from DC. After four months in Thailand/Laos, he wrote me, "Bill, this is a really good deal; much better and safer than flying for the Marine Corps in Vietnam, and the pay is much better, too. Come on over." I applied and was hired. Our last bit of correspondence consisted of two one-word letters. I dropped him a note that said, "Inbound." His response was, "ETA?"

June 14, 1970 to December 30, 1972
Air America, Thailand and Laos

I flew for Air America, the air arm of the CIA, from June, 1970 until December 1972. I flew out of Udorn, Thailand, flying H-34s and then Bell 204/205s, working almost entirely in the small country of Laos. While with Air America, I flew some of the very same H-34s that I flew for the Marine Corps.

"Death-defying adventure, big money, world travel, sex, booze, this true tale has it all. Captain Collier teamed up with his best Vietnam helicopter pilot buddy, Gary, and the two rascals shared true adventure enough to make any novel seem lame. Flying combat in mountainous and weather-hostile Laos was some of the most challenging ever experienced by any pilot, any time, any war. Making fabulous money and having airline benefits allowed them to live an exotic lifestyle, to travel the world on their monthly R&Rs and to chase and catch more than a few stewardesses from various airlines."

Chapter 10
1973
Return To Real Life

While passing through Taiwan on my way to Thailand, I bought a book, *How To Make A Million Dollars In Your Spare Time In Real Estate,* by William Nickerson. I knew I would earn some good money in Asia, and I thought I wanted to become a real estate agent/investor upon my return to California. I wanted to wheel and deal with the small fortune I would make in Asia and turn it into a larger fortune. Upon my return to Sacramento in early 1973, I studied for and passed the test for the California Real Estate Agent's license. I went to work for a real estate company in downtown Sacramento; I never made a sale nor got a listing unless I count the small three-bedroom house I bought for myself in south Sacramento.

Chapter 11
Reserves Again

Upon my return from Laos, I slipped right back into my billet with my reserve squadron. While I was gone, the squadron had transitioned from the H-34 to the giant Sikorsky CH-53A, the largest helicopter in the "Free World." I flew to Southern California for two days of ground school to learn about this huge beast. It was much more state-of-the-art than anything I had flown previously, and it was more like flying an airliner than a helicopter. I had flown a couple of hours in it before getting out of the Marines in late 1968, but now I was a qualified co-pilot.

This picture is of a more recent model of the H-53 Super Stallion, part of HMH-362 flying off the coast of Camp Pendleton. (Photo courtesy of former Marine Corps Photographer Dan Moore, Visual Media Group).

Humongous twin turbine engines powered the H-53 driving a huge rotor system made it a heavy lifter. Still, most of our training missions consisted of drilling more holes in the sky. One day, my friend Frank Moore had an H-53 filled with long-range fuel tanks to extend our flying range. We departed Alameda and flew up the coast of California beyond Eureka. From there, we turned east and flew across the Cascade Mountains to the Great Central Valley, followed it south until near Travis Air Force Base in Fairfield, then returned directly to Alameda. We flew more than four hours nonstop, burning more than 1,300 gallons of jet fuel.

I flew with Major Ansley Horton one day on a real mission. We were tasked to fly up to the Mare Island Navy base and work with some government scientists. They rigged a heavy load on a cable and had us hover at about two hundred feet to let the weight slide down the cable into the muck of the tidal salt flats near where the Napa River empties into San Pablo Bay. We repeated this exercise dozens of times, accruing six hours of flight time, almost all of it in a hover. We made a quick turn-around to Alameda for fuel twice, expending a total of 1,800 gallons of fuel. No one ever told us what the experiment was about, but we surmised it must have something to do with anchoring submarines to the bottom of the sea.

This was during the first of the two great fuel crises when auto fuel became scarce. People could only fill up their cars on odd or even days, depending on the last digit of the license plate on their cars. Some months I had to scrounge enough gasoline to drive myself to reserve meetings. Once I got to base, I could strap on an H-53 and go burn three hundred gallons of jet fuel every hour drilling holes in the sky. Getting home was no problem because the gas station on base had no alternating-day restrictions.

Our 53As were equipped with radar altimeters that had an "altitude hold" feature to help pilots hold a constant altitude. This was a good tool for flying over water, especially at night or in bad weather. One day my good friend Tom Sullivan and I were flying up the center of San Francisco Bay, we decided to test this new gizmo. We set the altitude for five hundred feet and headed directly for two small islands called "The Brothers." When we flew over the island, the H-53 jumped abruptly, almost violently up to compensate for the perceived loss of altitude, so quickly that it frightened us a bit. On this same flight, we decided to break the squadron rule against flying above two hundred knots. We put the aircraft into a mild dive at full speed and exceeded the speed limitation. Just because we could.

Flight out to the Farallon Islands

Thirty miles outside the Golden Gate is a group of islands, the Farallons. Named by the early Spanish explorers, the name means "pillar" or "sea stack." These islands are also sometimes called "The Devil's Teeth" because many a ship has run aground on them in the coastal fog that is common at all times. The islands belong to the City of San Francisco and hold a research station for the US Fish and Wildlife Service, which maintains a small population of people on the southernmost island to study a myriad of sea birds nesting there. The islands are closed to the public and have a no-fly restriction around them.

I flew out there and landed on the largest island legally. There was some kind of emergency, the researchers needed a lift right away, and we were available. We made it a point to approach slowly to give the many birds a chance to see us, hear us, and get out of our way. We landed amid a huge cloud of seagulls, terns, and other birds too numerous to count but didn't hit a single one with our rotors. Our mission completed, we proceeded to bore more holes in the sky on the way back to Alameda.

We took our summer camp at the Marine Corps Air Facility Base in Tustin, California. The base is sometimes referred to as LTA (Lighter Than Air) because during WWII, its two huge wooden hangars housed dirigibles. The hangars still exist even though the base has been closed for decades. Our duties were to support a Marine grunt operation out at Twenty Nine Palms USMC desert base. Every evening, we made sure that there was always something wrong with our helicopter that needed maintenance, requiring our return to Tustin, so we wouldn't have to stay overnight out in the hot, dusty desert. I got stuck as squadron duty officer for one night and had to stay over that night, the only night I ever spent at "29 Stumps."

One late afternoon, we passed by Palm Springs on our way back to LTA. The pilot I was flying with knew that in the hills above Palm Springs, Bob Hope had built a huge multi-million-dollar, 29,000-square-foot house overlooking the valley. Unfortunately, just before the house was completed, it burned to the ground. We flew over and surveyed the charred wreckage.

We were a rowdy bunch. We flew during the day and drank hard at the club at night. There were always young ladies hanging around the bar looking for love. One night, in the Officer's Club returning from Twenty Nine Stumps, I picked up one of the lonely ladies and took her over to the barracks right next door. These barracks were called "splinterville" because they were left over from World War II, and even though they were well beyond their demolition date, they still stood. When I got to the door of my room with my new friend, I tried and tried to get the key to open the door, but somehow, the key just wouldn't fit into the old lock. Frustrated, I stepped back and gave the door a mighty kick. When the door flew open, I realized that it wasn't my room. Much to my surprise, it was my commanding officer's room and he was not alone. Our CO was in the midst of enjoying the company of a young lady he had just met at the bar. Needless is to say, he was a bit surprised that I kicked in his door. The next day, all he said to me was, "You know, Bill, you really oughta not kick open your commanding officer's door when he is in the middle of a blow job." He was cool.

That bit of violence scared my date away.

Chapter 12
1974-1975
Calicopters
Stockton, California

After earning my California Real Estate License, I barely had a start in the Sacramento real estate business when I received a phone call from a fellow named Ric Eccles. He ran a small helicopter company, Calicopters, out of Stockton Airport, about fifty miles south of Sacramento, and he asked me if I was available to fly for his small company. He needed someone to fly an Alouette III (AL III) the French-built machine, on a US Forest Service (USFS) contract. I couldn't resist; the lure of adventure was too strong. I immediately went to work for him, flying primarily the Alouette III, with a few hours flying Bell 47s.

The US Forest Service contract was at peppermint Helicopter Attack Base, (Helitack) located in the Sequoia National Forest, west of, and sitting at an elevation of 7,200 feet above the small town of Porterville, California.

I had to have 100 hours of experience in that machine before I would qualify to fly on the Forest Service contract, so Eccles put me to work doing whatever to build the required flight hours. The USFS also required that I attend Aerospatiale Company training in Grand Prairie, Texas, near Dallas. In Grand Prairie I had three or four days of classes and a few hours of instruction in the AL III. The instructor instilled in me a lot of confidence in the abilities of the AL III. On one flight he told me to nose over violently. That terrified me because I knew that in a Huey, to push over abruptly could snap the rotor mast, and the rotor-less machine would then fall out of the sky like a greased brick. The AL III had no such limitation.

(Google "Alouette III" to see videos on YouTube of them starting and flying.)

The French have a different philosophy than US helicopter builders. Because their primary mission of the AL III was to fly rescues around the Alps, they installed a powerful engine that allowed them to fly at high altitudes, so the main limit in an AL III is the torque on the transmission. Another feature I loved about the AL III is its built-in circular calculator around the altimeter. All I had to do was twist the outside bezel until the pipper was at my altitude, then the torque gauge indicated what my torque limit was, no guessing. Humidity and temperature were not factors of concern. I never came near over torquing the AL III, even when I later flew to the top of Mount Whitney or when I externally lifted 800-pound propane tanks to lookouts at 10,000 feet of elevation.

Another adaptation for me was that the French built AL III's blades turned in the opposite direction of all US-built machines. Because of that, the tail rotor control pedals worked opposite from what I was accustomed to. On my first take off in the AL III after returning to Stockton, I anticipated the torque and pressed in some mild left pedal, as usual. As soon as I broke ground, the helicopter made a violent ninety-degree left turn. After that cheap lesson, I only inputted tail rotor pressure as needed.

The office staff at Aerospatiale had a cute girl assistant with an outrageous personality, helping to orient the guys to the area. One day she pulled up her skirt and exposed her panties. Printed on them was the note, "What you see is what you get." I did not check further into that message. While I was there the Aerospatiale Company divorced from the Chance-Vought Aircraft Company. I witnessed aviation history as a big cyclone fence gate rolled closed, signifying the end of that business relationship forever.

While I was in Texas training, Eccles had gone to the local bar and injured his knee in a vigorous bout of Indian wrestling with another patron. When I returned, he had a cast on his left knee. He was the main crop duster pilot for the company, and he was out of commission, so he wanted me to learn to spray and dust. He took me out to a nearby field and introduced me to crop dusting turns under less than perfect conditions.

Because of his injury, he couldn't use his left leg. He had our mechanic create a stirrup for the right rudder pedal, so he used his right foot to both push and pull. In pain, taking pain pills and flying the Bell H-47 with one foot, he showed me the wild and crazy pedal turns that crop dusters do while spraying and dusting. I was petrified! I eventually did some of this kind of work, but very little, more slowly and less efficiently than Eccles.

January 23, 1974
My First Precision Lift Job

One of the first things I did was lift a huge air conditioner to the top of a local post office. I didn't know the new machine very well yet, and it seemed to me that the huge box, an eight-foot cube, would be too heavy for me to lift with the relatively small helicopter. When I balked a bit, Eccles didn't hesitate to put my mind at ease. At my request, our mechanic, Bob Johnson, removed the battery from the machine after my start. He even removed both lightweight doors from the helicopter to give me more peace of mind. It gave me an enormous feeling of accomplishment when I easily lifted that air conditioner to the top of the post office without using anywhere near maximum power. Workers on the rooftop grabbed ropes that trailed from the box and guided it right down onto its anchoring bolts as I slowly and gently lowered it. All there was left for them to do was put nuts on the bolts and connect the plumbing.

I had done thousands of external loads in Vietnam and Laos and three most challenging heavy lifts while flying for Air America, but this first high-precision lift was a real confidence builder for me.

Frost Control

In the great Central Valley of California, agriculture is king. One of the main crops susceptible to frost damage during bud development is almonds. In the past, old tires or smudge pots were burned all night to warm up the air. These methods are no longer used because of environmental considerations. Helicopters are now used to protect the almond buds. They fly low and slow over the trees, blowing warm inversion air down over the fragile almond buds to protect them.

Usually, the growers will contract with the helicopter operators in advance, ensuring the helicopter will be available. The large growers and the helicopter operators watch the weather closely during the four to six weeks of springtime when the threat of frost is highest. The growers place recording thermometers throughout their large commercial orchards. On cold nights, the foreman of a particular orchard drives continuously from station to station all night checking the thermometers. When the temperature starts to dip towards freezing, the helicopters launch.

Sometimes, I was able to standby at my home in Sacramento, two hours away. Thanks to advances in weather forecasting, we always got several hours, if not a whole day, warning before a hard frost. When called upon, I would then drive to the company office at the Stockton Airport and continue to wait there. I would pre-flight my helicopter and be ready to launch on short notice. Then it was just wait, and wait, and wait some more for the call, which often did not come.

Sometimes the helicopters were pre-positioned in the orchard; having been left from the previous call out. This was the slow season for helicopter flying, so the helicopters weren't needed anywhere else for weeks on end. In this case, I would drive to the orchard near Snelling, California, and standby there. This was a good filler job for the helicopter and crews because it gave a little income for the operators and pilots during the time of the year when nothing else much was happening.

Some clever person calculated how many acres a helicopter could protect. The weight of each machine determined how much air it displaced while flying, and therefore how much warming air it could blow down on the almond trees, and each machine was assigned a particular section of orchard proportional to its weight. Usually we had a chance to drive around our section in the daylight, to get a feel for its size and shape, and to see the location of any potential hazards like power lines. Smudge pots, roads, and other landmarks were used to delineate sections.

Flying around above the orchard in the dark air, I could actually feel the difference between the freezing air at my feet and the warmer inversion air around my head as I cruised slowly at a speed just above translational lift (thirteen knots). The first time out, I didn't know this, and I didn't wear warm socks. My feet were freezing before the night was over. It was possible to snack on small finger foods to help stay awake, but with the constant turning and flying at such a low altitude, it was impossible to drink coffee. I would grab a quick cup of coffee whenever I refueled, which happened only on the longest nights.

I would fly down a five-tree wide row to the next smudge pot marker, turn 180-degrees to pick up the next five rows. I flew back and forth, back and forth over my section of the orchard, until it was covered. The warmer air blown down would take about forty-five minutes to dissipate. At that point, it was time to go back to the beginning point and start the circuit again.

Frequently we launched just before dawn when the air reached its coldest. Only one time I launched just after midnight and flew until half an hour after sunrise. These were the hardest nights, simply because after hours of droning along over the same treetops again and again, with no change in the dark scenery to stimulate me, fatigue and boredom set in. The hardest part for me was simply staying awake. I flew with the aircraft heater off so that I wouldn't get drowsy.

Once in a while, one of us flying low and slow over the orchards would blow over a tree. The first time each one of us did that, we went to the foreman and apologized for flying too slow or too low or whatever it was that caused us to kill his tree. The farmer assured us, "You are helping to cull the weak and dying trees from the herd." The average pilot might get called out four or five times in a frost season and fly only one or two of those nights. We just sat around in the barn office with the mechanics drinking coffee and swapping lies all night.

The Hershey Company owned several large orchards to grow the almonds for Hershey candy bars. The name of the ranch where we worked was called "L.D. Properties." When we asked what the "L.D." stood for, the ranch manager told us: "Loss Deductible." The almond orchards and the frost chasing helicopters were a tax-deductible business expense.

Another very unique use of the helicopters I learned from Eccles was using the crop spraying capabilities of helicopters to spray whitewash on the glass of greenhouses. It was perhaps not so neat as a hand-applied application, but it was many times faster, easier and cheaper. Eccles had done this in the area of Fremont, where there were once thousands of greenhouses. I never did this.

To build more AL III hours, I spent some time in the field spreading synthetic ammonia fertilizer and seeds of wheat and oats in the farmland east of Stockton. The system that Eccles used was simple but most practical. A large funnel-like spreader bucket attached to the cargo hook on the bottom of my Alouette. The bottom of the bucket was strapped to a pallet with a small lawn-mower engine ("putt-putt") fixed to it. The little engine ran full time and drove a belt that turned a small impeller just below the outlet of the bucket. My way of controlling the release of the synthetic fertilizer, which looked a lot like small, white plastic BBs, was to toggle a switch on the control stick. That would open and close the valve in the bottom of the bucket, feeding the material into the impeller, starting or stopping the spreading of whatever material we were spreading.

I would fly patterns across a field until my bucket was empty, then return to the rig for a second bucket. Each bucket was in turn filled while I emptied the other, so it was a continuous process. I used the same technique for spreading wheat seeds on a farmer's field. On my first attempt, I failed to take into account a strong crosswind, so I spread a lot of seeds on the adjoining road. This particular farmer was fairly mellow and didn't seem to care. He spent his days driving his tractor back and forth over his fields, with a big jug of red wine next to him to fight off the cold and boredom of his job.

I flew the H-13s for a few hours and did little crop dusting and spraying with it. I had an aversion to spreading chemicals. The last major thing I did before leaving the Marine Corps was take the US Army's month-long class on Nuclear, Biological, and Chemical (NBC) Warfare in Fort McClellan in Anniston, Alabama. I was, and believe I still am, a certified expert on NBC Warfare. I didn't like spraying chemicals and being exposed to them. I am sure that most, probably all of them, are harmful to our health in the long run. (Re: Agent Orange.)

At one point, Eccles was flying the AL III, using it to spread fungicide on almond trees at L.D. Properties. Adverse to the chemicals, I alone among the crew decided to use a protective dust mask. Soon all the rest of the crew decided they must have masks, too, which cost Calicopters a bit of money. The boss was not pleased with me that I had started the trend. Too bad; I felt safer.

While we were spreading the fungicide on the almonds, a new crew member was an older, recently retired USAF lieutenant colonel. His job was to load the hopper with the fungicide mixture and watch Eccles, who would give him the signal to stop filling when the hopper in the rear passenger seat area neared full. Somehow the colonel failed to see Eccles signal and over-filled the tank, bursting it open at its forward, top seam. The noxious fluid spewed up to the ceiling of the aircraft, then splashed forward into the cockpit, covering Eccles and the entire instrument panel with the yellow, chalky mixture. Fortunately, it didn't do any obvious harm to Eccles or the machine. The colonel was fired right away.

February 27, 1974
Surveying the Geothermal Fields

In the hills of northern Sonoma County, overlapping into Lake County, lies an active geothermal field. From Santa Rosa on crisp, clear winter days, one can see steam from the fumaroles in the hills. Energy companies decided to explore these geothermal wells as a commercial source of energy production. The highest is Mount St. Helena, (not to be confused with Mount Saint Helens in Washington State). I met up with a group of the energy company officials at Santa Rosa Airport and flew them around the area so they could get an overview of what might be done to exploit the natural steam energy. This was one of the initial aerial surveys of the area. A few years later, I would be working out of Santa Rosa Airport carrying surveyors up to this area so they could establish the location for each plant.

One of my job requirements was obtaining a California Crop Dusters Apprentice license. Eccles gave me a few old books to study. I was less than excited about crop dusting and spraying. Reluctantly, I drove to Sacramento to the state agriculture department office to take the crop duster apprentice exam. I had not studied the material very hard and didn't care if I passed. I hurried indifferently through the 175 true-false questions. When I handed it to the woman behind the desk for grading, she looked at me and said, "So, you really want to be a crop duster?" I lied and said yes. She glanced at my exam and placed it in her inbox, and said, "Okay, you passed," not grading my exam. I walked out with my apprentice's license.

March 3, 1974

Some entrepreneurial person came up with the idea of pollinating cherry trees to improve the crop. Somebody in the small farming community of Linden actually climbed ladders and used a fine paintbrush to collect pollen from cherry blossoms. After he had collected an ounce or two of pollen, it was mixed with a few cups of wheat flour to give it some bulk so it could be handled. A small hopper in the center of the Bell 47 floor dispersed the pollen mixture out the bottom of the helicopter as I flew over the cherry treetops. That was a challenge for me in that I didn't have a lot of Bell H-47 time and trying to control the manual throttle while doing crop dusting turns at treetop level was challenging. A time or two, I feared I might crash into the cherry trees

March 30, 1974
TURLOCK TIMES, Turlock, California

I have rewritten the script from the article because it is hard to read the aged news clipping:

LOCAL AIR LIFT

"An International Paper Co. sign points the way as a Stockton-based helicopter prepares to lift a scrap collector-ventilator into place on top of the local paper company's roof. Plant officials hired pilot Bill Collier and the Calicopter crew after figuring the distance to be traveled as well as the weight to be lifted. The sheet metal construction, weighing a total of 3,000 lbs., was manufactured by Bainbridge International Paper Co. employees were evacuated from the building before the lift."

The reporter who took this picture immediately left the scene, missing a much more exciting story. This routine lift job immediately turned into an exercise in survival.

The job was simple enough. Pick four bulky but light metal pieces from the parking lot next to the building and place them on the roof. The first piece was a large iron frame (visible in the picture), which would be the base for the rest of the pieces. I lifted that piece into place without breaking a sweat. The second piece was a large funnel, which I picked up and placed perfectly down into the center of the square frame. The third and fourth pieces were the dome-shaped top to the large conical hopper and the top frame to hold it all together.

After placing the funnel, I flew back across the edge of the building to start the third lift. This blustery January 30 day, the wind was gusting strongly, so it did not alarm me that the AL III rocked a bit and the nose of the helicopter jerked a few degrees off to one side. *Just a gust of wind bouncing off the edge of the building.* After I had moved about 100 feet more to the right, as I hovered for the third lift, the Alouette made violent attitude changes. The nose swung quickly about thirty degrees to the left, and the helicopter rocked about twenty degrees from level. As quickly as it happened, the situation reversed itself, jerking the nose back to center. With this second violent maneuver, I knew something was drastically amiss. The second jerk was so violent, I felt that should there be a third, the helicopter would start to self-destruct. Perhaps the tail would come off, leaving me drastically out of balance, without directional control. I didn't want to be in a machine that was coming apart in the sky. It was time for me to take emergency action.

I knew I had to get the machine on the ground as soon as possible. My first impulse was to slide forward and make a rolling landing in the plowed field right ahead of me. But then I thought better of that. I feared the wheels would sink into the soft dirt and trip the machine into rolling over. I chose to cut the engine and settle straight down from about thirty feet.

Here is where, in my opinion, I encountered a major flaw in the engineering of the controls of the AL III. In order to cut the engine, I had to let go of the collective, reach down to the floor and pull the throttle lever backward. This maneuver cost me a second or two of having my left hand on the collective lever. In every other helicopter I have ever flown, the throttle is on the collective, right in the pilot's palm at all times. A simple twist of the wrist can reduce throttle instantly. Having to remove my hand from the throttle and reach down delayed my pulling in full collective pitch to soften my inevitable impact with the ground. By the time I got my hand back up to the collective, the helicopter was preparing for yet a third violent torque change. The RPM had deteriorated to the point that I could count the blades as they circled overhead. Because of the lower RPM, my hydraulic pump stopped working and I no longer had hydraulic boost to help wrestle the controls. When I pulled up on the collective to cushion the impact, the control was stiff and almost un-moveable.

I was aware that sometimes, when an Alouette III lands hard, the rotor blades can flex down through the cockpit, decapitating the pilot, a not uncommon occurrence with Hueys in Vietnam. In addition to pulling up on the collective, I simultaneously was attempting to duck my head forward to avoid losing it. I also knew that if I impacted the ground too hard, my chest could be impaled on the cyclic (control stick). That could be painful or even fatal, too. SPLAT! CRUNCH!

I impacted into the ground with a good rate of descent. Fortunately, I didn't smack into the ground hard enough to lose my head to the blades or get punctured by the cyclic. I had contorted myself to avoid both potential disasters and walked away with just a slightly strained back. My landing was less than perfectly level; the Alouette rocked backward, and the tail rotor blades struck the parking lot pavement. But I was alive and intact.

We figured out the reason for this incident. Our mechanic, after checking the oil level, failed to replace the cap tightly on the engine oil reservoir. In the early morning dark before departing Stockton, while doing my pre-flight inspection, I didn't see that the oil reservoir cap was loose. During my flight to Turlock, enough oil blew out of the reservoir to deprive the hydraulic engine governor of oil.

The hydraulic boost system worked off the same oil reservoir as the engine. A standpipe in the reservoir, denied oil to the boost system should the oil get below a certain level in order to protect the engine from oil starvation. The engine governor being intermittently deprived of oil caused the torque swings. With no governor, the rotor system lost rpm causing the swings because of a loss of torque to the system. A slug of oil would get into the system, causing the engine governor to try and regain normal RPM. This is what caused the massive torque corrections and subsequent violent swings. At the Aerospatiale school for the AL III, no one had talked about these particular features.

April 3-4, 1974
Measuring The Snowpack

Calicopters had a standing contract with the City and County of San Francisco to transport surveyors to measure the snowpack in the California Sierra Mountains. The city contracted with two Norwegians, Don Paulson and Lee Dahlin of the small town of Columbia, California, to measure the snowpack in late spring, when the snow depth was at its maximum, before spring run-off began. Snow was their environment. To these guys, this was an occasion to party because, during the next two to four days, they were going to earn a substantial amount of money for their efforts. They treated me to dinner at one of the best restaurants in the area and plied me with liquor. Too much liquor, I am afraid. After dinner, they insisted that I sit up with them and drink coffee until about two in the morning, even though we had scheduled an early morning take-off. After a while, I was not only a half-drunk, but a wide-awake half drunk. Finally, I was able to retire to the guest room. Mrs. Paulson then came into the bedroom after I had gone to bed and offered to bring me more coffee. I declined her offer. I'd already had way too much coffee. I barely slept before the two Norwegians called me out of bed the next morning to go fly the survey. I hauled the men, their snowshoes, a few supplies, and a little equipment, including minimal survival gear.

The way these men measured the snowpack was quite ingenious. They carried a long, segmented aluminum pipe about two-and-a-half-inches in diameter, which would screw together to a total length of about 30 feet. Whenever we landed in one of their pre-determined measuring points, they screwed the pipe together and forced it vertically down into the accumulated snow until they struck dirt. Pulling it up, they measured how many inches of snow was in the pipe and weighed the pipe. Over many years of doing these measurements at the same places and the same time each year, the city was able to compile statistics that gave it a pretty good idea of how much water was retained in the snowpack. We measured snow at places called Dodge Ridge and Early Intake near Yosemite. Some of the places were as high as 8,300 feet.

The scenery and cold mountain air were absolutely breathtaking. The weather could not have been more perfect, with bright sun illuminating the bright sky-blue heavens. If you have not seen the blue sky from a higher altitude, you have not really seen a *blue* sky. Pristine Alpine meadows of glistening snow surrounded by stands of tall coniferous trees and snow-covered granite mountains with majestic rock outcroppings as far as I could see pleased my eyes.

At one measuring point sat a small cabin. Don told me that several cabins had been built years before, especially for the survey crews who had done the surveying on foot for years prior to the use of helicopters. In those early days, they hiked miles in snowshoes over the snow from trailheads, and it took them two weeks to do the job. In case the weather turned bad, the crew could hole up in one of the cabins until the weather cleared. I felt more secure knowing that if the weather turned to worms, we had a secure place to hole up—provided, of course, that the bears stayed in hibernation. More than once, Don told me, bears had broken into a cabin and trashed it, eating all the emergency food supplies.

My Alouette III was on snowshoes. I had never flown on snowshoes before, but it was not a challenge. I learned in Alaska that it was wise to bring in just a little power, and then wiggle the nose of the aircraft left and right, to break it loose from the snow, in case the shoes, skids, or skis had frozen to the ground. A lift-off with one ski frozen to the ground can result in a rollover-type crash. I also learned in Alaska how to take off and land in blowing snow. Taking off and landing had to be planned a little more carefully than usual because blowing snow could easily cause a pilot to lose sight of the landing area around the helicopter. On lift-off, it is necessary to keep moving so that you can fly out of the cloud of your own making. It is very much like an instrument take-off (ITO) we practiced in flight school during instrument training. Failure to do these things could result in impacting trees or hills or getting vertigo and rolling over to either side.

April 9, 1974
First Long Line Experience

My first longline experience was before I ever even heard the phrase "long-line," and it was nearly a disaster.

"**Hawthorne Nevada Airlines Flight 708** was a domestic non-scheduled passenger flight between Hawthorne Industrial Airport, Nevada (HTH) and Hollywood- Burbank Airport, California (BUR/KBUR), that crashed into the tallest mountain in the contiguous United States, Mount Whitney, near Lone Pine, on February 18, 1969, killing all 35 passengers and crew on board.

"The aircraft, a Douglas DC-3, was operating on a visual flight rules plan. It departed at 3:50 A.M. PST and last contact was made at 4:06 A.M. when the flight spoke with the Tonopah Flight Service Station. One hour later, at 5:10 A.M., the plane hit a sheer cliff face on the east side of Mount Whitney at 11,770 feet. The main body of the wreckage then slid down the cliff and stopped some 500 feet (152 m) back from the cliff, where it caught fire. All 32 passengers and all three crew members were killed." Wikipedia.

Calicopters got the insurance contract to remove the debris. All the victims' bodies were removed years before. Contrary to the report above, the wreck was on the east side of the Owens Valley, and it didn't hit Mount Whitney. As the airplane hit hard and exploded into thousands of small pieces, much of the scattering debris bounced past the top of the peak and fell into the next ravine. Ground crew gathered up all the bits and pieces of the aircraft, put them into bags, which they then put into cargo nets. I then slung these full nets to the desert floor. Some of the bigger pieces I lifted individually, but there were few of these; only one piece was bigger than a Volkswagen. The heaviest piece left was one of the 1500 pound, nine-cylinder radial engines, that bounced over the peak and rolled down into a narrow ravine.

Because of the narrowness of the ravine, the engine was inaccessible by the normal short external cable. Bob Johnson asked me if I thought I could do this pick with a 100-foot line. I told him I thought I could. I also thought, *One thing to my advantage is that this aircraft has already crashed, it will not do any great harm if I have to drop this engine.* I flew up the draw and hovered 100 feet above Bob, who used a portable radio to talk me down to the load. In this case, my external mirror was absolutely worthless. I had to take all my directions from Bob. After giving me a few "Left, right, down, back," directions, he was able to grab the end of the dangling cable and connect it to the load. He jumped clear of the load, and radioed me: "Go ahead, Bill."

I had never done a load with such a long line before, and I got a bit over-eager. I didn't yet know that I should hover up gently and let the weight of the load center me over it before I lifted the engine. I pulled in power, and in one smooth motion, lifted the heavy piece of junk into the air, just like I had always done with the thousands of short-line external loads in the past.

Because it was off-center, both longitudinally and laterally. It began to swing uncomfortably, and I felt I had a tiger by the tail; or, rather, it had me. I had to guess which control maneuver to input. I inherently knew somehow that I had to get into harmonious synchronization with the oscillations of the load, but I didn't know where the load was, I couldn't see it, and I didn't know which control motion to make. It seemed every control input I made was wrong and exacerbated the situation.

With each oscillation, the swing became more violent than the last. The load was not only causing my helicopter to sway out of balanced flight but was dragging me down towards the desert floor, too. I was extremely uncomfortable and I began to feel fear. I knew that within a short time, I was going to have to drop the load or crash. But I also knew that if I could hold on for one more oscillation, when I dropped the engine, it would, with just a little luck, fall onto the flat part of the desert floor, where the salvage crew would be able to pick it up with their truck. I didn't want to have to repeat this terrifying experience.

I held my breath until I felt that the broken engine was at the extreme of its forward swing. It was pulling the AL III into a high nose-up attitude that no amount of forward stick would correct. With the centrifugal force added to the already too-heavy weight, my rate of descent was increasing alarmingly. I was only 300 feet above the ground and descending rapidly. I had to jettison the load soon. I knew that the centrifugal pull on the belly hook had to be exceeding the structural limits of the hook. To rip the hook off the helicopter would be much more embarrassing than dropping the load. Not to mention possible safety ramifications of ripping structural bits off my aircraft during flight.

With great relief, I punched the button and jettisoned the load. As I had hoped, it fell about twenty feet past the fence, onto the flats, and buried itself well into the desert sand, accessible by truck. Whew! I was glad to be done with that one.

I always found it a little spooky lifting out the wreckage of another aircraft. You wonder how it happened, how the craft splattered as it did. What did the pilot do—or not do—that caused his violent and instant demise. I don't tend to be superstitious, and I am not particularly religious, but at times thoughts of ghosts and spirits hanging around the wreck, trying to communicate frustrations of unfinished worldly business or perhaps vengeful resentments for lives cut too short, came to mind.

* * *

Rick Eccles, like Peter Defty, was completing US Navy flight school when WWII ended. He, too, was greatly disappointed that he never got to fly combat, but he immediately joined a Navy reserve squadron at Stockton Airport. When the Korean War broke out, his commanding officer, without consulting any one member, immediately volunteered his entire reserve squadron to go to that war. They all unanimously agreed to go.

While flying an McDonnell F2H Banshee off an aircraft carrier near Korea, Eccles got a "cold cat shot." The catapult that was supposed to hurl him off the end of the ship to flying speed failed as he rolled forward, and he splashed into the frigid sea east of Korea. As he was being hoisted up into the rescue helicopter, he said to himself, "You know, I believe there is a future in these things." After Korea he returned to California and started his little company, Calicopters, and he did very well for himself. At one time, he had several aircraft all over the world on various contracts, but by the time I worked for him, he had only two Bell 47s and the Alouette III.

* * *

A Lift Job Goes Lousy

One day I was simply moving a ventilator from point A to point B on the top of a paper factory near downtown Stockton. It was to be a single, routine lift, and the weight was supposed to be well within the limits of the AL III. It was scheduled for early in the morning to complete the lift before the workers would occupy the factory beneath me. FAA rules are that no one can be in a building when a helicopter is lifting things to the top of it.

I got to the airport early and did my pre-flight. While doing so, I noticed that my convex mirror was gone. Mechanic Bob had taken it off for some reason. Confidently I told myself, *I don't need it...Bob will be there to guide me with hand signals.* I started up and flew over to the factory, only about two miles away. Sure enough, as advertised, there was Bob on the factory roof. I circled around, made an easy slow approach to the unit, hovered, and Bob hooked it up. This was going to be an easy thing; I only had to lift the machine and reposition it to a new location about thirty feet away.

I pulled the cable tight and pulled in power. Strange; I pulled in full power, but the unit didn't seem to go anywhere. I looked at Bob, and he was still giving me the "UP" signal...continue he was saying. I couldn't. I didn't have enough power. I checked the computer encircling my torque gauge and made sure I had set it correctly. I pulled power again, and with no better results. The unit was obviously heavier than everyone thought.

I backed off on the power and allowed the unit to settle back down on the roof. I thought I had not moved it at all, but the unit had come off its base enough for it to pivot on one corner, so it was balanced but not quite lifting off the platform. Because I didn't have my mirror attached to the helicopter, I couldn't see what was going on underneath me.

Then Bob realized what was going on, and he signaled me to let the unit down. I saw his signal, reduced the power, and I felt the unit settle back down on its pad. That is what I felt, but what I didn't realize was that the heavy unit had pivoted enough that its center of gravity was beyond the edge of the platform. Without even looking at Bob, I tripped the release button, releasing the load and flew away.

As I did, I saw a serious scowl on Bob's face and watched him shaking his head. What had I done? The ventilator unit tumbled off its platform and punctured the roof of the factory. Fortunately, it didn't pass through the roof and fall into the factory. A few hours later, with my mirror attached so that I could see what was happening underneath me and lower on fuel, I properly placed the ventilator in its new position. A little roof patching corrected my mistake.

May 4, 1974
To Mojave To Fly Two H-34s

Eccles got a call from someone who had procured two US Army H-34s, and he needed someone to fly each one and evaluate it. Word was out that I was an H-34 expert, so Eccles, my new wife, Michele, mechanic Johnson, and I flew to Tehachapi Municipal

Airport in a rented Cessna 182. There we met a fellow who was short, had a patch over one eye, and had an uncanny resemblance to Moshe Dayan, the Israeli military leader and politician. For this bit, I will just call the man "Moshe."

Moshe had procured the two H-34s from an Army reserve unit in Arkansas and wanted to trade one of them to someone who would convert the other one to a twin-turbine S-58T in exchange. The story about how he became the owner of these two H-34s is one of legend.

Sometime in his past, he had bought into a partnership with another person, and together for only $5,000, they bought a surplus WW II Marine Corps Hellcat. After they had owned it for a while, the other owner died, leaving his half to Moshe. Moshe then again sold half to another fellow for $2,500. That person then disappeared out of his life somehow, and Moshe then owned the entire P-40 all to himself, with no money in it.

A Lieutenant Colonel of Marines who was shopping for the Marine Corps Aviation Museum approached Moshe. The colonel knew that Moshe's particular Hellcat had some significance to Marine Corps history, and the colonel wanted that particular aircraft. The colonel asked Moshe, "What do you want for your Hellcat?" After giving it some thought, he said, "An H-34." "Done," said the colonel.

The colonel directed Moshe to go to a particular Army reserve squadron somewhere in Arkansas and, "Just pick one off the line." So, Moshe goes to the base and walks up and down the line, eyeballing which H-34 he would like to own. Then he has an idea. He phones the colonel at Quantico and says, "Hey, Colonel, how about you give me *two* H-34s for my Hellcat?" Without hesitation, the colonel agreed; he wanted that Hellcat.

Moshe returns to the flight line, once again looking over the H-34s, when an officer in the reserve squadron approaches the smallish older man in civilian clothes with the patch over his eye and asks, "Who are you, and what are you doing here?" Moshe simply hands the officer the business card of the Marine colonel in Quantico. The officer calls the colonel, comes back, and says, "Which two H-34s do you want?

Moshe had no idea which ones to choose; someone said that perhaps he might look at the logbooks. After evaluating the logbooks, Moshe chose two H-34s that had minimal hours on their airframes. Then there was the problem, how was Moshe going to get these aircraft out west to Tehachapi? Once again, the colonel helped. He arranged for two pilots from the reserve squadron to fly the two helicopters to Tehachapi. Moshe had only to pay for the fuel.

At Moshe's request, I took each of the H-34s out onto the Mohave airport and flew them both for a total of half an hour. Both were in perfect condition. On-lookers were amazed when I did full touchdown autorotations with each aircraft. No sweat for me; I had done hundreds of autorotations in H-34s. At Air America in Thailand, every check ride and route check included full-down autos. In my logbook, I recorded only the side number of one of the H-34s, US Army number 64333.

I have reason to believe one of these H-34s may have been the one converted by Winnebago Industries into a flying camper for the RV convention in 1977. It was on the cover of the September 1977 Popular Mechanics magazine. I believe I flew that one later in life after it had been reconverted to standard configuration.

Camper H-34 on floats

About this time, I was spreading ammonia nitrate fertilizer over a field near the small town of Linden, just north of Stockton. As my circuits took me past a small crop-dusting airport, I observed a small crop-dusting airplane making practice landings and circuits from that airport. We passed close enough to wave to each other. I found out later that the pilot was my good friend Gary. I knew he was in the area, and he even stayed over with us for a few days. He was my great buddy, fellow Marine Corps pilot, Vietnam roommate, fellow Air America pilot, travel buddy, and all-time best friend. Sadly, he had only months left to live.

May 7, 1974
Another Challenging Lift Job

East of Reno, Nevada, a new power plant was under construction. Materials for construction were lifted up to the top of it by a small, portable crane which crawled itself up the walls that it had just built. This was a clever idea, and it worked well, but there naturally had to be a limit to the construction, at which time the small crane had to somehow be retrieved from the top of the tower. They couldn't just push it over the edge. That is where I came in.

I flew to the site and looked at the 160-foot tall chimney. It didn't look so tall from the ground. I climbed up the inside ladder to the top to see what the job looked like from there. On the top of the tower, looking down was a frightening experience. Don't ever let a pilot tell you he is not afraid of heights; most pilots are as afraid of heights as anyone else. It is just that when we are sitting in the cockpit, strapped in and our hands on the controls, with our fate in our own hands, we don't feel that apprehension because we feel we have control.

The little crane had been broken down into three pieces, each of which weighed less than eight hundred pounds. According to the nifty calculator built into the altimeter of the Alouette, I would have plenty of power to make this lift, even though we were well above sea level.

I climbed back down to the Alouette III, cranked it up, and flew to the top of the tower, where mechanic Bob awaited and he hooked me up to one piece of the crane. This was once again before I had learned visual reference, so I was doing this with my mirror. (At least I had the mirror this time.) With nothing nearby to give me any good ground reference, I had difficulty holding a solid, stable hover. The owner of the crane had said that he wasn't too concerned about whether the crane arrived on the ground in good repair, "I just want it down." I took this as license to drop the load if I felt I had to. Of course, if I felt I had to, I would drop the load anyway, regardless of what he might have desired.

Alouette III at Nevada power plant lift job.

I pulled in power and picked the largest piece of the crane off the tower. Once I was away from the tower, the piece slid under the helicopter and flew comfortably, just like any other external load I had ever hauled. I flew down and placed the piece gently onto the ground and returned to quickly complete the remaining two lifts. Job complete. No sweat.

June 1, 1974

Eccles hired another pilot, Lee Lemke, primarily to fly the Bell H-47s on spraying and dusting jobs. One day Lee was spraying noxious weeds alongside Highway I-580 east of Livermore, when his engine quit. He did a superb job of planting the little machine in the only available tiny spot on a steep hillside, barely big enough for him to set down, and it sloped at about thirty degrees. I lifted the disabled H-47 from the hillside and placed it on a waiting trailer.

June 3, 1974

I rescued an injured hiker from hills east of Stockton and flew her to the hospital.

June 15, 1974
Power Poles, Power Plays

I flew the AL III to Huntington Lake to set some power poles. Eccles had briefed me on how to set poles, "Lift up slowly until the pole is vertical and the line is tight. Then lift straight up to bring the pole off the ground." (He should have told me that before the engine lift!) Mike Eccles, the boss's nephew, rode in the back and directed me. We picked up a pole from a rack of them. Nephew Mike in the back then directed me for the approach to the hole, where linemen awaited each pole. As soon as they could reach one, they pushed it into the hole as I slowly lowered it. The terrain here was steep, and it must have been a challenge for these workers just to stay on the hillside, much less dig a ten-foot-deep hole into the hillside. We set twenty 55-foot-long poles over two days at an altitude of 6,600 feet.

Mike worked with his uncle to become a crop duster. His uncle instructed him until he was able to get his commercial and crop-dusting licenses and then allowed him to fly to build up his experience level. It was an unspoken agreement between them that Mike would work for Eccles once he got his certificates. At least that was what Eccles thought. As soon as Mike got his license, he branched out on his own in direct competition with his uncle and even hired Eccles' primary spray/dust pilot to work for him. What a rotten nephew he was.

Daydreams, Nightmares

While flying through the sky, I always tried to be very observant of things around, above, and below me. At times, when the sun was right, I could see my shadow beneath me, following along in perfect formation with my aircraft. I loved watching it match my speed, flitting along at zero altitude, seemingly flying through solid obstacles with the greatest of ease. Nothing was an impediment to my shadow…not tall trees, buildings, wires, rocky outcroppings…nothing. A few times, I was alerted to the presence of another aircraft in my part of the sky when I saw another shadow near mine. For certain one time, and almost for certain a second time, observing the shadows helped me avoid a mid-air collision.

One fine spring morning, Eccles asked me to play tour guide for a group of four people. They were Norwegians, the parents and an uncle and aunt of his beautiful Nordic wife, visiting from "the old country." I loaded up the two older couples and departed westerly towards downtown Stockton, to show them our city before flying east into the Gold Country, Sierra Nevada foothills.

As I leveled off from my climb out, I caught the motion of my shadow below, to my left. I watched it for a few seconds, sliding effortlessly over every obstacle in its path like a spirit. Then I noticed another shadow on the ground. This second shadow, coming from my left, about ten o'clock was on a perfect collision course with my shadow. My head swiveled quickly as I looked to the left, where I would expect to see the conflicting traffic headed my way if it were on my level. I saw nothing. "Must be up higher than me," I thought, and relaxed a bit.

I continued to scan, looking up, but saw nothing. I looked down at the shadow and checked low, mentally creating a line from the shadow to the sun behind me to see if I could spot the approaching aircraft lower than me; nothing there either. Now the shadow was getting quite close to my shadow, still on a perfect collision course. I again looked frantically to my left, but still saw nothing. I quickly decided that if something was approaching me at my altitude, I better make an avoidance maneuver NOW.

I rolled into a hard left bank, just in time to see the bottom of a Cessna 172 making a hard left bank to avoid me! The little airplane passed so close that I heard the sound of its engine as he veered abruptly away. I am sure that if I had not turned into him, we would have collided. All five of us in my Alouette, plus all occupants in the small airplane would have perished. The people in the back sent out a chorus of oooh's and aaah's as I banked abruptly, but I doubt they saw the Cessna. I kept my cool and flew the folks out to and around the foothills.

I gave them the two-dollar tour of the Gold Country. The best part was when I found a small valley that was carpeted golden with the blooms of zillions of California Poppies. The four Norwegians loved it. I hovered down to about five feet from the ground to give them a cow's eye view of the beauty. Departing the field, I had to make another slight left turn to avoid a small hillock, and with the banking of the helicopter, the folks in the back oooh'd and aaah'd again as I came to a rather high angle of bank. They had their cheap thrills for the day, and so had I.

Eccles never mentioned anything about the near mid-air incident, and I never mentioned it to him. I never knew if his wife's folks ever realized how close they came to death that fine spring morning. A few years later, flying a Hughes 500-C for another company, I had a very similar incident, only this time, I used what I had learned from my previous experience. I turned into the shadow bogie a little sooner and had more time to react. This time we missed each other by two hundred feet from what had been a perfect collision course. Who says it doesn't pay to daydream a little now and then?

A midair collision is every pilot's nightmare. I always made it a point to be quite aware of where I was, to keep my head swiveling and my eyes constantly searching for air traffic. I did have several mid-air collisions when I was a young teenager. When I was about 14-years old, I built a plastic model of a B-17. My cousin built a B-24. We found that if we tied strings to them, we could make them fly by swinging them around in a circle. We got bored with that and decided to swing them into each other, creating midair collisions. After each crash, we glued them back together and did it again. Then we got bored with that, so we soaked them with lighter fluid and set them ablaze before running them into each other. That was the end of them.

Chapter 13
May, 1974
Peppermint Helitack Base
Sequoia National Forest

In preparation for the Forestry contract, I was required to be certified under FAA Part 135 for the Forest Service. Eccles set up an appointment with me to fly with the local FAA examiner. We had a nice flight around the airport. I showed him I could fly the Alouette, and I shot a couple of autorotations. It was all quite casual. He signed me off without any grilling about FAA regulations. He just wanted to make sure I could operate the machine safely.

I also had a check out in a Piper Cherokee PA-32 Arrow, so I could fly myself home while on breaks. I liked that small, low-winged airplane. Most of my fixed-wing flying experience was in the Beechcraft T-34C Mentor and the North American T-28 Trojan in Navy flight school. I landed a T-28C on the USS *Lexington* on September 7, 1965, in the Gulf of Mexico, to qualify as a Naval Aviator. To me, the Arrow was a miniature version of the T-28. I don't like high-wing aircraft. I am tall and have a long back. When I sit in a Cessna or similar aircraft, my head is up between the wing roots, and I can't see a thing.

"The three best things in life are: A good landing, a good orgasm, and a good bowel movement. The night carrier landing is one of the few opportunities in life where you get to experience all three at the same time."

Ready room sign, USS *Enterprise*, Gulf of Tonkin, 1969.

Once I arrived at the Peppermint Helitack Base at 7,200 feet, I had to have yet another checkout with forestry check pilot Harold Dickey. We departed Peppermint and flew around the mountain peaks. I shot landings at the Needles Point Lookout helipad at about 8,200 feet in altitude and Jordan Peak Lookout helipad at 9,200 feet. Visibility was CAVU (Ceiling and Visibility Unlimited); the scenery was spectacular.

My very first fire was named the "Lloyd Meadow Fire." The siren wailed; we filled the AL III with the helitack crew and jumped off the mountain towards the fire, about ten miles southeast. I was a wee bit nervous, this being my first fire, and I wanted to do it right. We arrived at the fire, a small brush fire burning in the high desert scrub. There was plenty of room to land nearby, and I deposited the crew. They went to work fighting the fire; I went back to base for more firefighters. I never had a bit of nervousness or doubt in my ability to do this job after that first landing in the high desert.

The Peppermint Forestry Base Helitack Crew in full battle regalia. Author's photo.

Someone asked me once, "How do you find the fire?" "Well," I replied, "Dispatch gives us the general location of the fire, we head in that direction, and from there, we follow the smoke signals."

Bambi Bucket Work

One of the most fun aspects of forestry flying is dropping water with the Bambi Bucket. This is a lightweight, portable, collapsible plasticized canvas bucket that can be unfolded and attached to the belly hook in a flash. The pilot has a switch that actuates, through either compressed air or hydraulics, a trap door in the bottom of the bucket, and he can open or close the door in a half-second. This is what you usually see when the evening news broadcasts "film at eleven" of a helicopter dropping water on forest fires.

Once the bucket is hooked up, the helicopter is hovered up carefully until the bucket hangs directly below, centered and stable. Once this is accomplished, the bucket will fly rather nicely along but at reduced speed. Then the fun begins.

Contrary to Hollywood depictions, pilots of firefighting aircraft do not get right down into the heart of a forest fire and, with Pulaskis in their teeth, engage in hand-to-hand combat with the flames.

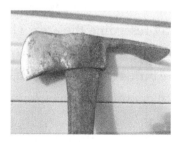

Pulaski: A fire-fighting tool that is an axe on one side and a hoe on the other. Named after Ed Pulaski the firefighter who invented it. This one is quite worn.

Helicopter water drops are primarily used to douse smoldering debris left behind after a fire has passed over an area and to put out hot spots where embers have blown away from the main fire and kindle a secondary fire. A secondary fire reflects poorly on the management skills of the fire boss.

The pilot flies to where there is a pond, lake, or slow-moving stream. He carefully slows down and descends until the open bucket sinks into the water, filling it. Lifting the bucket from the water closes the trap door and has now captured anywhere from 250 to 800 gallons of water, depending on the capabilities of the machine and the size of the bucket. The pilot then gets to play bomber pilot.

Pilot technique comes into play here, as it depends on what effect is needed from the water. All the water can be dropped on one spot to saturate a single smoldering hot spot, or the pilot can fly at varying speeds to spread the water over larger areas. Altitude also is a factor. If a pilot really wants to drench something, he drops low, and the water cascades onto the target. Dropping the water from a higher altitude will cause the water to separate into finer and finer droplets as it falls more rain-like.

The huge fixed-wing tanker-bombers fill their tanks with a slurry of water mixed with fire retardant and grass seeds. When they drop on a fire, they are also instantly reseeding the area. The pilots of these huge fixed-wing aircraft drop the retardant in strips well ahead of the fire so that when the fire burns its way to the strip of retardant, the fire stops or slows down enough that the ground crews can then attack it.

When I wasn't flying on a fire, I did things like take external load supplies to the lookouts. I remember slinging a load of personal belongings to Julie, the lookout lady at Mule Peak. She admonished me to be careful with her load as it included her sewing machine, and she didn't want it dropped. Her husband was a local ranger, and every night after a hard day's work, he had to climb about 300 steep steps to the lookout to be home with her.

When we began to prepare for this gig, we phoned the local real estate agent and tried to rent something for the summer. Too late; there was nothing available. I really wasn't looking forward to commuting ninety minutes each way up and down the hill every day. Ranger Sherman had the solution. He owned a small travel trailer and rented it to the company. There were RV pads right next to the helipad. Our temporary home was fewer than 100 feet from my helicopter. There was no long mountainous commute for us, and we got free electricity, water, and propane from the USFS. More than once, when things were slow, we closed the door and exercised our "honeymoon rites" during work hours.

June 28, 1974
Another Near Mid Air-Collision

A huge fire began burning the grassy hills just east of Bakersfield. We dispatched and went to work on the fire. After dropping some firefighters near the fire, I pulled up and almost ran into a small civilian airplane. There was a no-fly order in the area for civilian aircraft, and this guy nearly killed us all by violating it. He knew he was in the wrong and took off in a southerly direction, trying to make good his escape. He failed because my helicopter could fly faster than his little puddle jumper. We flew right up beside him and got his side number and reported him to the proper channels. We never got any feedback, but I hope he at least got a letter of reprimand from the FAA.

At sundown, at the end of a hard day's fire-fighting, we landed in the base of operations and bedded down for the night. Someone handed me a disposable paper forest service sleeping bag, and I prepared to sack out on the ground with the troops. I liked that; it made me feel connected to them. Some higher-up forest service person decided that it was improper for a pilot to sleep out on the ground, out in the open. This pilot must have a motel room. We drove about ninety minutes before I was able to get to a motel room. Then, in the morning, I had to get up about 4:30 to make the return drive to the camp so I could begin flying again at first light. I was more tired from lack of sleep than I would have been had I slept on the ground.

We flew into Bakersfield Airport for fuel. As we crossed the neighborhoods east of the "Oklahoma City West," someone pointed out Merle Haggard's house. He knew it was Haggard's house because there was a huge, colorful tile guitar inlaid on the bottom of the famous country western music star's swimming pool.

The last weekend of June, it was time for me to go to Alameda for my monthly reserve drill. I flew the AL III down to Porterville, and the boss traded aircraft with me. He took the Alouette back up to Peppermint, and I flew the Arrow right onto Alameda Naval Air Station.

June 30, 1974

Departing the NAS on Sunday afternoon, fog required me to call for a "Special Visual Flight Rules" departure. As I departed east, the weather just got foggier and foggier. I did not want to scud run further into the east Bay Area. Clear of Alameda tower, I said to my wife, "Heck with this," pulled back on the stick and blasted up through the one-hundred-foot thick overcast and popped up into the clear, bright air above the clouds. That was illegal, I knew it, but I was happy to get above the fog and have unlimited visibility. We flew home to Stockton for the night, took care of the few errands that needed our attention, then flew the Arrow back to Porterville Monday morning before showtime.

July, 1974

I carried a medevac to the hospital in Porterville. Then I carried an external load of supplies to Baker Point Lookout at 10,000 feet. Another medevac: a camper managed somehow to shoot himself, so I carried him down to the hospital in Porterville. One fellow was arrested nearby by the park rangers when he showed up at the local store bragging about the three mountain lions he had just heroically shot...three cougar kittens.

One hot summer night, we had a big lightning burst. Ranger Sherman showed me a computer printout, a satellite download of the hundreds of lightning strikes that had just that night occurred in our vicinity. These kept us busy for a few days. I happened to look at the top of the hill west of our base and saw smoke coming from the top of a tall pine tree. I asked the ranger if they had that fire in their system. He said no, and we immediately pounced on it, putting it out. Because I spotted it, they named the fire in my honor, the "Collier" fire. In most cases, the way the firefighters kept lightning struck trees from creating a bigger fire is by simply cutting down the tree, and then hacking the top of the tree to bits, spraying a fine mist over every spark or ember with what they call a "Piss Pump," a backpack rig that gave them the ability to spray a fine mist to put out the slightest ember. Sometimes a crew of two or three firefighters would spend several days putting out one of these smoldering treetops.

Another time I was resupplying the Pinnacles Lookout when I spotted smoke about five miles to the north. I asked the Pinnacles Lookout, Lauren, if he had that fire in his system. He did not. That fire became quite a big project for a few days, what we called a "campaign" fire. We were the home base for several crews fighting this fire. The Peppermint crew needed all the help they could get to provide food for all the firefighters that came from other areas, so Ranger Sherman asked my wife if she would like to work in the camp kitchen to help prepare the food. After two days of getting up at 4:30 a.m. to work for minimum wage, she just decided to not go to work anymore; the pittance she earned was not worth it. Weeks later, she received a nice paycheck. Even though she had not gone to work after the second day, the ranger had kept her on the payroll, and she got paid for two whole weeks of work. We talked to the ranger and tried to return the pay, but he said it didn't matter; "It's all a part of doing business."

Early July, I got a call from my reserve squadron. They needed someone to take a ninety-minute flight. I explained that I was eight hours away and had no relief pilot. I was getting low on flight time at my reserve squadron, but I knew as soon as the season was over, I would be working nearly full time at the squadron, and I hoped that by the end of the year, I would be the high-time pilot for the squadron.

Chapter 14
July 17, 1974
Atop Mount Whitney
The $4K Flush

Three forestry fellows from outside our station arrived for a ride to the top of Mount Whitney. This was exciting because I knew it would be challenging to land in the rarified air at that altitude. Mark Johnson, the helitack chief, and I calculated the weight and balance, fuel required, and off we went.

The top of Mount Whitney is 14,497 feet above sea level. The Alouette was a good machine but couldn't take four people to the top, with the equipment the fellows brought along, plus the fuel required to get back home, plus reserve. It was a warm day, making the air even thinner. I had never landed higher than about 10,000 feet.

We first flew to a beautiful grassy field called Trout Meadow at 10,000 feet. This was a pristine alpine meadow surrounded on three sides by steep cliffs with a perfectly crystal-clear stream running through it. I could see trout dashing about in the water as I flew over. We would stage out of here and break the load for the peak into two parts. We put out the biggest two of the forestry guys and most of the equipment they had brought along. Mark, the helitack foreman, and I then flew up to the top of the peak with a single passenger. The Alouette climbed pretty well at first, but as we gained altitude, the air became thinner as the rate of climb diminished.

The top of Mount Whitney is about a third of an acre, not quite flat, but strewn with lots of rubble and boulders. I circled a couple of times to reconnoiter a landing site. I was careful coming over the edge of the cliff to make sure I didn't get caught in any updrafts or downdrafts. I picked a spot and landed with adequate power to hover in ground effect. I had to be very careful to avoid landing on any loose rubble which might make the aircraft slide around, and I also didn't want to land on any big rocks that might damage the bottom of the helicopter. Getting a maintenance crew and spare parts to the top of Mount Whitney could prove to be a challenge.

I dropped off the first passenger, returned to Trout Meadow, picked up the other two, and transported them and their gear to the top. I shut down the AL III to wait...and watch.

On top was a small stone structure about twelve by fifteen feet. Originally built by the government to shelter equipment for cosmic ray studies, it was no longer used for scientific uses. It became a shelter for people in case of bad weather. Outside the door of the building, under the eaves, I found a shelf with a registry book in a hinged metal box for people to sign in. I looked in the book and saw that people from all over the world had signed their names and made comments. The hike to the top of Mount Whitney is not really a bad hike. The trail is fairly easy and well used. It is the altitude that gives people problems because at that altitude, it is easy to suffer anoxia, the lack of oxygen to the tissues. Many people had written in their comments. Examples were: "Joe Jones, from Needles California, six hours from Trout Meadow," and "May Smith, LA, 18 hours from trailhead at Someplace Falls." People had signed in from several foreign countries. I couldn't help myself; I had to sign in: "Bill Collier, Stockton, CA, 10 minutes from Trout Meadow by helicopter."

In the meantime, the forestry people were preparing to accomplish their mission. Most hikers camped out overnight once they got to the top. Over many years, people had been simply doing their businesses all over the place, and the top of the mountain had become one big stinky mess. The forest service had solved that problem by building a two-hole outhouse, no roof, enclosed by stone walls, looking like something you would expect to see in a *National Geographic* special about Afghanistan. The two-holer had indeed solved the problem of people pooping all over the top of the mountain, but it had created a new problem. All the human excrement was deposited into two regular-sized fifty-five-gallon garbage cans, which eventually filled up. These "toilets" needed to be flushed.

The three forestry fellows dragged the full cans of shit out from under the crapper seats and placed them about fifty feet away from the edge of the northeast side of the mountain...a sheer cliff straight down for about 3,000 feet. The forestry fellows then tied a long length of rope to one of the shit-cans and a second rope to the third forestry guy. The two remaining fellows each grabbed a safety rope while the third fellow carefully edged a full shit-can to the edge and dumped fifty-five gallons of raw human excrement over the cliff, then repeated the procedure with the second can. They slid the empty cans back under the outhouse seats, and our mission was accomplished. Because of the fuel burned off during the two earlier round trips from Trout Meadow, I was light enough to lift off with all four people and all the equipment. I returned directly to Peppermint in time to refuel and be on call for the rest of the day.

I often have wondered what it would have been like if there had been some mountain climber coming up that sheer cliff...fortunately, rock climbing did not become popular until years later. Can you imagine…a rock climber getting pummeled by 110 gallons of shit? "Whatever I said or did Lord, I am sorry, I didn't mean it! Please forgive me!"

Counting the three hours of helicopter time at $457 per hour, the labor of the four forestry persons involved, and the administrative work necessary for this mission, I would not be surprised to learn that this double "flush" cost the taxpayers in excess of $4,000.

Chapter 15
July 27, 1974
FAA Pioneer

It came time for my reserve squadron deployment to summer camp at the Naval Air Station Fallon near Reno, Nevada. Eccles showed up with a Cessna 172 and said I could fly it to the meeting. I could only attend for the weekend, but I needed to go. Arriving at Fallon, I did not compensate for the hotter, thinner air at the higher altitude, and I pranged the airplane rather hard. *Oh, well.* Nothing broke off the Cessna, so I locked it up and went to my squadron area.

When I arrived, I was told some dreadful news. One of our H-53As had crashed the day before, July 26th, with no survivors. Fortunately, the machine that crashed had only the crew aboard and no other personnel. It easily could have had twenty or thirty passengers as we deployed the entire squadron for summer camp. It seems that the H-53 had been flying for several hours, hot refueling on stop-overs, which made it impossible to inspect the rotor system between legs. Part of one of the rotor blades departed the rotor system. The ensuing drastic imbalance caused the helicopter to instantaneously rip apart, rotor blades chopping the huge hulk to bits as it tumbled down out of the sky onto a grassy hillside beside and partly onto Interstate 80 just north of Vallejo, California.

I am sure that the entire crew died instantly as the terrific violence of the rotor tearing itself from the fuselage probably snapped their necks. Killed in this crash were our squadron executive officer, Major "Buzz" Sawyer, and copilot Captain Gary McClasky. Gary was roomies with my brother in the house I bought in Sacramento. His instantaneous, violent death hit close to home. At least one of our squadron pilots quit reserves because of this mishap.

The rest of the squadron had been flying sorties between Alameda and Fallon to bring squadron equipment and supplies to summer camp and were grounded elsewhere. As the senior officer present at Fallon, I became the acting squadron commander. I had a most competent group of senior NCOs, so I really didn't have to do much, and I didn't have to make any command decisions except to "continue the march." After a couple of days, one of the majors showed up to take command of the squadron. I headed back to Porterville and my forestry contract.

Departing, I discovered that someone had broken into my locked Cessna on the Navy base in plain sight of the control tower, and they did a sloppy job of duct-taping the door shut…but why would they even bother to tape it shut again? A quick inspection showed nothing missing nor any damage. Puzzled, I pressed on.

Hours later, at Peppermint, mulling over this, I realized why my Cessna had been broken into. Upon my arrival at Fallon, my hard landing must have activated the Emergency Locator Transponder (ELT), which automatically activates a rescue beacon when an airplane crashes to lead rescuers to the crash scene. I surmised that the Fallon tower heard the crash beacon on their radio and tracked it down to my Cessna. Base personnel broke into my plane to turn it off. Because it was not uncommon for the ELT to activate erroneously, the FAA soon promulgated a directory that every pilot should tune in the frequency of his or her ELT upon shutdown to make sure he or she had not activated his own. Can I say I was a pioneer and that I helped create a new FAA directive?

Chapter 16
Peppermint Soup

It was while at Peppermint that I perfected a recipe that has been one of my favorites. I call it "Peppermint Soup." It is not named for its ingredients but for the place. I know this soup has many other names, and this recipe has been "invented" by many other people spontaneously. A friend, self-proclaimed "World's Greatest Helicopter Pilot," Andy Campbell, invented this on his own, and he calls it, "Stuff."

About once a week, my wife, Michele, would travel down the mountain to buy groceries. She would usually be gone most of the day and get home about suppertime. It became my duty to cook supper those Fridays. My simple solution was to simply dump all leftovers from the fridge into the pot and simmer it all together for a few hours. I liked to throw in a few jalapeno peppers. Not a lot of talent involved, but it was the beginning of my culinary efforts, which have gotten much better over the years.

My wife occasionally complained a bit that she was the one that had to drive the pickup ninety minutes down the mountain and back up, while it took me only fifteen minutes to fly the Alouette the same distance. One day we were driving up the hill together, and we came across a highway sign that said, "Elevation 5,000 feet." I teased her, "I don't know why you complain so much about driving up this hill, Peppermint base is only a little more than a mile" (7,200').

Fire Choppers

IT'S COSTLY - and taxpayers foot the bill when careless visitors cause forest fires in the Kern Valley. In this case, it took manpower and a good deal of equipment to squelch a fire across from Camp 3 north of Kernville Thursday and Friday. These two helicopters cost about $349. per hour each to operate. Common sense and caution in preventing such fires is far more economical and safer. This fire, which destroyed about 45 acres, was caused by the illegal use of fireworks. SUN Photo

Article from Kern County SUN

August 2, 1974

A Mr. Ralph Smith came to Peppermint before duty hours. He had pre-arranged for me to haul two full helicopter loads of food and supplies out to his isolated cabin. His family owned an entire square mile in the middle of the National Forest; the property had been in his family for decades and was grandfathered in for them to retain ownership. His extended family was riding horses out to their cabin for a week. When I finished, he gave me a twenty dollar tip, the only tip I ever received in my entire flying career.

One day, we were dispatched north to a small section of the Sequoia National Forest that is separated from the rest of it. Flying north, I saw, off to the east, a large fire burning vigorously. I asked the helitack foreman why we weren't fighting that fire. "Oh, that fire is in the National Park. It will burn itself out naturally." That gave me cause for thought. Fires have been burning for millions of years in forests, yet forests still thrive. Could it be that, in her innate wisdom, mother nature knows that fires don't need to be extinguished but should be allowed to burn? That question has been debated by the forest service for decades and still persists today. The big problem is mankind. People insist on building homes and towns in the forest. When a fire gets going, it is up to the firemen to save the structures and the people.

August 26, 1974
Another Life Saved

A teenage boy was stung multiple times by yellow jackets, putting him in danger of anaphylactic shock. I rushed him to the hospital at the China Lake Naval Air Weapons Station about forty miles to the southeast. Another life saved. I liked this part. In Vietnam, I carried approximately six hundred wounded, dead, or dying Marines to field hospitals.

We acquired a puppy dog, a German Shepherd-Border Collie mixed mutt. Pasha loved to ride in the AL III. Instead of having her ride in the truck with my wife and get motion sickness, she would ride down the hill with me in the AL III. All I had to do was open the door and command, "Get in the truck," and she would hop in and place her paws on the front lower bubble window and look out at the view. On start-up, the AL III made a horrific howling noise. Pasha would raise her head and howl along with the engine until the start was complete.

We took the AL III to a place called Pinehurst for a needed bit of engine maintenance which required mechanic Johnson to stick a long probe into the engine and scrape carbon build-up off some inner part of the engine. Bob made a mistake, twisted the brittle tool too hard and broke it off inside the engine. We were hard down; the engine was not damaged, but the piece of the tool had to be removed. We were out of service for a few days until that work was completed.

I noticed where the machine was parked for repairs that there were lots of scrap metal and other bits of junk on the ground. This is called FOD because Foreign Object Damage will ruin an engine and damage rotor blades. A small herd of children had gathered and were enthralled by my Alouette, so I said to them, "Hey guys, you like my helicopter?" "Yes," they responded enthusiastically. I asked them if they would like to help me keep the helicopter safe and make some money doing it. They were all ears.

I showed them a few of the nails, bottle caps, and other objects I found on the ground, near the aircraft. I explained what FOD is, and told them, "I will give you a penny each for every bit of FOD you pick up from the area around the helipad. I'll back in about three days and pay you." They were excited about that. Upon my return, I was amused by how much FOD they had collected. They must have stolen every nut and bolt and screw and nail from their father's workshops. I paid them $10. for all the FOD they collected.

After returning from my August reserve meeting, I continued a task that Eccles had begun in my absence, carrying the remainder of a truckload of plywood sheets to Jordan Peak lookout, so forest service could enclose the tower's frame. I knew that I wouldn't be able to go very fast with such a flat load, as it would begin to fly around uncontrollably at any speed higher than an air taxi. I made several loads, flying quite slowly for more than two miles with each load. It was challenging to stay slow enough so that the plywood bundles wouldn't fly out of control, carried either vertically or horizontally. Eccles had lost control of a load the previous day and dropped it into the woods, never to be seen again.

Hauling external loads of plywood...a challenging feat. Author's picture.

September 1, 1974
Ping, ping, ping

Nearly the last relief period of the season, it was getting dark by the time we could make the crew change. At Porterville airport, I pre-flighted the sweet maroon and white Cherokee Six and pulled off the ramp into a dirt area to do my run-up. I heard what I thought was the engine make a few beats of a most extraordinary pinging sound. Ping! Ping! Ting! After about three beats, it stopped. I did another run-up and listened again. I heard nothing new and checked all my instruments; all seemed okay. It didn't occur to me to get out and inspect the aircraft in the dark. We proceeded home without incident, only to find out the next day that the pinging sound I heard was my prop cutting up a strand of barbed wire that was sticking up out of the dirt where I did my run-up. There was quite a bit of damage to the propeller of the Cherokee Six.

I shudder to think what might have happened if there had been enough damage to the propeller that a piece of it had separated under power in flight, especially on takeoff. The imbalance would have instantly shaken the engine right off its mounts, and it might have departed the airplane entirely, leaving us without any semblance of aerodynamic balance. Oh, well, lesson re-learned: pay attention to wayward sounds, something we helicopter pilots are usually very good about.

The owner of the airplane was not happy with the damage and refused to rent to us again. Consequently, for the next relief period, the boss showed up in a Cessna 182. I had never flown a 182 before, but I had time in the 152 and 172. *Heck, just go for it.* We flew home in the dark and I had my wife read the landing checklist. I took a long, slow approach, giving myself plenty of room, landing midfield on Stockton's longest runway. No incidents this time, except Pasha vomited on the back floor as we touched down.

October 11, 1974
I Save a Heritage Sequoia Tree

During one of the lightning storms over the previous summer, lightning struck the top of a giant Sequoia tree near our base. At its 200 foot-high blasted-off top it was still seven feet in diameter; at its base, it was about twenty-three feet in diameter. When lightning struck the tree top, it started a small, smoldering fire which, over winter, burned down through the center of the tree and then burned a hole out at the bottom, creating in effect a giant chimney. The winter's rain and snow had not been enough to put out the fire. Every time a bit of wind blew, the wind drew sparks out of the chimney-tree and spewed them all across the surrounding forest, creating the risk of a forest fire.

This "heritage tree" was considered too valuable to simply cut down and hack to pieces as is done with ordinary trees. What to do? The forestry crew came up with a novel solution. The fellows set up a portable square pool, much like a backyard plastic swimming pool, filled it with water from tankers, and added a magic chemical to make the water "wet."

This chemical compound, called "wet water," when added to water, breaks the surface tension that holds water together so that water no longer bonds to itself. If you have ever seen water skeeters skimming over the surface of the water, or if you have ever seen the meniscus clinging up the sides of a test tube in a science class, you know what that means. I was told that a duck placed upon a pond full of wet water would sink.

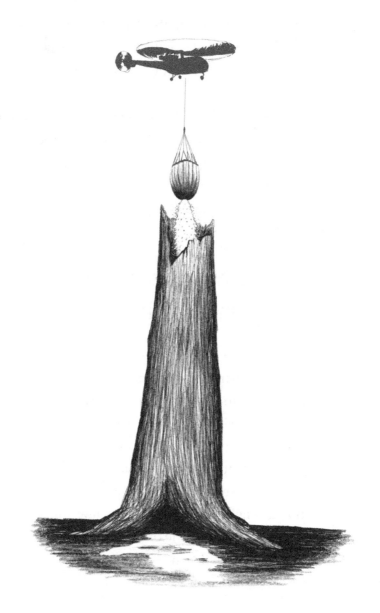

Saving a Giant Sequoia tree.
Illustration by Jacob Greiff, Sandpoint, Idaho.

We attached the Bambi Bucket to the Alouette, and I delivered seven loads of "wet water" to the top of the tree. When water started running out the bottom of the tree through the lower hole, we felt we had saved the tree.

Mid-October, we returned our AL III to Stockton for a routine rotor head replacement. As I was flying back to Peppermint, I circled my friend Buzz Baiz's grape farm in Selma and landed in his barnyard. We spent the night with one of my best friends—fellow MARCAD, Vietnam veteran and Air America pilot—his wife Phyllis, and their son Keith.

October 15, 1974
Quickie Stop

Returning to Peppermint the next day, we took our time. When we finally arrived at Peppermint 15 minutes past our ETA, the forestry fellows had begun to get a little concerned about us. Where had we been? When the helitack foreman asked me, I just smiled and walked away, muttering something about, "Doing a little sightseeing." We took advantage of having our very own helicopter to use as we wished, and we landed at a remote and secluded LZ in the woods, shut the helicopter down for a few minutes, and enjoyed a stand-up quickie on the side of a big rock, right out there in Mother Nature's pristine wilderness. Just another part of our honeymoon.

October 22, 1974

A SikorskyS-64 Skycrane had been logging a few miles south of the base near a place called Greenhorn. It crashed, killing the entire crew. I remember flying over the crash site and seeing puddles and streaks of molten aluminum that had run down the side of the hill, cooled and solidified.

October 23, 1974

It was getting late in the fire season. I helped the fire lookouts decommission their posts. I carried two loads of 800-pound propane tanks to Jordan Peak Lookout at 10,000 feet. This was right at the power limit of my Alouette. Curious, I wondered how it compared to the mighty twin-turbine CH-53A I flew in reserves. I consulted the flight charts in the back of my CH-53A handbook and was astounded to learn that the CH-53A could not lift any more than my AL III at these altitudes. Yeah, Aerospatiale! Yeah, Alouette III!

October 30, 1974

SNOW! Lots of snow. The fire season was definitely over. We moved ops to Porterville airport, cleaned the travel trailer, returned it to Ranger Sherman, and returned home.

The Alouette III in the snow. The Jordan Peak Lookout covered by snow.

Chapter 17
November 9, 1974
Last Reserve Meeting – Fired!

Unfortunately for my reserve status, the late snow caused me to miss October's reserve meeting. I had already missed the September meeting due to work. I was low on my flight time requirements, but I had repeatedly told my CO and operations officer, "As soon as my summer contract is over, I will go from being the low-time pilot to being the high-time pilot before the end of the year."

Early November, I rushed to Alameda for my reserve meeting. Usually, our meeting was the last weekend of each month, but the November meeting was near the tenth of the month, so all us Marines could gather and celebrate the Marine Corps birthday, November 10th. I packed up my dress blues with my captain's bars, my highly shined black shoes, and all my medals, badges, and ribbons, ready to celebrate.

Saturday morning I was eager and ready to start flying and catch up on my flying hours. Even though everyone knew I was trying to make up lost time, I was surprised and sad to see that I wasn't on the morning flight schedule. *Oh, well,* I thought, *I will be on the afternoon schedule.* I sat at the operations desk, monitoring the morning's flight activities, when a good friend, Major Hal Zamora, came through operations in a huff. He said, "Bill, I can't make my flight this morning. I must attend a staff meeting. Find someone to take my place." I jumped at the chance to replace him.

I scurried downstairs to the locker room to get my flight gear, only to find that my lock had been cut and all my flying gear was gone. My flight suits, helmet, gloves, everything...all STOLEN! I was upset, but I had a flight to make. I rushed to the flight gear supply (paraloft) and asked the sergeant to quickly scrounge me up some gear so I could go flying. His response was, "Sir, I have been instructed to not give you any gear." This is how I learned that I had been fired.

A few weeks prior to this day, the Marine Corps decided that there would be a RIF, (reduction in force) of the reserves. The only fair way to enact a RIF was to cut the lowest time pilot. Guess who? The same full-time officer who had twice called and asked me to drive a sixteen-hour round-trip to take a ninety minute flight couldn't be bothered to call me and tell me I was fired. To say that I was just a bit miffed would be a gross understatement.

I countered by borrowing some gear from another friend and took Major Zamora's flight anyway, as a copilot for someone else, even though I figured I wouldn't get paid for it. (I don't know that I ever did.) At the end of the flight, we flew past the control tower in the slot in the base of a diamond formation. To me, that was a grand exit, and it was my last flight with the US Marine Corps.

That night at the birthday celebration, the more I drank, the more I steamed about getting RIF'd. I decided to publicly demote myself. I started by taking off my aviator's wings as I no longer felt valued as a Marine Corps pilot. A little later, I removed my shooting badges. Then I took off my ribbons and medals. Next to last, I took off my captain's bars. Finally, I removed the Marine Corps insignia from each side of my collar and hat. As I walked out of the pavilion, people stared at this Marine wearing an unadorned uniform. I was done with the Marine Corps. I felt I was no longer a Marine. As we used to say in Vietnam, "One good deal after another."

Under President Clinton, Alameda Naval Air Station was decommissioned and is now an industrial park.

Chapter 18
November 25-26, 1974
Flying For Bing Crosby

Flying south in California's Central Valley, my instructions were simple: go to the Visalia Airport, meet up with some folks from Hollywood and do as they request. A film crew was shooting a commercial for Bing Crosby, who owned all or most of the Minute Maid Corporation.

I usually dressed casually for work, in blue jeans and plain shirts. In this case, I packed a nice leather sport coat, slacks, shirt, and tie, hoping I might make an impression on the glamorous people...and perhaps find a chance to break into the Hollywood flying business...and maybe meet a starlet.

We started the day with introductions. It was fun to meet Bing Crosby in person. He impressed me with his gregarious nature and welcoming smile. What a treat it was to hear his sonorous baritone voice.

The TV crew had me fly to a place east of Visalia, where I landed the helicopter on the edge of a bluff overlooking hundreds of acres of orange groves. The weather and visibility were perfect for filming. The camera crew set a tripod beside the helicopter to shoot through it, to film the orange groves below the plateau. With Crosby and his family sitting in the AL III, I would simply turn on the starter just long enough to get the rotors turning. To keep the battery from discharging fully, I did a full start about every third take and ran the engine for a minute or two, knowing the efficient NiCad battery would recharge quickly.

*Bing Crosby and family in the Alouette, Visalia, California.
"Look, Nathaniel, there are the orange groves!"*

The director wanted close-up photos of Crosby and his family flying over the orange groves. To do this, we had to fly in close formation, with the camera ship flying in front of mine. I didn't know much of the background of David Jones, the other pilot. I did know that he was former Army and a Vietnam veteran; but I had no idea if he was an experienced formation flyer. From what little I had seen of the US Army's formation flying in Vietnam, I thought it erratic and wobbly. I was hesitant to trust him with my life and the lives of my very important passengers. Many aircraft have crashed due to inexperienced pilots trying to fly in formation. It has been well established that a mid-air collision will ruin your whole day; this is true even more so in helicopters than in airplanes.

During pre-Vietnam training in North Carolina, I had done a lot of formation flying to build coordination and confidence that I would need in the war. We played a game called "tail chase." The lead helicopter would fly ever-increasingly difficult maneuvers, and the second helicopter would try to keep on his "wing." It got increasing more challenging as the lead pilot introduced more difficult maneuvers. At times the second helicopter would have to break away to avoid smashing into the lead. Sometimes we flew with over-lapping rotor systems. After a lot of practice doing this serious game, we could keep up with the lead no matter what he did...with one exception. The only way for the lead to dump a good chase pilot was to pull back hard on the cyclic "stick" and make a zooming climb, gaining altitude and losing airspeed until he was at zero airspeed and a high hover. Then he would do a pedal turn to face the chase helicopter. There was no way for a chase to stay on the lead's tail when they came face-to-face, nose-to-nose at a high hover.

Could this Army pilot measure up? I offered to fly formation on Jones, but he said, no, he had lots of experience flying formation on someone behind him, and he knew what the cameraman wanted. I reluctantly agreed, knowing that I would be able to see him well in front of me and rationalizing that I could break off in an instant if something went amiss.

We took off, and I flew the required course straight and level and *very* smoothly over vast regiments of orange trees. Sure enough, Jones was able to fly in quite close, off to my left, his rotors less than twenty feet from my rotor, which allowed the cameraman in his back seat to shoot directly into my helicopter. His camera could see Mr. Crosby and his family as they pantomimed the words of the commercial. The audio was dubbed in later. This is the worst possible way to fly formation in helicopters, for if Jones' engine were to fail, he might fall directly into my rotors before I would even have a chance to react. I was nervous about this, as was Mr. Crosby.

After a short while, Mr. Crosby told me he had had enough. He insisted that I tell Jones that we should, "Stop this nonsense, NOW!" I radioed Jones, who then told the cameraman Crosby's concerns, who then said back to Jones to relay to me to tell Mr. Crosby, "Just one more take." We did this relay conversation several times before Mr. Crosby finally resigned himself to submitting to the wishes of the cameraman. Soon we were done. Safe.

Back at the motel, I showered and dressed up for my big debut with the Hollywood folks. I was a little disappointed that they had not invited me for drinks at the hotel bar, where I felt sure the crew would surely be after such a hard day's filming. I went to the hotel bar, but no one was there. I sipped a couple of drinks, waiting. Finally, I went to the front desk and asked the desk clerk if he knew where the crew had gone out to dinner, thinking I could catch up to them—no such luck. As soon as the shoot was over, they had packed up and gone back to Hollywood. Drat.

We saw the commercial later on TV. Part of it consisted of the shot of my AL III from Jones' as we flew over the orange groves. Dubbed in, Crosby says to his son, "Look, Nathaniel, there are the orange groves." From there, it was a quick cut to the sales pitch of the commercial. If I had not known from the beginning that it was me flying, I wouldn't have recognized myself because my helmet and aviator's sunglasses hid most of my face. Two of my friends did ask me later if that was me flying in that commercial with Bing Crosby, so it seems I was recognizable.

That's it. My entire Hollywood-flying portfolio is wrapped up in those two seconds.

December 14, 1974
Another Naval Death Experience!

Calicopters won a contract to spread synthetic fertilizer on the Concord Naval Weapons Station grounds about forty miles to the west of Stockton. Nuclear weapons were stored in underground bunkers on this base, but the surface ground was leased to local cattlemen to graze their herds; this kept the grass down to help prevent grass fires.

I departed Stockton airport in my Alouette III helicopter at first light. My support crew had departed an hour earlier, a small parade of vehicles, including a fuel truck, a larger tank truck full of ammonium nitrate synthetic fertilizer, and a conveyor belt device on a trailer used to deliver the fertilizer from the bottom of the larger truck to my spreader buckets. We had briefed to meet at the guard shack at the entry to the base. I flew to the designated rendezvous point, but my crew was nowhere to be seen, and I saw nothing resembling a guard shack. I thought I must have misunderstood, so I began a search for them. I followed the road between small hills onto the base and started searching, flying low-level around the base. After about five minutes, I observed a Military Police (MP) vehicle following behind me, lights flashing, but I thought little of it. I did a U-turn and flew to the other end of the base. I noticed that the MP vehicle shadowed me, lights still flashing.

Finally, I saw what I thought to be the guard shack. It was about twenty by thirty feet, bristling with antennas with several official-looking vehicles parked beside it. *This must be the guard shack. I'll land here and ask the MPs if they have seen my crew.* As I shut the helicopter down, the MP truck rattled to a halt in the gravel about fifty feet in front of me. When I walked towards the guard shack, a Marine corporal, with a rifle in his hands, approached me briskly from the MP truck and commanded smartly, "Down in the dirt on your face!" I tried to explain why I was there and that I was looking for my crew, but I could tell from his demeanor that he was quite serious. If I didn't get down, he was going to put me down hard. I felt that he was aching to give me a vertical butt stroke with his rifle. I saw him shift his body stance, getting ready to deliver a blow, but he checked himself and instead gave me a second firm order, "Down, now! Facedown in the dirt!" I flopped down onto the cold, muddy soil.

Prone on the cold, sticky soil, I slowly reached back and slid my wallet out of my left rear jeans pocket and handed up my pink reserve ID showing that I was a Captain of Marines. *This will get me a little respect.* None! The corporal didn't care; he was focused on protecting his nuclear weapons from my heinous threat. I stayed put, getting muddier, wetter, and colder. After a few minutes, a US Navy Lieutenant Commander arrived. I was allowed to get up off the ground and speak with the corporal's superior officer.

I learned that my crew had a mechanical problem with one of the trucks and never made it to the base. Of course, they were difficult for me to find because they weren't there. Worse yet, I learned that no one had ever bothered to inform base security troops that we were scheduled to do the job. I had put the whole base on high alert by flying low and slow over the base.

After things got all settled out, we distributed tons of fertilizer to the grasslands atop the bomb storage bunkers. Grass fires were prevented, so the Navy was happy; the cattle got fat, so the farmer made money, and I wrote a nice letter to the commander of the base, commending the Marine corporal for his no-monkey-business professionalism. I hope he got promoted... and I am eternally grateful that he didn't rupture my skull with his rifle butt.

Chapter 19
Early 1975
Return to Peppermint

We prepared for our second year of the Peppermint contract. I went through the series of casual check rides again. I flew a lot of small jobs like the snowpack survey again with Don and Lee, up to 9,800 feet. I flew some frost control and a small TV gig. I took Diamond Walnut Company executives on a sightseeing tour of the Stockton area. I did a lot of crop dusting, seeding, fertilizer application, and just simple waiting around, idle.

I flew a power line survey starting at Hetch Hetchy Reservoir, following the power poles all the way to the edge of San Francisco Bay. I flew low and slow, bobbing up and down, so that the two observers on board could look at every transmission tower and inspect each one for damage from windstorms or lightning…or bullets…sometimes foolish people shoot at the insulators on transmission towers. At one point, we spotted a coyote in a large open area. To give the observers a bit of a break, and myself a respite from the demanding flying, I chased the coyote across the open dirt until he fell over from exhaustion. Then we returned to the patrol.

April 12, 1975

I flew to Bear Valley and carried several loads of parajumpers up to 13,600 feet so they could jump out of my perfectly good aircraft in a parajump/ski competition. I looked away as they jumped out.

Captain Bill and mechanic Mike Tulley at the Bear Valley Para-Ski meet.

Late May, 1975
No Room at the Inn

We deployed back to Peppermint, but only for a week or two. The forest service contract bids had been "re-evaluated," and we were somehow squeezed out of the lucrative Peppermint contract. Eccles swore it was politics, but he couldn't prove it. It looked like we would not have a contract at all that summer, but then we were assigned to Markleeville, California, just south of Lake Tahoe.

Markleeville, the county seat of Alpine County, was barely a wide spot in the road. It had no stoplight at its one T intersection. I flew the Alouette to the nearby forest service pad. My mechanic Mike Tulley and his girlfriend picked me up, and we went to the nearest—and only—bar/restaurant/hotel in town, had dinner, then adjourned to the bar. We had made no provisions for accommodations, but we were in a hotel; it wasn't busy, and we felt confident that we could get a room at this hotel. After a few drinks, I had made friends with the bartender, who was also the owner of the hotel. That was even better; I was sure I could get a room because I was a now friend of the owner.

About midnight, I asked the bartender/owner to rent us rooms. He said. "No, I can't do that." Uh-oh! Even though the old building had been a hotel in the past, and there were empty rooms upstairs, it was not a licensed hotel, and he couldn't rent us rooms. Drat! What to do now? It was after midnight, there were no other hotels or motels in town, it was at least twenty miles to the next nearest motel...and we were drunk.

Finally, he said to us, "You know, I can't rent you a room, but I can let you sleep in a room for free." We spent our first night in Markleeville on metal cots in the tiny bedrooms of a former gold-rush whorehouse. The next day my wife arrived with our pickup, and we found a house nearby to rent.

July 2, 1975
The Worst Possible News!

I was there only about three weeks, doing very little flying, when one of the forest service men told me I had a phone call in his downtown office. When I answered, it was Eccles, and his cryptic message was, "Go to a phone booth and call me back from there." Thoughts of mystery and intrigue crossed my mind. What interesting and exciting event was happening now? I was seriously not prepared for the actual message he conveyed.

He told me that my great buddy Gary Connolly, fellow Marine Corps pilot, Vietnam roommate, fellow Air America pilot, travel buddy, and all-time best friend was killed that morning in a crop-dusting accident near Napa! I dropped the phone and ran out of the building, across the road and down the riverbank, seeking solace at the riverside. I needed privacy so I could cry...and scream! I was utterly devastated by my good buddy's death.

Several of our mutual friends came to our cabin that night, and we had a bit of a wake, with lots of good stories about Gary and copious amounts of booze, which helped ease the pain of his loss. A few days later, I helped carry Gary's closed casket to his grave. I was, and still am, grieved by his loss. That huge void in my life has never been refilled.

After only a month in Markleeville and very little flying, something happened, and we lost the Markleeville contract, too. There was no more work for the Alouette, but the company expenses continued. Eccles asked me if I would be willing to return the Alouette to the dealer in Grand Prairie, Texas. He said he would pay my return airfare back to Stockton, after which I would be unemployed. I said, sure, if I could take Michele with me, and we would pay her return ticket. He said okay.

The next afternoon, we blasted off to return the Alouette III to the Aerospatiale factory in Grand Prairie, Texas. We got a late start the next day and intentionally covered only 130 miles. We dropped in to visit my good buddy, Buzz, and his wife again. We had landed in his barnyard before, and I knew that if we showed up unannounced, he and his wife, Phyllis, would welcome us. We flew a few circles around his farmhouse to announce our arrival, and he waved us down to land. Over drinks and dinner, we persuaded Buzz and his wife Phyllis and their ten-year-old son, Keith, to join us on this epic journey.

August 1, 1975
We Revisit Peppermint

The following day we departed Selma early. The next stop of our trip was Las Vegas, except that leg was too long a stretch fuel-wise for the Alouette. We would have to detour through Bakersfield just to buy fuel. I noticed that the straight line drawn to Las Vegas on the air chart passed directly over Peppermint, so I called and talked to the pilot of the company that had taken over *our* contract and arranged to buy a tank of fuel from his fuel truck. We refueled at Peppermint and proceeded to Las Vegas.

We landed at McCarran Airport and spent a memorable evening in Las Vegas. On the second day of our journey, we departed Vegas at a leisurely hour and flew right over Hoover Dam. I was amazed at how many wires stretched through the air just below the dam, and I was appreciating just how many wires when I realized that we were right above the middle of a great steel spider web. Should the engine fail, we might be caught in the wires! I had my wife, my two best friends, and their son in my machine. A huge lump grew in my throat and stayed there for the next few seconds until we cleared the area.

We crossed over the dam and flew right up the middle of Lake Mead until the canyon narrowed, and we entered the Grand Canyon. The towering cliffs closed in on us until there were only a few hundred yards between them. At one time Buzz saw on the air chart a cable tramway, but when we arrived at the particular spot, we could see no cables, nor any signs of such construction activity, towers, cables, gatherings of autos, nor any other sign of such a hazard. It must have been something that was projected but not yet built. I doubt that all ten of our good eyes could have missed it.

We spent that night in Albuquerque, had a nice dinner, and another leisurely start again the next day. The summer days were long; we flew until 9:00 p.m. or later every day. I figured that since I was going to be laid off as soon as I delivered the helicopter anyway, I didn't have to be in a great hurry. What was Eccles going to do, fire me? This attitude was a carryover from Vietnam. Whenever we thought we might be in some kind of trouble while flying around the war, we used to say, "What are they going to do to me? Make me a helicopter pilot and send me to Vietnam?"

When we passed through the great meteor crater in Arizona, we really did pass through it. I circled down inside the crater and hovered at the bottom. We could have easily landed at the bottom. We hovered out slowly and got the best inside view of the meteor crater, all for free.

In New Mexico, navigator Buzz noticed on the chart that there were some Indian cliff dwellings on our path. "Let's go see!" We had a good close look — three passes, too close it seems. That night when I called in to Eccles to report our progress, he asked me what I was doing so close to the cliff dwellings and, "Who are the other people in the helicopter?" Oops, busted! We had been low enough for a Park Ranger to get my side number and see the passengers.

I explained to Eccles that I had brought my friend Buzz along because Buzz was an aviation (A&P) mechanic, and I thought he wouldn't mind if Buzz and his wife joined us. Eccles said, "Oh, okay." Neither of us mentioned the boy, and I let the subject drop. So, what's he going to do…he has already laid me off, effective touchdown in Arlington. I had not broken any FAA rules, but the AL III was a very loud machine, and we had disrupted the tranquility of the park.

By my charts and guides, I knew that there was no jet fuel at the Gallup Municipal Airport. But I also knew that in a pinch, I could burn truck diesel. I saw a convenient truck stop and landed atop a small bluff overlooking the station, a hundred yards away. I shut down, and we walked down to the office and talked to the manager, telling him what we needed to do.

"No problem, go ahead."

Buzz stayed below to keep trucks away from the pumps on the outboard row of pumps. When all was clear, I started up, flew down to within fifty feet of the pumps and landed. After I shut down, we manually pushed the helicopter up to the pumps, turning the rotor blades by hand as we went in to keep them from striking any pumps or posts in the way. We filled the tank, then reversed the process, and were soon on our way.

*Refueling at a truck stop in Gallup, New Mexico.
My good friend and fellow pilot "Buzz" Baiz at pumps.*

Crossing a corner of Oklahoma, I landed in a farmer's field so Phyllis could hop out and grab a handful of Oklahoma soil for her father, an Oklahoma native. We arrived in Dallas the same day, delivered the Alouette to Aerospatiale, and had a short visit with my good friends John and Sherry. Returning to Stockton by commercial air, I read the inflight *TIME* magazine. There was an article about clusters of cancer in California's great valley. Every city along the valley highways had a cancer cluster. This confirmed my aversion to crop dusting and the chemicals involved.

My good friend Buzz died in 2017 of Agent Orange-related cancer. My good friend John died just before Christmas, 2019, of Parkinson's disease. When I attended John's funeral early January, 2020, I stayed with one of best friends, LtCol James B. Barr USMC

Retired in McKinney, TX. I am sad to report that LtCol Barr died of leukemia in early January, 2022, at age 80. (See Dedication.) All three deaths of my good friends I attribute to Agent Orange.

Chapter 20
Early 1976
Saudi Arabia

After being laid off from the Calico-peter, my wife and I decided to sell the old Stockton farmhouse and busied ourselves preparing it for sale. My reserve buddy, Tom Sullivan, phoned me from Alameda to say he had seen an advert in *TRADE-A-PLANE*, the yellow monthly newsprint magazine for real working pilots and mechanics. Someone needed H-34/S-58 drivers to go to Saudi Arabia. (The Sikorsky-58 is the civilian version of the H-34.) I sent a resume and promptly forgot it.

A few weeks later, I got a call from someone named Robert Boyd of Carson Helicopters Inc. of Perkasie, Pennsylvania. He asked me, "Are you ready to go to work?" I was puzzled at first because I didn't remember sending the resume, and I didn't recognize the name of the company, nor the name of this person calling. This turned out to be one of the all-time great capers.

The number one song in January was "Theme from Mahogany (Do You Know Where You're Going To)" by Diana Ross.

As a background, I must mention what was going on in the world at the time. The first great oil embargo had happened three years before, in 1973, and Saudis were gathering money in Midas-like proportions. With all their newfound wealth, they were buying enormous amounts of everything. Much of the spending frenzy was by the Saudi government for infrastructure upgrades.

This created a serious bottleneck at their main port in the capitol of Jeddah. Built years before, this small port was capable of unloading only three small ships at a time. Ships had to wait up to six months before their turn to get to the pier to unload. When I arrived, I could look out on the harbor and see dozens of ships, sitting at anchor, waiting. We were told that each ship received an average of $4,000 a day demurrage for loitering out there. Multiply this amount by dozens of ships, and it became a considerable sum, even for the filthy rich Saudis to pay. The obvious solution was to build more docks and expand the harbor. That had been planned. The cement for the project was purchased and was en route, but once the cement arrived, it would still have to wait at least six months before it could be unloaded. That is when Frank Carson proposed to the Saudi government that they unload the cement using helicopters.

The main problem with this idea is that there is no place to land a helicopter on most ships due to masts, cranes, and rigging. This created a market for those who have expertise with helicopter "long-lining," a technique that was in its infancy. Very few pilots had done it, and fewer still were proficient. Most of us had all done hundreds of hours of external load work, but when we heard about long-lining, most of us said, "No way! Not possible!"

At his company headquarters in Perkasie, Frank Carson gathered the greatest collection of pilots and crews (some might say, "drunks, misfits, shitbirds and derelicts") that I hadn't seen since Vietnam or Air America. Every day, two or three more pilots or crew arrived at the Philly airport. Carson rented an entire local motel to house and feed us.

It became old home week, as fellows I hadn't seen for years began to drift in from places all over the globe. Guys I knew from flight school, Vietnam, Air America, and one or two from Alaska dribbled in. At first, we had little to do but loaf around the motel and join up in the bar every night, drink beer, and swap lies. By the time our stay in Perkasie was done, I weighed in at 217 pounds, heavier than I had ever been, and thirty-one pounds above my flight school "fighting weight."

Learning long-line work was the most challenging thing I have ever done, a completely alien and unnatural procedure that was logarithmically more frightening than my first attempts to hover or learning to fly on instruments. My first impulse was, *This is not possible! How can a guy fly like this, maintain any semblance of normal flight, still see his instruments, and continue to manipulate the controls safely?* But when I saw other pilots doing it, ...a*nything any other pilot could do, I can do, too.* With my background of forty-three months of combat flying in Vietnam and Laos, I was confident.

Normally any aircraft feels well balanced as it flies through the air. Unlike an automobile, where one may have to lean into a curve to compensate for centrifugal force, in an aircraft, when a pilot induces an angle of bank in his turn proportionate to the rate of turn, a turn is a very comfortable, balanced maneuver. G-forces make him feel like he is sitting straight up, even if he is in a steep turn. Not so in long-lining. To pick up a heavy load at the end of a one-hundred-foot line was to throw every bit of balance and equilibrium out the window. To begin with, in order to control the load one hundred plus feet below, the pilot must be able to see that load. There is only one way to do that: lean over sideways, head out the open window and look straight down at the load. This position is completely contrary to everything I had done up 'til now. Most flying is done by looking straight ahead, using a visual reference to the horizon for orientation. I had to overcome years of experience to force myself to lean over and look straight down at the load. This was an uncomfortable, unnatural, alien situation.

In the early part of training, we worked right in the backyard of the Carson Helicopters Inc. They owned about forty acres in a wooded neighborhood near Perkasie. We first started practice with very small loads, if you can say a fifty-five-gallon barrel full of concrete is a small load. It was, relative to the lifting capacity of an S-58, and it was something we could have absolute control of as we learned.

Most of the fellows were Vietnam vets and trained to do external loads in flight school. We had all done thousands of external loads in Vietnam, taking supplies and ammunition to troops in the field, a very expedient way to move cargo in a hurry. Being fast was good, especially in those situations with a threat of getting shot at or incoming mortars. Most of the Carson instructors were not Vietnam vets and had learned their trade on the job. The students had spent many hours as before getting to fly on their own. We were being pressured to learn enough to fly solo right away.

To pick up a load was no different from any other external load, to start with. As we hovered low directly over the barrel full of concrete, someone would connect the line to the hook. Then we hovered straight up until the line was taut. It was very important to be absolutely straight up over the load, and gently pull the line taut. Now we are ready to begin. Adding power, we lifted the load off the ground. If I were directly over the load, it came off the ground straight up and felt okay. This was not the case for the first few attempts.

To lift off-center was to impute a swing to it. I was immediately reminded of my first external long-line load near Lone Pine, California in 1975 with the engine of the crashed DC-3.

In addition to all this, you have to occasionally glance into the cockpit and check your instruments, especially the torque gauge, or both the RPM and manifold pressure, to make sure you are not ruining your engine and drivetrain. A quick glance at the instrument panel doesn't seem like much until you are in the middle of a lift, and the quick turning of the head can make you dizzy.

Even with a balanced load, the chopper felt a lot different on the controls because the actual center of gravity of the machine was somewhere between the machine and the load, not at the seat of my pants where I was used to feeling it. (A friend calculated the center of gravity in this situation. He figured it was 38 feet below the pilot's bottom.)

Many times, trainees dropped (pickled) the practice load until finally we began to get a feel for how to pick up the load without imputing a swing. Flying straight and level was the easiest part, so long as we were gentle on the controls for any attitude change. In real life, straight and level flying was the thing we did least; in real life, everything was a pick up, a turn, a short run, and then another turn into a landing, and then the landing phase.

The landing phase was the biggest challenge. Of course, we could have simply come to a very gradual stop, coming to a high hover, and then let the load down to a landing, but this was not practical. For one thing, a helicopter at maximum gross does not hover well, and all of our flying was to be right at maximum weight limits. The name of the game in helicopter flying, as with most businesses, is that time is money, so we had to learn to be fast and efficient.

To land the load, we learned to come in fast, usually near cruise speed. A few hundred yards out, we began to reduce power to decelerate and descend. It was a rapid transition from flight to a hover, the goal being to reach 150-200 feet altitude and zero knots airspeed simultaneously right at the drop spot. Just before coming to a stop, we bled off the remaining airspeed with a slight flare-up of the nose of the helicopter and a simultaneous slight reduction of the collective pitch to avoid imputing a climb. This flare caused the load to swing out in front of the helicopter about twenty feet. Then a smoothly coordinated maneuver that combined a slight lowering of the collective and using the cyclic (stick) to level the helicopter, brought the load to a gentle stop just as it touched down on the ground.

Practice, practice, and more practice is what it took. We slung barrels of concrete all over the back forty acres at Carson's heliport until the neighbors complained about the noise. In more than one case, a helicopter hovered over a neighbor's back lot for several minutes while someone hopped the fence, found the load in the woods, and re-connected it to the long-line.

We had three safety backups which allowed us to drop the load instantly if need be. At the bottom of the long-line was an electrically operated cargo hook, just like the one built into the bottom of the helicopter. The hook at the bottom line had an electric release switch on the collective stick. When a load was safely on the ground, I had to just flex my left thumb and mash that button to release the load. There was a second release on the cyclic control stick that released the upper hook. It was not desirable to use the upper release because that jettisoned the entire long-line and lower hook assembly.

The second safety backup was a manual release. If both electrical releases failed, or in the case of complete electrical failure of the helicopter, we could always drop the entire rig with a manual release. In the S-58T, the manual switch was a spring-loaded pedestal right by the pilot's right foot, which could be stomped in a flash to drop the load. (I have always wondered why something that you stomp with your foot was called manual release. Why not "footual"?) In some other helicopters, the emergency release handle is by the pilot's left hand. A good preflight inspection always included a function check for all three releases.

After a few weeks of training in Perkasie, we all boarded a Boeing 707 and flew to Jeddah, Saudi Arabia and began to unload the ships. The company put us up in a hotel in downtown Jeddah. Later we moved to an apartment building that Carson had built specifically for our crews.

For the first two weeks, it seemed we were trying to build a cement causeway from the ships to the shore, we dropped many loads of cement bags into the harbor. At least thirteen hooks and long-line assemblies (at $13,000 each!) went into the salty bay. Management whined but eventually we got better and better, and hook losses diminished. I am pleased to report that I never dropped one.

The ships to be unloaded were anchored a mile offshore. We would get two or three helicopters working the same ship in a "daisy chain" sequence, one machine easing into position over the ship as the one ahead lifted his load away. It was important to keep a good rhythm going because that way, everything went smoothly and efficiently. Once in a while, someone would get balled up and take longer to lift his load out, and the other helicopters would stack up behind, waiting a turn, but the normal interval would soon reestablish itself as each guy slid off with his load.

We got so proficient that we could literally place the hook into the hand of the young fellow on the deck of the ship, 115 feet away. He was standing there with the load cable loop in his hand; as we handed him the hook, he slapped the loop into the hook. We then gently pulled the line tight, which centered us over the load. In a continuous, smooth movement, we pulled more power until the load was off the deck. We then swung the load between the ship's riggings,—the reason for doing all this long-line business in the first place.

Carson's S-58s line up to pick up loads off a ship.
(Picture courtesy of Carson Helicopters Inc.)

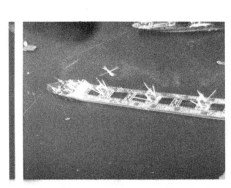

Clockwise from top left:
Carson Photo of S-58 over a ship.
An S-58 touching a load down.
The Somali laborers loading the cement into a truck.
S-58 hovering over a ship to pick up a load.
(Top left picture courtesy of Carson Helicopters Inc.
All others by author.)

As soon as we cleared the riggings and attained safe flying speed, we had to make an immediate 200-degree left turn around the ship's bow to head for shore. You could usually follow the helicopter in front of you by a track of cement dust in the sky. This fine dust was to cause some problems later on. We never got above 200-feet in altitude.

It was about three-quarters of a mile straight run to the beach, then a 120-degree turn to the left to get lined up for the landing. It was then a matter of technique: decelerate, descend to minimums, rock the nose back to swing the load out front, as the load reached its apogee of swing, rock the nose over to a hover, simultaneously setting the load down the last few inches onto the pavement, mash the release button, visually insure release, and go. To try and take off with the load still attached would have been a disaster. At best, we would have dragged the load down the landing, tearing open many the sacks of cement and creating a severe hazard for all the laborers on the landing. At worse, the load might drag the helicopter down to a crash.

On the final approach to the landing there was an open place on the seawall, directly under our flight path, where the Saudis gathered several times a day to pray towards Mecca, and we couldn't avoid flying directly over them. We were concerned that if we dropped a load or even a single bag of cement, the cement could squash someone like a bug. I wondered what would happen to one of our pilots should he accidentally kill someone? Would that pilot be executed for murder by beheading in the public square? Or would the company support him and argue that it was an "Act of Allah," and then get that pilot out of the country as soon as possible?

This was not something any of us wanted to challenge in this strange and foreign land. Jail of any sort has never appealed to me. We complained to the management; they consulted the port authorities, who in turn talked to the praying men, but nothing changed. The Saudis kept praying to Allah right under us, and we kept flying right over them. Their prayers must have worked, for no one was ever injured.

Billy Miller, a senior Carson pilot, had the most spectacular incident of all. As he lifted a pallet from the deck of a ship, he lost control of his load and swung it through the windows of the ship's bridge. He completely wiped out all the glass in the bridge, destroying the captain's wheel, all the navigation gear, and instrumentation, and the teak paneling, not to mention putting several hundred pounds of cement powder into the captain's "office." Carson bought the captain a new bridge. I have always wondered if it had been one of us new hires if that pilot would have been fired, but since Billy was an "old hand" with Carson, he stayed around.

The cover of the ARAMCO company magazine January-February 1977. Used with permission from ARAMCO. Notice the cloud of dust at the water behinds the load.

"Dead Man's Curve"

In the back of every helicopter handbook there will be a graph similar to the one below. It depicts that a helicopter cannot usually make a safe landing unless it is flying above a certain height or at a certain airspeed. Outside those parameters, a pilot it will not likely be able to convert an engine failure into a safe landing. We worked in the lower-left shaded portion of "Dead Man's Curve." In the manual, the left bulge and the lower right mound are both in red ink.

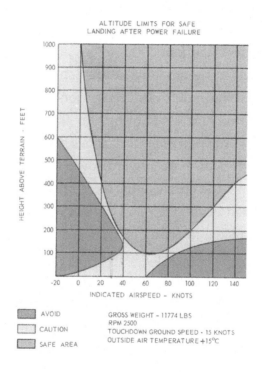

This Chart is from the back of my H-34 NATOPS manual.
(NATOPS: Naval Aviation Training & Operations Procedures.)

The Worldwide Adventures of a Helicopter Pilot ... the rest of the story

The Saudi project was funded by Carson's bankers in Perkasie. One day, Frank Carson told us, "Look sharp today, the bankers are in town, and they are going to be observing the operation. Give them a good show." By now, we were most proficient, and no one felt any problems with that. Besides, we were too busy flying to worry about mere bean counters. Of course, this was the day I made a bit of a mistake and embarrassed myself and the boss.

We all had developed the procedure of using our altimeters to check off certain altitudes during our approaches to the landing pad. I had a set procedure that was working well for me. I came across the beach at the 200 feet (over the praying Saudis), crossed the fence at 170 feet, and flared at 130 feet, all the while using my altimeter to judge my altitude. With the long-line being 115-feet long, this allowed the load to clear the cyclone fence by a few feet. On a normal approach, when I finished my flare, my airspeed was zero; my load was about three feet above the ground. It was a simple matter to rock the nose forward, lower the collective a touch, place the load onto the tarmac, punch the release button, visually confirm separation of the load and go. All this took about three seconds from crossing the fence.

On the day the bankers were to be watching, I came in from the ship, crossed the beach, set myself up to slide down and cross the fence at my usual 130 feet on my normal path. As I approached the fence, I glanced out to the side and saw a group of men in business suits, one of whom was Frank Carson. *"The bankers. Oh well, no problem, I'm doing fine."*

At the time my load should have cleared the cyclone fence below, I made my usual slight flare to swing the load out front and touch it down just past the fence. Instead of a smooth transition to a hover, I felt a slight lurch. OOOPS! I looked down, and sure enough, my load had bagged into the fence instead of passing over it. The fence, which had been a straight line, now had a great big U in it, the size and shape of my load. My load was indeed in the landing area but still outside the fence. And with the boss and the bankers watching!

Nothing I could do would undo the mistake. Hesitating would only interfere with the next helicopter close on my tail, so I punched the release button and rejoined the daisy chain, leaving the mess for the Somali laborers to cleanup.

Other pilots reported having this trouble, too. We realized that cement dust was getting inside our altimeters, causing them to register altitude change more slowly than usual. After that incident, we started using visual reference more diligently. Cement dust was a factor in two subsequent crashes, we suspect. Herman Goering, a friend from Air America, was hovering over the hold of a ship when both of his engines quit. Fortunately, all the young kids below him managed to scamper away from his crashing, thrashing, and crumpling machine as it fell into the hold of the cargo ship. Happily, it did not burn or explode, but Herman died of internal injuries on the way to the hospital. I was home on a month's leave during his crash. Captain Billy Pierson, former Air America hand, had a dual flameout a few weeks later as he crossed the seawall, but, despite his low altitude, he was able to get his S-58T down on the ground near the landing zone. Cement dust had somehow penetrated his hermetically sealed fuel controls.

* * *

Jeddah was an exciting and exotic place. For the first few weeks, we lived in a hotel right downtown. We had a view of a major traffic circle. It seemed to us that to the Saudis, the horn was the primary control of the car. They'd aim the car down the street and blast away on the horn, trusting Allah to keep them from harm. I am surprised there weren't more accidents. Car windshield wipers were used only to remove the desert dust from cars' windshields.

Carson rented a new apartment complex a few miles from the airport, and we had better living conditions. It was two guys to a room, and two rooms shared a bathroom. We had young houseboys clean our rooms and do our laundry for us. The houseboys had trouble keeping our laundry separate. I was frequently losing my socks and getting someone else's. To counter this, the first time I had home leave, I made it a point to buy red socks so that I would know they were mine. Comically, one of the other pilots did the same thing, so I was back to square one.

Being a bit further from the airport, we had to take local taxis to get around. I learned enough Arabic to say our address and, "Turn left. Turn right. Stop here. Thank you."

There was no social life in Saudi and no legal alcohol.

Not long after we arrived in Jeddah, we were approached—nearly assaulted—by three young, exuberant American men from Arizona who wanted to know all about our operation. They had come to Saudi to sell their very own concept of helicopter, called, "HONCHO." It was small machine with hollow blades. Instead of the turbine engine driving a transmission, it drove a powerful air compressor. The concept was that the air would be forced up the drive shaft into and out the ends of the blades to turn the blades. To increase lift at critical times, or to lift heavier loads, they planned to place small ramjets at the tip of each blade and fire them off as needed. It was a clever concept.

HONCHO Brochure cover.

They were not having much luck in the USA. marketing their idea, so they thought they would appeal to the rich Arab's egos to fund their project. Doing business with the Saudis at this time was an exercise in mega-frustration. Getting a meeting with anyone important took weeks, and then the person might not show up or would say, oh, you need to talk to my cousin, so-and-so. Then wait another few weeks for the next appointment. The process was tedious and frustrating for them, and living in Jeddah was expensive. To stay alive and to be able to continue marketing the HONCHO concept, they created another job for themselves. They imported and were selling QUIP machines, an early version of the fax machine that transmitted a copy of a document one line at a time.

The HONCHO fellows taught us about Sadiki (the Arabic for "friend"), or "White Lightning," which was almost the only booze available to us. I believe some Americans working for Aramco were making a fortune distilling moonshine in their American compound homes.

Social life was non-existent. There were no nightclubs or bars. There were no available single Saudi women. But the young fellows from Arizona had found a fix for that, too. Somehow, they had weaseled their way into the international nurse corps that worked at the hospital operated by Whittaker Corp. The Arizona kids had met them, and the leader of the three actually had a steady girlfriend, a sweet young RN from Denmark. She invited some of us to a quiet party one night at her apartment. For hors d'oeuvres, she served a tasty horse sausage and Danish cheese. The first round of drinks, she poured from an expensive bottle of Scotch. Everybody got a thimble full of the nice Scotch, then we switched over to some rot-gut cheap stuff. The expensive whiskey was treasured and hoarded.

The main entertainment for us was going out to dinner, but there were only about three restaurants in town, and they soon became repetitive and boring...and expensive. I remember going to a nice seafood restaurant that did a good job on shrimp and lobster. Interestingly, Muslims are not allowed to eat these animals because the Koran says that to be eaten, a fish must have gills.

Rather than go out to eat a lot at the expensive restaurants, we went downstairs to the little coffee shop eatery on the ground floor of our building. We found the people there to be friendly, and they welcomed us warmly. None of us read or spoke Arabic, and there was no menu. The waiters would escort us into the kitchen, where we could see everything that was cooking. We would point and nod our heads, and the waiter brought us whatever that we had pointed at. I remember lots of tomato sauce over garbanzo beans and falafel bread, all with some kind of meat. One day I brought a tablet, and I had the young waiter write in Arabic the name of each food in each pot. I then wrote down an English description of the same food. We now had a menu. We learned later that the herds of camels we saw being off-loaded from ships in the harbor were imported as food. Was camel on our menu? Probably.

The senior of the three kids from Arizona was young, handsome, blonde Dan. He went to the airport frequently to gather the QUIP shipments from the USA. Eventually the airport security got to know him and just waived him through security so that he could roam around the acres of cargo sitting on the tarmac to find his own shipments. Dan said that he saw actual kitchen sinks out on the tarmac that had been flown in. One night he was sitting around with us drinking Sadiki, and he told us that several times he had seen enough information on the shipping labels of some pallets, to realize that some contained bales of Eurodollars or shipments of gold bullion.

We procured some mechanic's calipers and measured a stack of twenty-dollar bills. Using that as a rough gauge, we figured out that the bale of Eurodollars he described must be worth at least a billion dollars—in cash. This got our juices flowing and we sat around many nights figuring out how to snatch a pallet of money or gold, which became one of our major forms of entertainment.

There were two US-style supermarkets in Jeddah catering to the many Americans working there. We liked shopping for food, but alcohol wasn't available in any form. The stores did, however, carry excellent grape juice in bottles that looked just like wine. We learned that if we opened a bottle and placed a little yeast in it, and let it sit around for a couple of weeks--voila—halfway decent wine. We also found we could mix some starches of almost any kind with yeast in a plastic garbage can and let that ferment, creating our own beer that way. That was disgusting and tasted of plastic

* * *

While working, we landed on the opposite side of the warehouse to refuel every 90 minutes, and the young troopers from Pennsylvania refueled us. I made friends with one of these fellows, Roy Fluck, and felt I had to look out for this young, naive teen just out of tech school and his friends.

Our S-58Ts had lockable controls, which made it possible to secure them and leave the helicopter turning. The rules we worked under said that if we had to get out of a helicopter for anything, we should shut down the engines and rotors because helicopters have been known to somehow become unlocked and roll over, or a strong gust of wind might roll one over. Such a mishap could kill my young friends. One day I observed another pilot getting out of his S-58T without shutting down. I have always been a safety freak, and I didn't like this situation, so I admonished him for putting the kids at risk.

He said, "Okay, I won't do that anymore." The next day, he did it again. Angry, I reprimanded him in public in the office trailer. He shoved me; I shoved back, pushing him out the door of the trailer office. We had just moved into the hangar, and there were not yet steps outside the door, so he fell about thirty inches to the concrete floor. Before he could regain his balance, I was on him. I pushed him up against the side of the trailer with my left forearm against his throat, pinning him to the wall, pummeling him with my right fist. He was trying to fight back, but we were too close to each other to really do any harm, then the other pilots pulled us apart.

Usually, in a work situation like this, fighting was a reason to be fired, but our chief pilot had seen the altercation and knew I wasn't to blame. But neither was the other pilot fired. I think they wanted to keep us around as we were now both highly experienced members of the team, and the name of the game was "tonnage hauled." To fire us both and have to train our replacement would have cost the company a lot of money.

The altercation made me so angry that I hopped back into my machine and flew and flew and kept flying until I had flown five hours straight, stopping only to refuel. I was the first pilot to fly five hours in a row. I have often wondered if the other pilots resented what I'd done because I showed that flying five hours straight was doable. Later our regular routine settled into flying just four hours between each shift, with three shifts a day, sunrise to sunset.

I remember one morning we arrived at the port and we couldn't fly because of fog. The outside air temp was eighty-six degrees.

Before I left, I had a tailor make me an authentic Arabic daily dress costume, called a *thobe*. It makes a great Halloween costume but has been sometimes mistaken for a wedding dress.

"Sheik" Collier in his authentic Arabian "Thobe."

Pilot Herman Goering had crashed while I was home on leave. Upon my return to Jeddah, Herman's destroyed S-58T lay in a crumpled heap at the opposite end of the hangar. When I inquired about details, no one seemed to know the reason for his crash, and no one seemed to be making any effort to determine why he had died. Feeling like this job was no longer safe, I quit and returned to Santa Rosa. PTSD struck again.

Chapter 21
Santa Rosa, California

We took the equity from our Stockton farmhouse and bought a defunct winery sitting on ten acres in the Bennett Valley area of Santa Rosa. We began a massive repair and remodel of the derelict 1917 Victorian house. The main house had been unoccupied for years. Blackberry vines grew up through the kitchen floor. It had no running water, no electricity, and no gas. I had to dig up the clogged sewage lines and replace them. There were six employee cottages that were rented, and two huge barns.

Months later with old farmhouse remodel job under control, I became restless and wanted to fly again. I became aware that the local sheriff department contracted with the owner of a Bell-47 out of Sonoma County Airport (STS) for their occasional helicopter needs. I phoned the owner of the company, but he was a one-man show and didn't need any assistance. A few months later he ran out of fuel, swerved to miss a power line and crashed, killing himself and badly injuring the female deputy sheriff observer.

WAYco.
Santa Rosa, California

Shortly thereafter, a local US Army Vietnam veteran Huey pilot and native of Sonoma County, started up a small helicopter company, WAYco (Company and personnel names changed for reasons soon to be obvious.) He picked up on the vacuum of the sheriff's need and was flying a Hughes 500-C on-call for the sheriff. I looked up WAYco in the phone book and asked the owner (whom

I shall call Vetfella) if he needed a pilot. He invited me to his office for an interview. My wife was at work, and I was babysitting my infant daughter, so I asked Vetfella if he minded if I brought my baby to the interview. In the middle of the interview, I changed my daughter's diaper. A father himself, he understood and hired me.

Vetfella checked me out in the company's Hughes-500-C. We did practice landings and autorotations at the disused Santa Rosa Army Airfield in the Roseland district of southwest Santa Rosa. At an Air America reunion soon thereafter, one of the old-timer fixed-wing pilots told me he flown P-40s out of that base during WWII. That airfield has since become an industrial park.

Early December, 1977
A Life-Saving Rescue at the Geysers

I checked out to be the Sonoma County sheriff backup helicopter pilot, "Angel 2." During my check ride with Vetfella, dispatch sent us up to the geysers to rescue a construction worker who had been injured. The man was in great pain, seemed terrified, and had probably never been in a helicopter before. Vetfella suggested that I climb in back and comfort the injured man, which I did. I held his hand and told him that we were on our way to the hospital at lightning speed, and he would soon be in good hands. He seemed relieved. I never heard any feedback, but I believe he survived.

I must have had an FAA Part 135 check out about this time, but if I did, it was another easy, casual ride.

Being the sheriff relief pilot kept me out of jail one night. I was attending evening classes at Sonoma State College (later: CSUS Rohnert Park) studying geography just to burn off my GI Bill. The geography students had a club called the Radical Advocates of Geography (R*A*G). Typical college kids, they liked to party. When they found out that I owned two huge barns, they asked me if we could have a party in one of my barns. Why not?

There were dozens of cars around my barn, the R*A*G band was blasting, and everybody was having a good time. A crabby old lady, who lived 100 yards away, got upset with the noise and called the cops, reporting there was a bunch of wild people trespassing and having an out-of-control party in an abandoned barn next door to her property.

Luckily, I just happened to be walking back to my house from the barn when six carloads of law enforcement officers briskly drove in and halted in my circular driveway. Dispatch had sent three carloads of sheriff deputies and three carloads of city police because they weren't sure if my property was in the city or in county jurisdiction. Somewhat surprised, I greeted the leader of the officers and asked, "How can I help you?" I explained that it was my property, it was my party, and I was the sheriff's helicopter pilot. I showed them my beeper and invited them to call dispatch and have me beeped. They departed, mission aborted. Had I not inadvertently intercepted them, they might have raided the barn and discovered that my barn was full of underage students indulging in alcohol and marijuana.

Soon Captain Kelly of the Sonoma County Sheriff's office called me in to his office for an interview and to officially bless me as the sheriff relief pilot. He told me that I would be required to attend paramedic training to be a first responder. That sounded good to me; I liked that sort of thing.

He was a big bull of a man, all decked out in his perfectly pressed uniform, with black patch pockets on the khaki shirt, adorned with badges, captain's bars, and shiny decorations, most reminiscent of a senior officer's military uniform. He said they would have to do a full background investigation on me. These two bits of information tweaked my PTSD. I had nothing to hide. I had a sterling background, having had a top-secret clearance while in the Marine Corps. I had no criminal record whatsoever, disregarding a handful of traffic citations over decades. But somehow, I allowed my PTSD to convince myself that I didn't want to give up the $225 a month that the GI Bill was paying me to attend night classes. The sheriff job paid just slightly less per month, so I phoned Captain Kelly the next day and declined the job, using the excuse that it would cost me money. That was a huge mistake for more reasons than one. Coulda, woulda, shoulda. PTSD struck again.

Early 1978
I Meet a Legend of the Helicopter Business

WAYco dispatched me on a mission to carry a load of executives to survey the geothermal sites from the air. We rendezvoused with the people at the Sonoma County Airport coffee shop. The weather was atrocious, with pounding rain and high winds all day long, and we never got off the ground. Several other pilots from other companies and I sat around, drank a lot of coffee, and told war stories. It was here that I met yet another of the great characters in the helicopter industry, Ron Garlick. I soon began to work for him part-time doing heavy lift jobs all around the Bay Area.

His company was originally a heating and air conditioning company in Concord, California. Several times, Garlick had hired helicopters to lift air conditioning units to the tops of buildings. He didn't like the high prices they charged and decided that he would buy his own helicopter and cut out the middleman. He bought two surplus H-34s and put them to work. At first, he didn't feel confident doing the lifts himself, so he hired me. He eventually taught himself to fly the H-34s and did most of his own lift jobs. I don't know if he hired instructors to help him learn the H-34, but I was impressed that he was able to teach himself. The H-34 is easy to fly once you have some experience in it, but the learning curve is a challenge.

January 26, 1978

Garlick hired me one day to fly for him on a contract to string power line cables from post to post to bring energy down from the geysers to the grid. As we broke ground departing Lampson Field airport, I noticed that he shut off the electric fuel pump. I asked him why he did that, which was completely alien to everything I had learned while flying many hours in the H-34 in the military and at Air America. He said, "It will save me from burning out the fuel pump." He was so adamant about it, I didn't feel like arguing with him about it, even though we were headed off to fly in the mountains. I knew if we had an engine-driven fuel pump failure, our engine would quit, and we would crash.

A few weeks later, I heard that he had crashed into an orchard, killing a few pear trees and demolishing one of his H-34s because he had turned off the electric fuel pump. He had another crash on top of a school building in Alameda, but he walked away from this crash, too. Perhaps teaching yourself to fly H-34s is not such a good idea.

The Worldwide Adventures of a Helicopter Pilot ... the rest of the story

Garlick's crash atop a school building in Alameda, CA.

April 28, 1978
Carrying Surveyors to the Geothermal Sites

All the geothermal development in the hills required that the area be surveyed in detail. WAYco got the contract to carry the surveyors. I had flown power company executives over these sites a few years before while flying for Calicopters out of Stockton. Now I was in direct support of the surveying crews.

The surveyors would show up at the airport in the morning. First stop, I would drop off the guy with the transit on a hilltop. Then I transported a second man to a hilltop perhaps a quarter-mile away. I would then drop off the third man at another hilltop. By the time I got back to the transit man, he had taken two shots on the measuring sticks set up by the other two guys, and I would then move him to a new vantage point. By the time he was ready, I had moved the two stickmen to new points. Surveying in this manner was much more efficient than doing this job on foot.

Before using helicopters, the men had to start up before dawn and drive 90 minutes from Santa Rosa. Then they had to scale the hillsides, which were crumbly chert, where for every step they took, they slid back a half foot. It was hard, hot, arduous work just to get to the top of a single hill, and once they got the shot, they had to descend the hillside and climb up to the next hilltop. If there were lucky, they might get two sets of survey shots in a long day. Using our Hughes 500-C, they could do in a half-day work that would have taken them weeks to do on foot.

Another advantage was safety. Early one morning a trio of surveyors were driving up the winding, single-lane, dirt road in the dark to get to the trailhead so they could start their day. In the dark, they didn't see that recent rains had washed out the road, and they drove smartly into a mud slide area where the road had given way. Their truck tumbled to a stop, and the men scrambled out of their truck just before it was swallowed by the still-flowing mudslide, buried forever. Just think if they had not been able to get out in time!

One day I had a few minutes to wait because the surveyors were just redoing one set of shots. They asked me to wait for about forty minutes. I couldn't just fly around for that long; I would get too low on fuel. I searched for a flat spot to land, but these were scarce. Finally, I spied a perfect flat spot to land under the umbrella of a huge Valley Oak tree. I hovered in, landed, and shut down under its protective canopy. When the proper time had passed, I started up, hovered out of that natural hangar, and went on my way. Another time, I landed in a tight spot on the hillside that had a steep upslope to it. After I shut down, I stepped out of the 500-C to relieve my bladder. When I stepped off the skids, the machine started to tip over backward! I quickly hopped back onto the skids and competed my business from there. I sat in the cockpit to keep it stable until my wait was over. Several large geothermal power plants were eventually built in this area, and they continue to generate power to this day.

Our local fuel company hired cute young girls to drive the refueling trucks and pass gas to any aircraft that required it. A few times, whenever I had an empty seat in my 500-C, I would take one of the girls up to the geysers with me so she could see the work they were supporting. It was good PR, and I felt good about giving each girl a free ride.

WAYco attempted to become the Sonoma County air ambulance. I carried a doctor up the North Coast to the little village called Elk to demonstrate our capabilities. When I arrived, I couldn't resist landing atop one of the isolated sea stacks offshore from the tiny town. As I lifted off, I spied naked girls sunbathing on the beach below. On the return trip to Santa Rosa, I was astounded to see a huge copper-roofed Buddhist temple way out in the redwood forest. I was a native of Sonoma County and had spent many hours fishing and diving around on the coast, but I didn't know that temple existed. Further down the road, I was delighted to see that a carpet of apple blossoms brightened the entire Anderson Valley.

June 12, 1978
A Laminated Beam Becomes Toothpicks

WAYco got the job of lifting large, laminated wood beams to the top of a huge home being built on top of a small hill in the Napa Valley, just across the valley from Yountville. The driveway up to the home under construction was too narrow and twisty for the big truck carrying the 27-foot long beams, so the trailer parked at the bottom of the hill. The beams were fairly light, not a big challenge power-wise to our little 500C. This was going to be a piece of cake. When we arrived, the building contractor said he didn't trust *our* equipment. He *insisted* that we use *his* metal hooks on the ends of our steel cables to lift the beams. We tried to argue with him that we were experts at this, and we knew what we were

doing, but he wouldn't hear it. He again persisted that we use his cheap aluminum hooks he had bought just that morning from a local hardware store. I hovered over the truss and pulled tension on the load. It was fairly light, and I lifted it easily off the truck and started slowly and gently for the hilltop. At about 100 feet above the ground, both hooks suddenly sheared simultaneously, dropping the expensive beam to the dirt road, barely missing two cars. It landed flat, disintegrating into a mass of splinters.

The laminated beam that fell to earth near Yountville, California.

Had not both hooks failed simultaneously, the heavy load would have swung like a pendulum, pulling my little helicopter out of control and probably slamming it into the ground before I could react. The contractor had no choice but to admit that he was at fault. The beam was custom made for this house, and it would take weeks to get a replacement, greatly delaying the job...and his paycheck. Fortunately, the contractor was able to modify some other beam he found in stock, and a few days later, I flew back over to Yountville and finished the job. This time the contractor allowed us to use our own steel hooks.

Replacing the beam a few days later.

WAYco was a shoestring start-up company and needed to do anything to stay alive. Even though they lost money on every trip, they found it better to have the helicopters losing a little bit of money every day rather than sitting idle and losing lots of money every day. We began to barnstorm fairs. I flew hundreds of passengers in the Hughes 500C and 269C at the Lake County Fair, the Contra Costa County Fair, the Kings County Fair, the San Luis Obispo County Fair, the Mendocino County Fair, and the Lassen County Fair, and several air shows and fly-ins around northern California.

At the Porterville fly-in, I was elated to meet one of my heroes, the famous WWII Marine Corps fighter ace, Pappy Boyington. It was a treat to shake his hand and buy his autographed book, *Baa Baa Black Sheep*. Returning to Santa Rosa, I plotted a direct line from Porterville. It was later that I realized in the dark I had busted right through a restricted area east of Concord protecting the Lawrence Livermore National Laboratory. I would legally return to this spot while fighting fires a few years later.

While flying an airshow in Ukiah, I saw an old friend fly by. The GOODYEAR Blimp had been in the large hangar at Tustin for repairs just before I got off active duty. After the repairs, the pilot was giving rides to base personnel. I got in line and was the last person to board the last flight. The pilot saw my aviator wings and asked me if I would like to fly in the copilot's seat. YES I would. After we flew around for a while, he said those magic words. "You got it." I took over the controls and flew the blimp for about 15 minutes.

Now the Blimp was flying over. I had to say, "Hello." I tried to reach them on the common radio frequency, but no luck. Nevertheless, I flew up to the blimp and flew formation on it for about two minutes, keeping a safe distance as to not give the pilot any reason for concern.

After the air show in Ukiah, I flew low over the entire length of the Russian River from the Coyote Dam to Healdsburg. I saw beautiful sights and many amazing homes perched on hillsides overlooking the river.

Flying county fairs was fun and challenging at the same time. We got to meet a lot of wonderful folks from all the rural areas and give them an aerial view of their hometowns. Sometimes a couple would show up and want to take their child for a ride. A problem was that sometimes both adults were very heavy, and we knew that there was no way we were going to get the little Hughes 269-C off the ground with that much weight. It took a bit of talking, but we usually split the heavy couple up and paired them off with lighter people.

One thing delighted us pilots at each fair. We were told to take the incoming and the outgoing county fair queens up for free rides. The newly-elected queen was always fresh and bubbly, aglow with the excitement of her new job, her new duties, and exalted position. The outgoing queen, on the other hand, was always tired and worn looking. It seems that a year of being the queen of a county was hard work.

For two years running, we also sold rides at the Bodega Bay Fisherman's Festival. That was great fun. We flew everybody around the Bay and over Bodega Head, all in three minutes of flying. It was amusing that the festival was always the most beautiful weather all year in this area, somewhat warm and sunny with light winds. The weather was so exceptional that some of the local real estate people refused to work the weekend, saying it would be unfair to sell property based on the weather that weekend, as the weather was usually much colder and damper.

In early May 1978, WAYco Director of Operations, Ms. "Whine," a flight instructor, took me flying and checked me out in a Cessna 182. We made steep turns, slow flight, stalls, and approaches. I now could legally fly people around in the 182 commercially should such a need arise. It never did.

August 20, 1978

When I flew to Susanville, Lassen County, to fly the Lassen County Fair, the local radio station announced to its audience that helicopter rides would be available at the fairgrounds, and that, "Vietnam veteran Bill Collier would be flying passengers." A former grammar school and high school classmate, Janet Sweet, was living in Susanville at the time. She heard my name on the radio and came to visit.

It was here that I made a mistake that could have been a disaster. The local USFS firefighters asked me if I could take them up so that they could display their rappelling skills to the fairgoers. The firefighters had arranged for me to rappel them down right into the middle of the fairgrounds. What they didn't do was institute any kind of crowd control.

As I hovered about fifty feet over the center of the fairground, a large crowd gathered beneath me. I was hovering directly over dozens of people, which is strictly forbidden by FAA rules. I knew better and wanted to terminate the exercise, but I had a fireman dangling underneath me on the rappelling line. I didn't feel comfortable moving off until he was safely on the ground. Glancing down, I saw a baby carriage shooting off across the pavement with a parent in hot pursuit! Fortunately for me, no one was injured, and no one reported me to the FAA.

A few years later, I attended the pre-dawn launching of many colorful hot air balloons at the hot air balloon festival in Windsor, California. The local REACH Air Medical Services helicopter was on display. I chatted with the pilot a bit; he seemed professional and competent. I was appalled when he departed low and slow over the balloons on the grass, some of them full, and some of them in the process of being inflated. Nothing awful happened, but I did hear that he was reported to the FAA and lost his license.

The whirlybird... ...gets the work (done)

Helicopter hauls roofing and insulation to the top of Santa Rosa's Bethlehem Towers housing complex for re-roofing job. The copter is also used to bring debris down

High Flying Roofers

An old man in the lobby of Bethlehem Towers chuckled an old man's chuckle as William Heyland walked past. "Hey. Ya oughta charge people ten bucks to take 'em up to the roof." Pause. "An' then charge 'em 20 bucks to bring 'em back down."

The old man broke up and William Heyland smiled. His helicopter was at that moment hammering the air overhead lifting boxes of roofing debris off the top of the building and setting them gingerly in the parking lot below.

The roofing job was being done by Al Cal Roofers, a Santa Rosa firm which had been momentarily stymied over the logistics of putting a new surface on the lid of the 15-story retirement complex. Al Cal department head Troy Linville says a helicopter was "the only way to do it." The biggest crane available couldn't negotiate power lines and other obstacles, while the Hughes 500 helicopter soared freely back and forth dangling boxes of old roofing material at the end of a long cable.

Heyland, who with his partners Bill Collier and Bob Walesh says construction jobs are the meat of their business. The Hughes helicopter can lift up to 1,000 pounds and for bigger jobs they use a larger chopper with an 18,000 pound load capacity. Heyland says his company will lift virtually anything anywhere and also offers rides at county fairs.

None of the elderly residents clustered on the sidewalk seemed eager for a ride but most were enjoying the show. "This is the most exciting thing that's happened around here in a long time," said a silver-haired woman with a happy sigh.

Clipping from Santa Rosa Press Democrat, August 31, 1978

August 29, 1978
High-Flying Roofers

Our company was hired to assist roofers to replace the roof on the highest building in Santa Rosa, the circular thirteen-story high-rise retirement village, Bethlehem Towers. The roofers had scraped all the old roofing off the top into wooden boxes. We flew up and attached the cables on the boxes onto the belly hook of our 500C, lifting the trash away to the parking lot. On the return trip, we lifted the replacement roofing materials to the top. This was great fun and very satisfying work.

We were hard at work when a petty local city government official arrived and insisted that we shut down. He was upset because we didn't have his permission to fly over "my city." He said that anything flying over his city was in his domain, under his control. I pointed up to a commercial airliner going overhead and said, "What about the airliners? Do they have to check in with you before they can fly over Santa Rosa?" He didn't like that question and continued to insist that we shut down. We tried to explain to him that he had no jurisdiction over our aircraft, that this work was under the jurisdiction of the FAA, and that we had notified the FAA of what we were doing. He still insisted we shut down and threatened to call the police. We shut down, and project manager, Bill H., called our office. Vetfella's uncle sat on the county commission, so a call from him to the Santa Rosa mayor got the petty official off our backs and we went back to work finishing the job.

From the weekly newspaper, "News-Herald" September 6-12, 1978

August 2-3, 1978
Engine Flame Outs!

While Bill H. and I took turns flying the 500C, selling rides at the Lake County Fair in Lakeport, the machine became difficult to start. Sometimes it would take two or three attempts to get the turbine to light off. Worried the engine might flame out during flight, endangering passengers, I decided to not fly the 500C anymore. We phoned in and complained to Director of Operations, Ms. Whine.

Our company mechanic soon showed up, inspected the engine, and declared the machine safe to fly. He said that there must be some contamination in the start-up cycle, but once the engine started, it would continue to run. I didn't trust him. I didn't know enough about the inner workings of the fuel system to know just how separated the two systems might be...or if they were separate at all. Could it be that whatever was clogging up the start-up cycle would soon be clogging up the fuel flow to the turbine as well?

The next day, the flameouts became more frequent. I again decided I wouldn't fly the machine. I walked over to a phone booth and called the home office. Reporting the problem to D O, Ms. Whine, I told her that I wouldn't fly the H500C anymore; she *ordered* me: "Bill Collier, you get your ass back in that helicopter and FLY it!" Just as I was trying to decide whether to say, "Come on up here and fly it yourself," or "You know where you can stick that helicopter," Bill H. walked up and said, "The question is moot; the 500 won't start at all now." I put him on the line with her.

Our mechanic showed up again and replaced the fuel filter, something he should have done the day before. It was seriously clogged with tiny metal particles. We determined that these particles came from a hand pump that we used to manually pump fuel from the fuel tank on the company pickup. This "molasses pump" was meant to pump heavy liquids and oils which would lubricate the pump internally. Pumping fuel removed all lubrication from the pump, causing it to gradually disintegrate internally, hence the metallic particles in our fuel filter and the subsequent flameouts.

The last night of the fair, Ms. Whine ordered me to fly the 500C home immediately after the fair closed, about 1:00 a.m. She said it needed to be at the hangar, "First thing tomorrow morning for maintenance." I refused. There is a high, dark, wooded mountain (Mount Saint Helena, 4,328 feet above sea level) between Lakeport and Santa Rosa. No way was I going to fly over that dark mountain on this moonless night. When I delivered the 500 to the hangar the next morning at about 8:30 a.m., there was no one eager and waiting to work on it.

Later that day, Ms. Whine phoned me and again *ordered* me to come into the office so that the office manager could lay me off. I refused this order, too. I'd had enough of this woman's orders. A few minutes later, the office manager phoned and politely requested that I come in. I was pleased to go to the office for him. I had had it with WAYco—and none too soon.

Early in 1978, WAYco won a contract to provide a Bell 205A to cover the California Division of Forestry (CDF) base near Willits, about seventy miles north of Santa Rosa. WAYco didn't own a 205A, so they had to hustle one up. Somehow, they found one for sale in Peru, transported it to Sonoma County, and outfitted it in time for the CDF contract. I wasn't privy to the details of this. Bill H. was the primary pilot because he had more Huey time than I did, though I met all the CDF Huey flight time requirements.

June 20, 1978, I had a check ride with the CDF check pilot in the company's tiny Hughes 269C. I embarrassed myself slightly when I lightly contacted the ground on a 180-degree autorotation. I corrected my mistake on the next three full autos, and the CDF check pilot gave me the certification I needed to be the Huey relief pilot. I doubled as the fuel truck driver. It promised to be a lucrative contract for the little company. I never flew the WAYco 205 because I was laid off.

The contract specified only that the WAYco 205A be on station from 10 a.m. until sundown every day. They could do other work with the machine in the mornings, just so long as the 205 was on the Willits pad by showtime.

And Compressor Stalls, Too!

Now, here is why I have changed the name of the company and of all the principals involved. I was a witness to this event, I swear it is true, and I could provide documentation and other witnesses to this should I ever be called into court. The maintenance logbooks of the 205 would be witness enough.

WAYco secured a contract to set some power poles high up in the Sierra Nevada Mountains. In order to get the job done in time to get back to Willits by show time, Vetfella launched the 205 in the wee moonless hours before sunrise. Bill H. was flying and the young copilot's girlfriend was along for the ride, too. In the dark, at altitude over the Sierra Mountains, the 205 began having compressor stalls.

There is not much that is more frightening for any pilot than having an incipient engine failure over mountains in the dark! They made a quick retreat to lower altitude and the flatlands of the

Sacramento Valley with plenty of room to land, should they need to. By then, it was daylight, so they limped the faltering Huey back to Sonoma County, but it was hard down. It could no longer be available for the CDF contract. Management tried and tried to find a replacement engine for the 205, but the only one available anywhere belonged to Evergreen Helicopter Company, and they wanted $175,000 for it. That amount was more than the company stood to make from the CDF contract.

The company had to give up the contract to the next lowest bidder, which just happened to be...Evergreen. No wonder Evergreen wanted so much for the engine. I believe WAYco was liable to pay for the difference between what they bid on the contract and what Evergreen bid. The company was now in dire financial straits.

The compressor stalls happened right after I was laid off, but it soon became known throughout the company that previous compressor stalls were well documented in the maintenance log of the helicopter. I talked to Bill H. and the mechanic; both confirmed the details. Could it be that because the records were in Spanish, no one had bothered to translate them? No excuse! What WAYco management did was criminal. They put the lives of the pilots and the CDF firefighters at risk because they wanted to reap the financial rewards of the contract. In aviation, to knowingly and purposely put the lives of crews at risk is the ultimate sin. I have never forgiven those people for doing that, and I never will. In 2017, I crossed paths with those despicable people at a social gathering, and I shunned them.

Now, desperate for money, the company had maxed out all of its credit and all the credit of its partners. There was no credit to buy fuel. When Ms. Whine got a call from a railroad executives to overfly railroad tracks in Mendocino County that had been washed out by a landslide, Ms. Whine insisted that the execs pay cash up-front...on a Sunday. Somehow, they managed to come up with the cash and got their ride.

WAYco folded soon after that.

Chapter 22
Garlick Helicopter Company

I went to work for Ron Garlick, doing heavy lifts around the Bay Area on a piecemeal basis. I liked this. I didn't have to report every day, but I was making good money doing interesting work. I lifted a lot of air conditioners, ventilators, and roofing supplies to the roofs of many buildings. The most memorable lift was in the up-and-coming Silicon Valley, where I made my heaviest lift ever.

November 7, 1978

I flew Garlick's H-34 to Silicon Valley to lift fifteen units to the roof of the QUME building. I lifted the first four loads, each weighing 4300 pounds, but I soon discovered that the rest were too heavy; my strain gauge read 5,250 pounds, more than the limit on the H-34 external load hook, 5,000 pounds. I decided to try and lift one anyway. Once I got it airborne, I couldn't keep it airborne. I didn't have the power to lift this thing, even at sea level on this cool morning with low fuel.

I said the heck with it, and did a hover-jump takeoff, and hopped the 5,250-pound load up to the top edge of the one-story building. I allowed the load to pull me down, then hovered over the load to regain my lost RPM, and once again rolled my power up to maximum-plus and repeated the maneuver. After two more hover-jump hops, I was able to hop the big article into place. I refused to do this again. I didn't like abusing the machine so much.

I had used this same technique while flying in Laos for Air America to lift a heavy portable sawmill engine off a hillside and another time to lift the undercarriage of a 155 Howitzer off a hillside. In these two cases, I had plenty of altitude to work with, and I jumped off hills into clean headwinds. Once I got translational lift, I flew the load to their destination airports, where each time I landed into a stiff breeze. In this case, I had no headwinds, and I was lifting the load up instead of taking it down. There was no wind to work with at the QUME lift.

I flew out to the foothills twenty miles west of Woodland, California, to lift the remains of a busted light aircraft (Mooney) that someone had driven partway into a hillside. I only had to carry it a short distance to a nearby road so a crew could put the remains on a truck. I never heard any details of the crash, whether anyone died in the crash or not.

February 9, 1979
The Worm That Ate Concord

Garlick called me one day to do some external lifting at the refinery in Martinez. The ships normally offloaded their products using long lengths of plastic PVC pipes that measured 200 feet in length and about two feet in diameter. Once the need for the pipes was completed, they had to be moved. The pipes were awkward and difficult to move by truck, so the refinery people called Garlick to see if this job could be done by helicopter.

The long pipes were lying on the ground on the west side of the Benecia-Martinez Bridge, and they needed to be moved to the east side. The distance was only about a half-mile, but it presented a couple of problems. The first problem was that the tubes could not be lifted over the highway on the bridge but must be carried under the bridge. Since the tubes were longer than the bridge was high, it was time to get creative.

I pulled up on one end of the first 2,200-pound pipe until it was about one-third of the way up, and I could see that it was about to kink. I then moved off so that I was no longer lifting straight up but pulling so that it slid along the ground. As it slid, I added more power until it came off the ground and was hanging vertically beneath me, a 200-foot snake dangling beneath the helicopter. Now the problem was how to get past the bridge.

*Pulling up the long pipe from the ground.
Laying it down in the water when approaching the bridges*

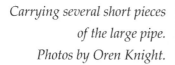

*Carrying several short pieces
of the large pipe.
Photos by Oren Knight.*

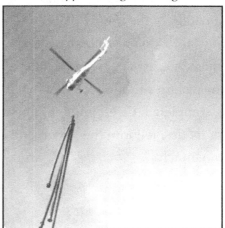

I was way too high to fly under the bridge, and I couldn't overfly the highway traffic on the bridge. I flew a gentle, slow descending 360 over the water until I again headed toward the bridge maintaining about twenty miles per hour of forward speed. I gently laid the big tube down in the water, reversing the process I had used to pick it up. The tube floated and I became an airborne tugboat driver. I wondered if the bridge was high enough for me to fly under it. I knew that I always had the option to abort the mission and take the tube back to where I found it.

There was plenty of room to pass underneath the bridge. I was careful to check for any hanging cables or other obstacles that might bring this flight to an abrupt halt. I proceeded towards the bridge, lowering the helicopter more and more until I had plenty of overhead clearance and was quite close to the water, and I cruised under the bridge towing the giant tube. A railroad bridge ran parallel to the first, but it was the same height as the auto bridge. It was a real thrill for me as I passed under the railroad bridge and saw that the drawbridge operator had raised the drawbridge for me. On subsequent trips, he did not.

Once through the bridge obstacles, I slid the tube out of the water easily as I accelerated and climbed away. When I reached the destination of the tube, I placed the lower end on the ground and gently laid it down while simultaneously sliding it forward placing it where the customer wanted it to be, without kinking it. I returned to the pickup site and repeated the lift five more times until the job was completed. One bundle of about five short tubes came loose from its ties, fell into the water, and disappeared. No one seemed to care much.

The drop zone was within the air traffic control zone of Concord Buchanan airport, so I checked in with the local control tower as I approached the drop area.

"Buchanan tower, helicopter November four seven eight niner Romeo,"

"Eight niner Romeo, Buchanan,"

"Buchanan, eight niner Romeo is doing external lifting in your control zone, at the south approach to the Martinez Bridge. I will be low, and outside the flow of your airport traffic."

"Roger, eight niner Romeo, we have you in sight. What is that thing that you are carrying?"

"This is the giant worm that ate Concord," I replied.

I did many more lifts in Silicon Valley around the Bay Area. One day I did sixteen lifts in thirty-six minutes.

Chapter 23
Summer, 1980
California Helicopter Company

I reconnected with one of my friends from the Carson/Saudi Arabia caper, Tom Balestreri. He had somehow gained control over two S-58Ts and created two small companies, California Helicopter and The Rotor Works. He was trying to work the two machines around the San Francisco Bay Area out of Oakland International Airport. Because they were both bright orange in color, his little company named them "Orange Julius" and "Clockwork Orange." Tom hired me.

At that time, the General Motors plant in Fremont was being retrofitted, and there was a lot of construction lifting to be done. Tom checked me out and signed me off in Clockwork Orange. The next week I found myself hovering Orange Julius over the GM plant, threading several 4,000-pound loads down through a maze of steel beams and cables to help the workers remodel the plant. I realized that, even in this twin-engine S-58T, should one of the engines so much as hiccup, I would be completely screwed. I would tumble down through the tangle of steel beams and cables and probably not survive. By now, I had two darling toddlers at home, and I didn't want to risk leaving them fatherless, so I told Tom I didn't want to work for him anymore.

Tom had a most stunningly beautiful and sassy girlfriend that could charm the chrome off a brass doorknob. When someone asked the beautiful blonde what part she played in the company, she replied, "I fuck the chief pilot." I heard years later that Tom went back to school and became an MD. I hope he married that perky blond.

1981

The Sonoma County Sheriff was hiring pilots to fly their new Hughes 500-D. I had pretty much blown my chance to be the sheriff pilot, but I applied anyway and flew a check ride in the 500D. Pilot Keith Gunderson called it a biannual flight review and signed me off, but of course I had burned that bridge, so I didn't get hired. Not too long after that, Gunderson came down with some dreaded disease, and his flying days were over. The full-time sheriff pilot job would have been mine had I stayed the course. Being the dashing, well-paid local Vietnam veteran hometown hero flying the local sheriff helicopter around the county would have been the ultimate dream job for me. DRAT! Shoulda, Coulda, Woulda!

Had I become the sheriff pilot, two lives would not have been lost. The sheriff decided to train deputies to be pilots. One dark and foggy night, a low time, inexperienced deputy sheriff and his observer launched out towards the coast on a mission of mercy. The pilot got disoriented and drove the county's brand new 500D into a big smoking hole in the ground, killing them both. I'll never understand why bureaucrats think they can save money by hiring amateurs for such demanding jobs.

Chapter 24
1982
Alaska Again
Bristol Bay Helicopter Company

Ron Garlick eventually moved his air conditioning company to Hamilton, Montana, and renamed it Garlick Helicopters. He took over a defunct plastics factory and created a very special niche in the helicopter industry. He bought crashed military helicopters, took all useable parts from each one, and then cobbled them together to make whole new machines. He built and operated the very first civilian Huey Cobra from the salvaged remnants of several army crashes. This Cobra could only be flown in the categories of experimental or restricted, but he was able to get USFS contracts to drop water on forest fires for it. Any movie you see from that era with a Cobra in it...it was his Cobra. Somehow, he even acquired mini guns and blank cartridges for the movies.

One year, he was dipping water out of Lake Pend Oreille near Sandpoint, Idaho, when his engine failed and he crashed into the lake. He sank with the machine and almost drowned, but a nearby fisherman pulled him out. Ron salvaged the Cobra and rebuilt it...again.

Early 1982, I got a phone call from a Mr. David Mahrt, owner-operator of a small firm called Bristol Bay Helicopters, Ltd. He needed an H-34 pilot. I asked him to give me a day or two to consider his offer and to talk it over with my wife. After a couple of days, I accepted the job.

Mahrt's H-34 was being rebuilt by Garlick in Hamilton, Montana. Mahrt wanted me to go there, check out the machine to make sure it was airworthy, and fly it to Anchorage. Mahrt had some contracts in Dillingham to support the salmon fishing industry. I trusted Garlick, and I felt that with my extensive H-34 experience, I could pass as a test pilot to check out the newly rebuilt H-34.

Eventually, after three weeks and under pressure from Mahrt, I accepted the H-34, even though it flew slightly out of rigging. I could either have the needle-ball instrument centered and fly in a slight crab, or I could have the helicopter fly straight and level and have the needle-ball instrument about half a ball out of balanced flight. I chose the latter. After all, my flying was going to be bush flying around Alaska in daylight conditions. That basic instrument slightly out of whack would not be a major concern.

On our trip north, the first and most exciting thing my crew and I did was fly across the tall, jagged Swan Range and the Flathead Range of the Rocky Mountains into the great plains of Canada, skirting Glacier National Park. It is amazing how quickly a pilot becomes attuned to the slightest whisper of the engine when flying over mountains, especially at night. We passed over these great aircraft-munching peaks without event.

We refueled at Calgary and flew on to Rocky Mountain House, with only one small glitch. When we passed through customs at Calgary, the Canadian customs agent asked me if we had an Emergency Locator Transmitter (ELT) onboard. I said yes, knowing full well that we didn't. I didn't want to delay us and spend more company money on something I felt was unnecessary, as we were going to follow highways all the way. Next day we flew to Fort Nelson via Dawson Creek and stayed over there. The third day we made it to Northway, Alaska via Watson Lake and Whitehorse, Yukon Territory. After four full days of flying, we arrived in Anchorage. These were days of grinding along over the road at cruise speed, watching miles and miles of miles pass underneath the chopper. So far as long-distance ferries go, this one was quite mundane. There are small dirt strips every half hour or so along the highway. At times, we stopped at one of these small strips for lunch or coffee just to break the monotony.

Fuel was easy to obtain, and the AlCan Highway underneath us for most of the trip made for a wonderful, never-ending emergency landing strip should we ever need one. At Anchorage, we spent the next three days going over the ship and making sure everything was acceptable for working in the field. I remember being impressed that at midnight Anchorage was light enough that I could read a newspaper outside. The next day I followed Mahrt in his second H-34 he lovingly called "Baby," to Dillingham. Along the way, we flew the length of beautiful Lake Clark. Dave radioed me that during World War II, a Navy PBY had sunk into that deep lake and was still there, awaiting salvage by some lucky divers.

The tidal surges in Bristol Bay are extreme. While unloading their catch at the Dillingham harbor, the local fishermen get stuck in the mud at the bottom of the bay and have to wait for the next high tide to get out of the small harbor to go fishing again. Time is money, and they would very much like to spend the next turn of the tide harvesting fish rather than sitting in the mud. Mahrt sold the local Martin Cannery on the idea that he could unload the fish quickly using the long-line technique. He convinced them that the boats could loiter offshore, the helicopter could unload a boat in a short time, and the boat could go right back to work.

Mahrt was a helicopter Gypsy. He had no qualms about flying into an airport, introducing himself, and then start borrowing things from the local operators. The local people were impressed by his two large machines and never questioned his ability to pay. I never saw him return any favor or pay anybody for the things he borrowed. He thought nothing of using the local's phone and running up huge phone bills while ordering parts and calling for technical assistance. It got to the point where I was embarrassed to go to any of the local businesses. One day in the cafeteria at Martin's Cannery, someone asked me, in a somewhat hostile tone, how long I had worked for Dave. I sheepishly told them, "Just a few weeks, and I hope not much longer."

On one of the very first lifts, I did something that inadvertently soured the program. I was hovering over a boat to pick up a cubic tote with 2,200 pounds of fish in it. The fisherman below was having trouble catching the hook. Looking at it from his point of view…here is a very big, noisy machine hovering fifteen feet overhead, and he is supposed to catch the swinging hook and latch it onto the tote. I made an effort to go a little lower so that he could grab the hook. The hook got to him, but suddenly his eyes widened in horror, and he frantically waved me away from the boat. I thought he must have seen something wrong with the helicopter, so I quickly flew back to the Martin Cannery landing pad.

Mahrt was there and motioned me to shut down. I climbed out of the H-34, expecting to see something major component falling off my aircraft. Dave told me that in dipping the hook down to hand the hook to the fisherman, I got just a little too low, and one of my rotor blades whacked the radio antennas off the top of the cabin of his boat and, he said, came within inches of the steel pipe holding the antennas in place!

Had the rotors contacted these steel fittings, the results would have been a disaster. I would have crashed into the small boat or flipped over into the freezing waters of Bristol Bay. Falling onto the fishing boat or falling into the freezing Alaskan waters would have been equally fatal. I didn't expect to survive a crash into the cold, freezing bay waters. I wore a life preserver under my safety straps so they could find my body should I drown. I don't recall why we didn't simply resort to a longer external line, but for some reason, we didn't. Perhaps the word spread among the fishermen that I had nearly crashed onto one of their boats, and they no longer minded waiting out the low tides.

We began to carry fish from the shores of the river. The native Alaskans used fish traps near the shore to capture salmon and sold them to the Martin Cannery. We had a regular route up and down the shore, bringing tons of fish back to the cannery. The fishing was all done by mid-July, and I went home. Never to return...I thought.

It seemed to me that Mahrt had a most unique way of handling his spare parts needs. He had a large green military box five feet square and about three feet deep, where he stored all the spares. What I observed, though, was that every time we changed out a part, he placed the old part back in the box. Since he was a very religious man, I finally figured out that he was not sending the used parts back for repair but was placing the old parts in the box and praying over the box to heal them. So it seemed. In reality, I am pretty sure that he sent the parts back to Montana for repair or replacement.

Chapter 25
A Temporary Career Change

I was partying at my old buddy Tom Sullivan's waterfront condo in Alameda. Talking to his neighbor, I learned that she was about to graduate from the local chiropractic college. After some discussion in which she learned that I was in a bit of a loose-ends quandary, she asked me, "Have you ever thought of being a chiropractor?" That had never crossed my mind, but right then and there I spontaneously and whimsically decided that I would become a Doctor of Chiropractic. Dr. Phyllis told me that when I finished school, I could come join her practice in Sonoma County. Perfect. I had a goal and a ready-made position waiting for me near home when I completed twelve quarters of school.

PTSD at work again! That is another of the major symptoms of PTSD: making poor choices and whimsically jumping into big projects without thinking them through.

I immediately began the challenging process to get admitted to Life Chiropractic College West (LCCW) in San Lorenzo, California. A college degree was not a pre-requisite, but some education was. I had an AA degree and nearly enough credits to have a bachelor's degree, but they were not aligned with any major. I was short two prerequisites, biochemistry and advanced physics. Fortunately, New College of California in San Francisco offered weekend classes to fill in those blanks. A bit short on cash, I decided that I would fly for the next summer to make some money for tuition and books. About that time, Mahrt called me and talked me into working for him again. This time he had, "A real contract doing serious construction work for a major company." He promised big money and good working conditions. I foolishly believed him. I went to Dillingham, Alaska again in late June of 1983, my third summer season in Alaska.

Chapter 26
June, 1983
Back To Bristol Bay

Before we could begin the huge construction project near Talkeetna, we had to finish the fishing season in Dillingham. I hauled many tons of fish from the shores of the river to the Martin Cannery.

One day while approaching the helipad near a fishing village on the shore of Nushagak Bay, I saw a crashed Cessna 207 on the beach, upside down. We got the full story from the natives. A young pilot, building his flight time to make himself valuable to the airlines, crammed at least fifteen people into his 207, which normally could take only seven or eight passengers. He had the entire beach for a runway, so it was not a problem to take an extended takeoff roll. I am sure he had done this before. As he rolled down the beach, he saw a fishing boat far out in front of him but thought he would be airborne before he reached the boat. Too late he realized he was wrong. He hit the boat; the aircraft nosed over, flipped upside down, and skidded backward to a stop on its roof. Fortunately, the passengers were so tightly packed in, no one was hurt badly. The aircraft was totaled, and the young pilot's career was badly mangled.

We filled up with fish from the natives and flew back to Martin's Cannery. I found it ironic that my mechanic, "Two Dogs," couldn't stand the smell of fish. All the while he was loading or unloading fish, he had to lean out of the H-34 and vomit.

July 7, 1983
Ground Resonance!

When we got back to the cannery landing pad, I approached the cannery LZ with my usual path, which was right over a huge stack of fish totes covered with plastic tarps. I had previously made a serious effort to insure that the loose ends and edges of the tarps were secured so that none of them could fly up into my rotor system. I had seen the disastrous results of tarps and shelter halves flying up into the rotor blades of H-34s and H-46s in Vietnam.

As I touched down, the helicopter made a pronounced lurch to one side and began to move slowly in an eccentric circular motion. I immediately recognized ground resonance! The out of balance gyrations rapidly increased in frequency and intensity with every turn of the rotors. Instantly the helicopter was shaking and dancing on its wheels in a frenzy, which grew more violent with every turn of the rotors.

There are two ways to counter ground resonance. Either will quickly move the rotor system back into balance. The first is to add enough power to the drive system so that all the blades are thrown back to their rear-most position on the blade dampeners, equalizing the distance between them. The second way is to apply the rotor brake, which causes the blades to hit the forward limits of the blade dampeners.

Somehow I convinced myself that the problem had been caused by one of the tarps coming loose and entering the rotor system, even though there was no corresponding TWACK, THWAK, TWACKING noise. Consequently, I did not want to add power and try to lift off, as that would complicate the problem by sucking more tarp into the rotor system. I chose to pump the rotor brake.

Since Mahrt's maintenance was not the best, when I grabbed the rotor brake and began pumping, nothing happened. The rotor system continued to rotate in its highly unbalanced condition. As the frequency and violence of the imbalance got faster and harder, the aircraft bounced around so much I was thrown against my shoulder straps. Even though I stood on the brakes, it danced towards the embankment of the small creek beside the helipad. I was about to dance over the edge of the bank and roll over into the creek.

Fortunately, just as the aircraft passed the edge of the helipad, I managed to pump enough pressure into the rotor brake system to bring the rotors to their proper balance and things settled down. No harm done, except a bit of embarrassment for getting into ground resonance and perhaps taking the wrong procedure to get out of it.

This incident was caused by four components of poor maintenance. The rotor blade dampeners were in poor shape, the oleo struts needed maintenance, the tires were probably not properly inflated, and the rotor brake was ineffective.

So why did I continue to fly for this Gypsy fly-by-night company? PTSD was certainly a factor. I was suffering from more than an over-developed sense of adventure. I lived with a sense of duty that carried over from my military experience, "Be loyal" and "Accomplish the mission or die trying." I did not question these attitudes for decades.

After the ground resonance incident, Two Dogs inspected the helicopter and found no obvious damage, so we returned to the river to pick up more fish from the native fishermen. At our first stop, I sat on the riverbank with the engine idling while Two Dogs loaded another cargo of totes full of fish, leaning out to throw up now and then. After he finished, he made a quick walk around the helicopter to inspect things before the twenty-minute flight back to the cannery. As he looked into the engine compartment through the intake screens, he looked up at me with a frightened look on his face and frantically drew his fingers across his throat, giving me the "cut engine" signal.

"Two Dogs." A truly strange name for a guy who looked like a tall, red-headed Viking. He claimed to be a Native American tribe member and said that in his tribe, babies were named after the first thing that impressed the mother after she gave birth. As a youngster, he, too, was curious about his name, so he asked his mother about his name. His mother explained, "When your older sister was born, the first thing I saw when I looked out of the teepee was a white fawn, so your sister's name is White Fawn. When your older brother, Standing Bear, was born, the first thing I saw when I lifted the teepee flap was a standing bear. Have I answered your question, Two Dogs Fucking?"

Two Dogs showed me damage to the drive shaft of the engine that he had missed after the ground resonance incident. The helicopter had danced around so violently that the drive shaft had bounced against a bolt on the edge of its housing. It was scored with a deep groove, like it had been turned on a lathe, making it susceptible to shearing. It could have easily snapped under a full load and caused the engine to immediately rev up to destructive speeds. Such RPM would have caused the engine fan to come apart, cutting fuel lines and electrical wires. Because of their magnesium alloy construction, an H-34 will burn to ashes in fifteen seconds on the ground. We would have exploded like a bomb, falling to earth in a shower of molten pieces.

As related earlier in Vietnam, I witnessed the horrible sight of a burning H-34 falling out of the sky. Five squadron mates were quickly incinerated alive when their H-34 was destroyed in flight by "friendly" fire," exacerbating the PTSD I had already acquired a month before.

Twenty miles from home base, we pondered what to do. This was before cell phones; the natives had no phones at their disposal, and no one nearby had a radio. We were too low for the helicopter's radios to be effective. After I thought about it for a while, I realized that since the H-34 had gotten us out here, it should get us home. I had not taken any special care on start-up and run-up or while adding power on the trip out. I decided to take the chance, and Two Dogs agreed. We dumped our cargo of fish onto the ground to lighten our load to reduce power needs. I made the gentlest start-up, run-up, and rotor engagement of my entire career. On takeoff, I applied power gently and slowly. We flew back to Martin's Cannery at a low altitude, praying that if the shaft did shear, I could be quick enough to reduce power before the fan disintegrated and hoped we might maybe make it to the ground un-roasted. We did.

Chapter 27
1983
Talkeetna, Alaska
Bouncing Beams and Collective Bounce!

The fishing was season over, and it was time to fly to Talkeetna. En route, I stopped at Lake Iliamna Airport, spending my last $40 for fuel for a few gallons of fuel because my fuel situation was marginal, and the last bit of this leg was over water. When I arrived at Talkeetna, I flew right down the main street at the minimum legal altitude to notify my crew I had arrived. There was no missing the full-throated roar of my nine-cylinder radial engine. By the time I shut down, the crew was there to pick me up. The boss was out of town, so we went directly to the bar and began serious drinking. Dave arrived the next morning and wondered why the helicopter wasn't ready to go to work...we were all still hung over and sleeping it off. I soon began to realize that my three mechanics were a bunch of drunks and might not be the most reliable. I wonder if they thought the same about me.

The state of Alaska had decided to build a power line intertie between Anchorage and Fairbanks. A transmission tower had to be built every quarter mile for a distance of more than two hundred miles. This required the transportation of hundreds of 2,200-pound I-beams out into the wilderness. Mahrt had bid on the sub-contract to carry them and got it. Good, this was a job I could sink my teeth into. My H-34 was a powerful machine; I could carry two of the beams each load. I loved doing external load work, and this was my favorite scenario: someone gave me a helicopter to fly, gave me a job to do, and then just got the hell out of my way and let me do it. (PTSD much?)

In Talkeetna, Mahrt furnished Two Dogs, the third mechanic Jim, and me a small travel trailer in a local trailer park. Chief mech Al lived nearby in Wasilla and commuted to work. Things were a bit tight financially, and Mahrt was unable to give us our subsistence pay. Two Dogs and Jim went down to the nearby river and poached some salmon. That was our dinner for several nights in a row. Finally, money loosened up a bit, and we were able to buy groceries. It was a great treat to go to the store and buy fresh veggies. I slept on the couch, next to the pile of spare parts.

One morning on preflight walk-around, I found one rotor blades had popped its Blade Pressure Indicator. This meant that blade had lost its air pressure from its sealed spar and might be in danger of coming apart. It had to be replaced. While changing the blade the mechanics had trouble getting one of the horn locking pins, which attach the blade to the rotor hub, back in. They studied the maintenance book and knew that it would be a tight fit, so they soaked the pin in dry ice to make it contract ever so slightly, so its diameter would diminish and it would slip easily into place. They didn't act quickly enough, and the pin seized up after going in about two-thirds of its length. They hammered it in the rest of the way with a small sledgehammer. Even though I knew their method was not exactly by the book and was not the way the Marines did it in Vietnam, I bet my life on it working properly.

My logbook shows that before we started hauling the heavy I-beams, I took the helicopter out with a 3,200-pound load on an eighty-foot long-line and practiced the long-line external load technique I had learned at Carson Helicopters. I could still do it.

The Worldwide Adventures of a Helicopter Pilot ... the rest of the story

For many days, I slung the huge I-beams out along the path of the soon-to-be power line. I couldn't hear it in the cockpit through my helmet and earplugs, but people in the area reported that I sounded like a gigantic wind chime flying through the sky as the beams bounced off one another.

One day I was delivering beams to the barren, rolling hills north of Talkeetna when the man on the ground began to wave frantically and motioned for me to land. I did and shut down. He showed me how my engine had dropped huge gobs of oil all over him and the beams. My big radial engine was in trouble, and I didn't feel safe flying the twenty miles back to base. A passing Jet Ranger pilot saw us and landed to see if we needed any help. Hell, yes, we needed help! We were stranded way out here on a hilltop, it was getting late in the day, and there be bears out here. We hitched a ride home. Mahrt hired the Jet Ranger to carry him and our two mechanics out to the H-34 to see how serious the oil leak was. They agreed that my decision to not fly it home was a sound one. They figured out what repair had to be done in the field so that it could be flown home.

That required yet another round trip back out to the stranded aircraft to install a jury-rigged tourniquet of sorts to put pressure on the source of the oil leak. That worked, and I was able to return the H-34 to Talkeetna for more permanent repairs. I flew carefully and watched the engine oil pressure and temperature gauges for the short flight back to Talkeetna.

One day off, some of the other pilots from another company chartered a Jet Ranger to fly us up to Clear Creek to do some trout fishing. After the Jet Ranger deposited us on a gravel bar and flew away, one of the guys told me to cast," Right there," pointing to a big snag that halfway blocked the stream. On about my third cast,

I caught a huge rainbow trout, the only fish caught on this expedition. It tasted great. Since money was tight and Mahrt was not forthcoming with pay, I took a hint from the Gypsy and never paid my share of the charter flight.

Another time, I went fishing where Clear Creek flows into the Susitna River. In the perfectly clear water, I could easily see hundreds of huge salmon, some weighing as much as forty pounds, swimming by. At this stage of their spawning, they were beyond eating and wouldn't strike on any bait or lure. That didn't stop the dozens of fishermen lining the banks from trying. It was very frustrating to see these huge salmon just a few feet away, tantalizingly unavailable. I wanted to be able to say I caught a forty-pound salmon in Alaska, so I put on a big treble hook, cast out and dragged the treble hook over the back of the biggest fish I could see and snagged his dorsal fin. He put up a good fight, and then I released him. Of course, I had no fishing license.

Another helicopter pilot dropped a portable generator just off the side of the Talkeetna runway. It weighed just a few hundred pounds at most, but when that dense load hit the tundra, it burrowed down about ten feet into the muck. An employee from that company, probably the pilot trying to make good his mistake, waved me down and asked me to try and extract the generator from the muck with my H-34. He had managed to dig down and find the cable attached to it, but couldn't pull it out with his Jet Ranger. Two different times I connected to that cable with my H-34, and both times, with my nearly brand-new engine barking its full 1,525 horsepower, could not extract that generator from the suction of the muck. So far as I know that piece of machinery is still stuck in the muck.

After a while, the company responsible for drilling the holes for the beams asked us if we could relocate their portable drill rig. This required using a one-hundred-foot long-line and picking up the parts of the drill rig one at a time, and then re-stacking the parts of the rig again in proper order with workmen underneath guiding the pieces into place. The heaviest piece was right at the power limits of my helicopter, but I was able to do it. When Mahrt went out to do the job, he couldn't come close to keeping the loads under control. The men refused to work under him as he swung the pieces wildly all around the drill site.

I had yet another problem caused by my acceptance of poor maintenance. I was setting a drill rig on a hillside when suddenly, the H-34 began to bounce up and down like a bucking bronco. I put the load down on the ground and returned to base to try and find out the reason for this and to inspect the machine for damage. We couldn't figure out the reason. There was no visible damage to the H-34, so I returned to the site and tried again…with the same violent results. The second bout of bucking was more frightening, so I decided I'd had enough of this out-of-control galloping. I wanted to get to the bottom of this problem.

Another pilot suggested it was "collective bounce." At first, I denied it because I considered myself an excellent pilot, and collective bounce is a pilot-induced problem. I didn't feel that there was anything I was doing that would induce such violence. Then I thought it over and realized that yes, I was inadvertently the cause of this problem—that and, again, poor maintenance. The collective friction on the H-34 had become dirty, making the collective hard to move up and down. To compensate, I had reduced the collective friction to the point where there was none at all. This made the collective too easy to move.

When I inputted a collective move, the inertia of the collective would make it want to stay where it was, i.e., when I reduced collective to lower a heavy load, the collective lever wanted to say where it had been before I put in the collective movement, and the loose collective friction allowed this. This imputed an upward command. When it corrected for the inertia, the collective once again wanted to stay where it was. The helicopter began to oscillate up and down around the static collective, causing the tremendously violent oscillation, shaking my H-34...and my confidence. We returned to base, gave the collective a good cleaning and lubrication, once again checked out the helicopter for damage, and went back to work. My logbook shows that we later had to change out the trunion blocks, as they had taken a beating. In the wilds of Alaska, all in one season, I had experienced the two most dreaded mechanical experiences a helicopter pilot can experience, short of crashing or being shot down--ground resonance and collective bounce.

I celebrated my 40th birthday in Talkeetna. As per my custom having a midsummer birthday, I went to the bar and bought a round for all the patrons. They reciprocated. The weather forecast for the next morning was lingering drunkenness with possibility of severe hangover.

After hauling hundreds of pilings into the woods we finished the job, and I returned to California to another case of AIDS, Aviation Induced Divorce Syndrome. After my wife picked me up at the airport during the drive home, she said, "You know, while you have been gone, I have been doing a lot of thinking." I questioned, "Oh, yeah, what about?" She replied, "I think we need a separation." My honest and spontaneous reply was, "Good idea." That was the totality of our hassles. From there, we worked out an amicable divorce with joint custody of the kids and agreed that neither of us would paint the other as the "bad guy" to our daughters. That has served us very well over the years. We remain friends and continue to share our two daughters and four wonderful grandchildren.

As divorces go, it was a California classic, a mutual agreement to no longer be married and to do what was best for the kids. I paid all my court-required child support over the years and then some. When the girls reached eighteen years of age, I discontinued sending child support to their mother, but I sent each daughter the equivalent of her child support and suggested that she give it to her mother for rent. I continued sending each a check monthly until they finished college.

Chapter 28
1984
CRANE Helicopter Corp.

Home from Alaska in early 1984, I began attending Life West Chiropractic College, San Lorenzo, California. Nearing the end of my first quarter at LCCW, I was getting bored and broke...again...not an unusual situation for me. The news had just come out that tuition would soon increase to nearly double for subsequent quarters. As class president, I was getting a lot of flack from the other students about the drastic tuition increase. It wasn't my fault, but they took their frustrations out on me. The Fight or Flight reaction simmered in my brain.

During a break from class, I saw an H-34 flying south over the Nimitz Freeway (I-880). Rather than follow that one home, as I did before my first Alaska trip, I broke out a phone book and looked up local helicopter operators. I called ARIS Helicopter Ltd. in San Jose and talked to Steve Sullivan. He gave me the number for CRANE Helicopters at what we kiddingly called Fremont International Airport, a former drag strip used only by private aircraft.

I called and chatted with Steve Lotspeich of CRANE. We met, and he took me out to the rolling hills east of Fremont and had me shoot some pinnacle approaches to hilltops and land in some tight confined areas. He hired me for the summer to fly the S-58s and a Hughes 500C. He needed me to endure another FAA Part 135 check ride so that I could carry cargo and passengers for hire.

Here is where I began to run into what I felt was the FAA Gestapo. My next check ride was a fiasco. The FAA examiner didn't like the autorotations I shot at the beginning of my check ride, and he failed me right away. I must admit my autos were less than perfect. I went back to Fremont Airport and shot dozens of autos with the 500C until I could almost do them blindfolded then I rescheduled the check flight.

On the next go-around, I dazzled the examiner with my autos, but then he failed me a second time because pinnacle approaches and confined area landings were not up to par! Why? I thought I flew perfectly and at no time did I place us in danger. I didn't understand until later, when I realized many of the FAA helicopter examiner positions had been filled by former U S Army helicopter pilots. I learned that Army training relied heavily on the student making a verbal description of every procedure as he executed it. I flew a good hop and did all the things that were asked of me, but I didn't verbalize each procedure. I hadn't reported that I was landing into the wind, that I was "scouting the landing zone for hazards and wires" and such. I had never been required to do all this before. With the exception of the two easy-going check rides while with Calicopters, I hadn't been subject to FAA check rides for a while. I had become a bush pilot, while the mentality of the FAA inspectors had changed from one of just making sure the pilot was capable and safe to one of making sure the pilot couldn't only fly by the book but recite the book while doing it. This is one of the times that I felt fortunate that I wasn't a trained killer. The examiner would still be recovering from a pummeling. I learned the new FAA mantra:

"We are not happy until you are not happy."

Steve took me out into the hills of Fremont and gave me yet a third check ride, giving me another okay. I realized I had to do it the FAA/US Army way, so I went to a local helicopter school and bought the booklet that gave explicit details on how to pass an FAA Commercial check ride. I memorized the book and passed the next check ride with no problem, flying a perfect hop while reciting in detail every nuance of every maneuver as I executed it.

I should have just bagged it entirely at that point and searched for a real job, but for a change, I wanted to finish something that I'd started. Besides, this being a student was a pretty good gig. I found studying easy, and there were a plethora of chicks to date and beer to drink.

CRANE lifted many heavy objects to the tops of large and tall buildings. If you were a giant frog and could hop from one roof to another of the large Silicon Valley factories, you would see hundreds of bright orange stickers reading:

Lifted into place by
CRANE HELICOPTER COMPANY
Fremont Airport

In the CRANE office, the radio was always tuned to the local California Division of Forestry base (CDF) frequency. As soon as we heard the radio traffic of a nearby fire, Steve would call and volunteer to fly on the fire. Steve knew about some obscure part of the state law said that if there was a fire and a helicopter company volunteered to fly on it, the state had to hire them. We got a lot of work that way.

Once we were working a fire out in the boondocks east of Livermore. The Lawrence Livermore National Laboratory was in the same Restricted Area I had busted flying home from Porterville while flying for WAYco. Of course, with a fire going on, we were allowed to fly around the area with impunity. Looking for a source of water to fill my Bambi Bucket, I spied a small, dark pond surrounded by a high fence. Perfect! No obstacles nearby, a good source of water, and near the fire. After I made two or three drops with the water from that pond, I was notified to not use that pond anymore. It was the sewer containment pond for the complex, and the firefighters didn't like me dropping raw sewage near them...or on them! I found an alternative source of water nearby.

Most of my work with CRANE was flying the Hughes 500C. I liked flying that machine. It was small, agile, sporty, and fast. I could cruise at 140 miles per hour, but I rarely did because most of our work was nearby. One morning when my daughters were staying with me, I took them to work. Steve's wife, Linda, brought my daughters in her car to watch me do my magic on a small lift job in Sunnyvale. After the lift, I landed in the customer's parking lot, and Linda loaded my daughters into the 500 for my return flight to "Fremont International Airport." I got to show them Marriott's Great America from the air. Sadly, I never took them to that amusement park in person.

July 4, 1984

On this Fourth of July, I launched out from Fremont to carry a photographer to film a spectacular event. A shipyard in Richmond had built a humongous tilt-up oil rig on a barge, and the barge departed to carry the rig to its future home, perhaps in the Pacific waters off Santa Barbara, California. My passenger was hired by the shipyard to capture pictures of the gigantic rig passing under the Golden Gate Bridge.

When we arrived, there were six other helicopters awaiting the barge, lined up like fish at a fish ladder, hovering into a strong wind just inside the Golden Gate Bridge. We communicated with each other on a common radio frequency. The barge was a no-show. We soon learned that the barge had broken loose from its tugboat and was adrift in the bay, floating with the incoming tide towards the San Rafael-Richmond Bridge. Should this massively heavy load strike the bridge, it could knock part of it down. The California Highway Patrol stopped traffic on the bridge, and everybody waited with anticipation while the tugboat personnel tried to reconnect the tugboat to the barge.

Just as the barge approached the bridge, it struck and stranded itself on Red Rock Island. The tugboat crew was able to wrangle it back under control and later tow it under the Golden Gate. As it passed under the Golden Gate Bridge, I found myself hovering just outside of the bridge, with a tailwind of about thirty knots. I began to worry about just how much tailwind the little 500C could take before the wind might blow out the fire in the turbine. My worry was for naught; it didn't happen, and later Steve told me that there was no limit to a tailwind for the 500C. The one photo that my passenger wanted, a picture of the barge passing under the Golden Gate Bridge from above the bridge, was not possible, because low fog obscured the top of the bridge.

July 6, 1984

While flying for CRANE, they occasionally loaned me to a small company at Oakland Airport called ASTROCOPTERS. Sometimes we worked jointly on big projects. On July 6th, I reported to the hangar for Channel 7 News. They didn't want to go anywhere; they just wanted to film a new introductory trailer for their program. I flew back and forth along the taxiway in front of Hangar 3 while beautiful news personality Suzanne Sanders pretended to be reporting. It was a thrill to meet her.

July 12, 1984

On this date, I carried a BBC news crew that filmed the Democratic Convention at the Moscone Center in downtown San Francisco. The next day, my girlfriend at the time, PJ, came to visit me in the hangar. She loved to sunbathe naked, so we climbed up the fire escape ladder to the top of Oakland Hangar 3 and got naked. After we made love in the sunshine, I fell asleep on my stomach. My backside got so sunburned I could barely sit for days afterward.

July 20, 1984

I flew a biologist who was tasked with collecting water samples from the south end of San Francisco Bay to measure what contamination might be coming from a sewer treatment plant in Milpitas. We hovered down and collected several samples, including one from directly under the Dumbarton Bridge. We continued, passing under the bridge.

July 28, 1984

South of San Francisco is the small town of Gilroy is world-renowned for its annual Garlic Festival. Tens of thousands of people attend the festival over a three-day weekend. As we flew down from Oakland in the 500C, we passed miles of backed up traffic as people queued up for parking slots. I carried TV Channel 7 reporter Aaron Edwards and his crew, and we landed in the baseball diamond at the center of the fair grounds. I became part of the crew, carrying the battery pack for the cameraman. Treated like royalty, we were escorted to the front of every line, interviewed all the big players, and were treated to garlic delicacies such as stir-fried garlic shrimp, garlic wine, and garlic ice cream. We were in and out and had the royal tour, all in about thirty minutes. We each left with a swag bag full of garlicky items. I bought a few jars of garlic jelly for my family, perfect for making garlic bread.

July 29, 1984

I flew two hours for Steve in his H-34 on a fire near Red Bluff, California. I was certified by Cal Fire to fly the H-34 on fires, but Steve usually flew the H-34 while I flew the 500C. I learned months later that Steve continued to use my name as a relief pilot for weeks after I'd returned to school. All he did was radio the CDF officers and tell them that he had been relieved and that I was now flying. I wonder two things. 1) How much money did he make using my name as relief pilot while busting the limits of his own flying, and 2) What would have happened had he crashed and been killed? Would the TV news report have said, "Helicopter pilot Bill Collier was killed today while flying for the California Division of Forestry near Red Bluff, California?" Could I have ever recovered from having been "killed?" As Mark Twain said, "The reports of my death are greatly exaggerated."

I didn't realize it until 2020 while putting the finishing touches on this book, but this day was my last ever flight in an H-34, my favorite machine. In late 2020, I created a spreadsheet of all the H-34s and S-58s I had flown. I was amused to find that with approximately 4,000 hours in H-34s, and I had flown more than 200 individual H-34s of various models. I flew H-34Cs, Ds, Es, Gs, Js, several models of S-58s and S-58Ts.

Six years after the fact, while still on active duty with the Marine Corps, I flew the H-34 (BuNo.148767) that had picked up astronaut Alan Shepard after America's first sub-orbital space flight on May 5, 1961. I also flew, after the film was made, the H-34 (N8294) used in making the movie, "The Right Stuff," depicting that pick up of Astronaut Shepard.

Chapter 29
August 1, 1984
Jeepers Jamboree

On a quiet Thursday afternoon, we were sitting around lamenting that it had been a slow week, and considering a three-day weekend, when the phone rang. I could tell by Steve's side of the conversation that someone needed the 500C. As the discussion went on, I knew it was going to involve me. *DRAT! There goes my three-day weekend with my girlfriend, Rhonda, and her daughter, Maria.*

After a while, Steve turned to me and asked me how I felt about going to the "Jeepers Jamboree." I replied, "I don't know, what's a Jeepers Jamboree?" He explained that a bunch of Jeep drivers get together and drive over rough trails, deep into the woods near Lake Tahoe, and camp out. I said I didn't mind, but I had some serious reservations. I imagined a bunch of drunken, red-necked, tobacco-spitting roughneck cowboys, and I wasn't too excited about the idea. I couldn't say no; after all, I worked here, and this is what we do. I had a concern about how my driver-mechanic, a black fellow named Gene, might be treated once we got into camp and mingled with the red-necks. We might have to fight our way out. I would not put up with any abuse of my friend Gene, and I was fully prepared to depart the mountain scene on a moment's notice, even in the dark of night, if need be.

As it turned out, I was very wrong about my pre-conceived notions of the Jeep people. It turned out to be one of the most interesting long weekends of my life. Mr. Mark Smith of Georgetown, had organized the Jeep Jamboree years before as a way for groups of people to go into the deep woods of the Lake Tahoe region, test drive their Jeeps over some challenging trails, and to do some nice socializing at the same time. The event had grown so big that it had to be limited to 400 jeeps. An overflow weekend was created just to handle those people who couldn't go on the initial trip each year. I was to fly support for the overflow weekend, with only 150 Jeep-loads of people. I heard that Chrysler Corp had given some thought to canceling production of the Jeep, but Smith's Jamborees heightened the interest in Jeeps to the point that the Chrysler decided to continue the line.

The trek started at Georgetown but immediately went to dirt roads, which soon turned into trails passable only by Jeep or horse. The trail passed close to Loon Lake, near the Jeepers destination at Rubicon Springs. This dam which would be my base of operations for the helicopter. Fuel truck driver, Gene, found his way to the dam.

In the 1930s, the Springs had been a destination resort visited by actors and actresses from Hollywood. At that time, there was a pretty good road over the hill from Lake Tahoe, but the resort had burned down, and the road fell into disrepair, no longer passable by anything bigger than a Jeep.

Over the years, Smith had put together a wonderful support system for this event. We flew over and scouted the trail from the air for problems or bottlenecks. If we spotted a problem, I landed nearby on the granite rocks. Smith would hike over to see what was happening. Smith would have the driver of a broken down Jeep get his crippled vehicle out of the way so the rest could pass. The broken Jeep would then wait beside the trail for help while the rest of the Jeeps continued on their journey. Smith had a pile of spare parts, a portable welder, and a mechanic on call at our base camp.

We could deliver a spare tie-rod, a tire, or whatever they might need in short time to keep the parade going.

This was not a race; it was more of a social event, an individual test of each Jeep driver and his Jeep. At one point, Smith asked me to land and shut down at a particular place while he went over and did a little trouble shooting at a bottleneck. I stayed with the helicopter and began to explore the nearby area. I had landed on a solid granite rock surface surrounded by some of the most beautiful and spectacular scenery in the California Sierras. What I was about to see enhanced that beauty a great deal.

A few yards from the helicopter were three most beautiful young women, running around the forest in short shorts and flimsy, braless white tops, tied together at the waist. They were sexy! What in the world were these three foxy women doing out here in the middle of the woods? Of course, I had to investigate. As I approached the young women, a Jeep approached. The girls had set up a photo shoot at a place where every Jeep had to pass. At this particular point, each Jeep crawled up a certain rock obstacle, and the front, right tire of that Jeep came off the ground, creating a perfect picture. These girls were from a local photography studio,

and the whole thing had been set up in advance to make and sell souvenir photos to the Jeep owners.

The girls came over and took a picture of me in front of my 500C. I thought, *"That was great, I would love to have a picture of me in that situation."* Unknown to me until the next day, they had taken one of me flying, too.

Above the camp, a flat-topped granite rock was the perfect helipad. Once, as I approached the pad, I saw a pretty blonde kneeling at the edge of the rock taking my picture. *I'd sure like to get a copy of that picture...and I sure would like to meet that blonde.* I didn't give myself much hope, however, for I figured no pretty blonde would be out here by herself, and she was sure to be with some tobacco-spitting, beer-swilling redneck. I was half right.

Another part of my duties was to carry supplies into the campsite for the cooks. I made several trips carrying frozen meat, bread, chicken, and other foodstuffs from the Loon Lake Dam. It was less than a five-minute flight each way. Among the many loads that I took from the dam into the woods, several trips included a group of eighteen men. They each had a lot of baggage, and the strange thing was that, although it was getting late in the day, I didn't take them directly to the main camp. I deposited them in a meadow about a mile away from the main group. It didn't make sense to take them way out there, but I was too busy to give it much thought. I was glad I didn't, for it turned out to be one of the most delightful surprises of my life.

The food in this camp was gourmet. I never had food like this when I went camping, and I certainly had never seen anything like this in Vietnam. To me, camp food was over-cooked hamburgers and hot dogs toasted black over an open fire, served with beans warmed over the fire in the can. This meal was prime juicy steaks, fresh salad, potatoes roasted to perfection, sweet fresh corn on the cob, and several choices of drinks.

There was even a full bar. Gene and I had an open tab and got all the drinks we wanted for free. I was careful to not overindulge because I knew I would be flying early the next morning. Breakfasts were eggs to order, pancakes, sausage, bacon, muffins, and Bloody Marys for those who wished them. It was first-class all the way. I was entirely wrong about it being a bunch of rowdy, drunken rednecks. I was pleased to learn that, for the most part, the people involved in the Jeepers Jamboree were accountants, airline pilots, small businessmen, and such. They all had in common a love of Jeep driving, camaraderie in the woods, and adventure. My friend Gene was perfectly accepted by everyone, and in fact, he was so personable, that he has a small group of friends in the crowd before we left, which was a big relief.

After the first day of flying, standing in the evening chow line, I realized that the attractive blonde I had seen shooting my picture at the helipad was right in front of me. It was a shock to me, and to her too, when I spontaneously said, "Hi, Julie." She was a long-term friend from Sacramento, and in fact had been living with my best friend Gary Connolly at the time he died in the crop dusting accident in Napa. We had a happy mini-reunion and caught up on old times. I had been right about one thing and wrong about the other. The blonde was with someone; he was not a redneck but an airline captain.

Standing in line for food, everybody's attention was captured by a shrill, high-pitched squeal emanating from the woods from the direction of the Desolation Wilderness. The immediate question was: "What could that be?" (Or, more likely, "What the hell is that?") Shortly that changed to the statement, "No, it can't be, not way out here!" And then quickly thereafter to "OHMigawd, it really is!" An eighteen-piece bagpipe marching band in full Tartan regalia, strutted out of the woods, playing *Amazing Grace*...the eighteen men I had dropped off in the distant woods a few hours before. This explained their strange baggage—the round suitcases—and why I had dropped them so far away from the main group. The bagpipe band marched in, circled around the gathered campers, and then marched to the cement dance floor in the middle of the camp. They entertained us with a delightful and wonderful bagpipe performance for an hour.

Earlier, I had noticed a baby grand piano sitting in the middle of the woods in the center of the camp. I had wondered two things. What was that doing here, and how did in the world did it get here? The question of why was soon answered, and the answer of how should have been obvious to me. What I didn't wonder was, "How is it going to get out of here?"

After the bagpipe show, we finished supper and started dancing. After a few hours of dancing and partying, a quiet hush fell over the campground. Then, as soft as a dream, beautiful classical music wafted through the camp. Notes of Brahms, Tchaikovsky, and Beethoven floated gently from the baby grand piano. I ambled over and took a look at the guy playing it. He was the one and only man I had seen all day who might fit the description of a redneck biker dude. He was bearded, scruffy-looking, and had that kind of beer-belly biker look about him, not a guy one would like to share a bout of road rage with. But this guy was wearing a tuxedo. A tux, yes, but in keeping with his unkempt, ruffian, biker appearance, his tuxedo would have been a definite Salvation Army reject. Dirty, frayed well beyond normal use and patched in places, it was the perfect ensemble for a biker pianist in the middle of the Jeepers Jamboree.

I pulled my sleeping bag out and slept that night under my Hughes on the warm Sierra granite. The next morning, at first light, as I was awakened by stiff joints from sleeping on the granite which had grown cold overnight, more soft piano music wafted to my ears. I can't think of a more pleasant way to be awakened than by perfectly played classical music in the woods. A gourmet breakfast introduced another day of adventure. I had no idea the adventure that lay in store for me that day.

As the Jamboree weekend wrapped up, I rode herd on the Jeepers as they crept up the steep trail toward Lake Tahoe and found their way to the South Tahoe Airport for a farewell luncheon.

I flew Smith to the airport and found that the cute photographer girls had framed nine-by-eleven pictures of each Jeep as they struggled over the rocky challenge with one front wheel in the air. The women also had two of my helicopter and me...one of me in the woods standing in front of the helicopter and the one taken while I flew low over them. Of course, I had to buy both. The picture of me airborne hangs in Steve's and Linda's garage to this day.

With the campsite evacuated, one small detail remained. The baby grand piano had to be hauled out of the woods. Smith and I returned, crossing the Desolation Wilderness for the third round-trip that day. I dropped the two passengers near the piano. Gene rigged the piano for lifting, and I hovered down over it as Gene attached the lifting cable to my belly hook. At about 7,000 foot elevation, it took all the torque I had to lift it straight up out of the tall pine trees surrounding the camp. I carried it across Loon Lake to the dam and placed it into the back of the waiting truck, no worse for the wear. I imagine anybody camping out in the nearby wilderness would have been quite amazed by the sight of a piano flying through the air under the helicopter.

I made my fourth and final trip across the Desolation Wilderness (Did I mention "There be bears there?) delivering Smith to the Tahoe Airport and flew back to the dam. *All I have to do now is re-fuel, zip home, and this adventure is over. I'll be home in an hour.* This adventure *was* over, but another was about to begin.

On the short final approach to land on the dam for fuel, I heard and felt a loud thump behind me in the engine compartment of the 500! The engine hadn't quit, I was still flying, and everything seemed normal, so I continued my approach for another ten seconds to land beside the fuel truck. Short of the dam, there was no place else to land anyway but large, uneven rocks.

I landed safely and quickly shut the engine down to determine what had caused the thump. Gene inspected the aircraft and found that the pulley that held the fan belt for the engine oil cooler had stripped its gears. No engine oil cooler, pretty soon no cool engine oil, pretty soon...no engine! The helicopter was hard down. I was stranded on the Loon Lake Dam until we got a replacement pulley.

We drove the fuel truck an hour to the nearest phone, called the CRANE office, and talked with Steve and the chief mechanic, John DeStories. Steve called Dallas and ordered a new pulley for the 500. Hughes Company put a spare pulley on the next available flight to San Francisco from Dallas-Fort Worth Airport. Gene and John drove immediately to San Francisco International Airport, got the part, and returned to Loon Lake, all in about six hours. We thought we were literally "out of the woods." We were quite wrong.

Somewhere in the evolution of this helicopter, the Hughes factory had changed the part. It was no longer a one-piece part but was now a two-piece part. We received only half of the part we needed.

After another trip to the phone and another consultation with the boss, we decided that I should try to fly the helicopter home. The plan being, I would start and run up quickly, take off as soon as possible, and keep a close eye on the oil temperature. The hope was that if I could accelerate to a high forward airspeed quickly, the ram air coming in the engine intake duct would be enough to keep the engine oil temp within limits. It seemed worth a try. I made a super-fast turn-up, jumped off the ground, and sped off, keeping an eagle eye on my oil temp gauge. No good! As soon as I started, and throughout my whiz-bang takeoff and acceleration, the little needle on the temp gauge crept closer and closer towards the red line. I made it about two miles over a ridge to where we had pre-selected a precautionary landing spot near yet another dam. I landed as quickly as I safely could and shut off the engine without the benefit of the usual cool down period as the engine temperature needle touched the red line of the gauge. I was again stranded, albeit in a new place.

Gene and John followed me in the fuel truck and came as near as they could to me, which was about a hundred yards uphill on the country highway. Again, we drove to the phone and conferred with the office. It was decided that John and Gene would drive to Fremont to get the necessary part, and I would stay with the helicopter. We went to the nearest tiny country store, bought some cans of Dinty Moore beef stew, some beans, and a *Cosmopolitan* magazine for me to read. That was the only reading material they had in stock, but I liked reading *Cosmo*...better pictures than *PLAYBOY*. We also bought some fishing equipment for me to help pass the time. They dropped me back at the helicopter and departed for the four-hour drive back to the hangar. I would be on my own overnight, as they would have to wait for the other half-part to arrive at San Francisco from Dallas and then make the long return drive.

I began to settle in for what would become three nights. To pass the time, I tried fishing, but that got boring right away. All the fish were on the bottom of the lake in the cooler waters, and I didn't got a nibble in two hours. I read the *Cosmo* for a while, but as it began to get dark, I figured I better gather some firewood from the huge pile nearby and build a small fire. I knew there was no great danger from wild animals, but a fire would be comforting and allow me to warm up my Dinty Moore Beef Stew. But I had no matches; no way I was going to try and rub two sticks together to start a fire. What to do?

Earlier, I had heard children yelling about a half-mile away, and I assumed that there were campers nearby. I decided I would walk over to their camp and borrow some matches. Just about that time, two pre-teen boys peddled by on their bicycles and stopped to admire the 500. I told them, "If you guys will bring me some matches, I will show you my nifty helicopter." They came back in about five minutes, not with matches, but with an invitation to their camp for dinner.

The place where I had landed belonged to the Sacramento Municipal Utilities District (SMUD). The campground was for the exclusive use of SMUD employees and their families. In this case, the boys' grandfather (another Smith) had retired from SMUD and had his entire extended family out for a week of camping. When Gene and John arrived back at the helicopter, they fully expected to find me hot, dirty, hungry, and crabby after spending three nights sleeping under the helicopter. They were right about that part; I did sleep under the 500 to guard it.

My note directed them to the Smith's camp where they found me with my belly full of good food, my feet up by the campfire, a cold beer in my hand, and in the company of one of Mr. Smith's granddaughters. Instead of being deprived for the three days it took for them to return with the spare part, I was treated like a prodigal son. Mrs. Smith was a fantastic cook and she prepared almost formal meals. The first night we had baked ham with pineapple and sweet potatoes. Roast turkey with all the trimmings the second night, and on the third evening she served steak and baked potatoes with baked beans.

With the proper part, the pulley repair was quick and easy, followed by a speedy jaunt home to "Fremont International Airport." I felt bad because I had promised all the Smith kids a ride in the helicopter in exchange for their wonderful hospitality, but once the machine was fixed, I reneged. I wasn't sure the problem was fixed perfectly, and I was hesitant to risk another forced landing with children aboard. I owe you, Smith family.

A follow-up anecdote: A few weeks after the Jeepers Jamboree, I was visiting with my brother Cal and his wife Eva at their home in Newcastle, in the foothills of Placer County. As I regaled them with stories about my recent adventure, they told me they had been camping very near Loon Lake the very same weekend. "The peace and quiet were wonderful," they said, "except for the noisy little red and white helicopter that kept flying over, buzzing back and forth, all weekend long."

Chapter 30
September 9, 1984
Firefighting Near Watsonville

We had another lull in activity, so we called it a three-day weekend. My girlfriend Rhonda was able to get away and join me. Linda is a fantastic cook, so the four of us had a lovely dinner and a few drinks at Steve's and Linda's house. We talked until well after midnight, and then retired. After a most satisfying romp of lovemaking, it seemed like we had just fallen asleep when Steve came knocking on the door and woke us up. There was a forest fire somewhere near Watsonville, and the CDF wanted both our ships on station at first light. After two hours of sleep, I kissed Rhonda goodbye, and we drove to Fremont airport, inspected our helicopters by flashlight, filled our fuel tanks, and departed south. I followed Steve with the 500C in loose formation to our destination.

By the time we arrived at the fire, the sun was up, and the CDF immediately put us both to work. Steve, with his bigger machine, was hauling firefighters around. I was assigned to do water drops. The fire boss assigned me to a particular hillside and said for me to "kill hot spots." There was a convenient pond right at the base of the hill. I went after those hot spots like a demented fighter/bomber pilot in a war. My aggressive but playful attitude was, *Kill all them dirty, pinko-commie, Anti-Christ, sexual pervert hot spots.* (I believe I see another hint of PTSD here.) This was a great game. I was having a blast.

A few hours and a few tanks of fuel later, after about my fiftieth drop, I slid down to the hill to the pond to pick yet another bucket of water. I was tired from the drunken debauchery and little sleep the night before, but I didn't want to stop. I was having so much fun, plus the more I flew, the more money the company was making. There was a good bonus for me at the end of the season if we had a good one. To call the fire boss and ask for a little downtime might invite to his attention that I was still dropping water where he had assigned me, even though those hot spots were long dead and no longer a threat. *Keep on going.*

I hovered down over the pond, dunked my bucket into the water to refill it, and made sure I was in a stable, stationary hover at the appropriate altitude. Exhausted, I saw an opportunity to grab a quick rest from the hectic pace of the last few hours. I took a deep breath and allowed myself to relax a bit, and…instantly fell asleep! My head falling forward woke me up with a start. I decided that I needed a short break, so I hopped over to the service area, shut down, crawled under the bigger helicopter, and had a nap on the dry, hard ground.

Before the nap, something unusual caught my eye as I flew these many drops, and after I had a little rest, I walked out into a nearby pasture for a closer look at what I had seen from the air. The pasture was covered with hundreds of small white pieces of debris of some kind, and I was curious to see what they might be. I walked out into the pasture and discovered something that was both very curious, and at the same time, rather disgusting. All over hundreds of acres of pasture, with one in at least each square foot of ground, were thousands of used tampon applicator tubes. What a mystery, what a surprise, and how did they get here? I had to find out the answer to this puzzle.

I found out rather easily as Linda had already made the same observation and sought out the answer before I did. We had seen water trucks dispensing water over the width and breadth of the field, but we had both assumed that it had something to do with dust suppression in support of our fire-fighting efforts. We were wrong. The trucks were spreading treated wastewater from a local sewage plant. At the plant, plastic products didn't dissolve in the treatment process and weren't filtered from the resultant treated sewage. They ended up in the truck to be dispersed over the many acres of pasture near us.

Even with the short nap, I flew more than eleven hours that day, which included .3-nighttime, my single biggest day of civilian flying ever.

I celebrated my forty-first birthday and the finality of my divorce this week. The number one song of the week was "Ghostbusters."

September 22-25. 1984

We got a contract to survey the routes of a proposed new powerline. I met up with another helicopter at Sacramento Metro Airport. For three days we each carried loads of executives (investors maybe?) and followed the track the proposed power line. We spent one night in Redding, California, and the second night in Klamath Falls. I don't know if the power line was ever built.

Chapter 31
September 29, 1984
Concrete Hauling

A telecom company was building a large transmission tower atop Signal Peak near Truckee. For the base of it, they had dug a huge hole in the top of the peak and steelworkers had laid reinforcing steel. The project was ready for concrete to be poured into the hole. There was no way for a cement truck to get to the top of the peak, so we staged in a meadow about a thousand feet below the peak.

We brought CRANE's 500C and a Jet Ranger from Astrocopters, each of which could carry the equivalent of a wheelbarrow's load of concrete, maybe a third of a yard. We started a daisy chain, each guy filling up his drop bucket while the other flew to the top and dropped his puny load into the hole.

This turned out to be a challenging but most fun job because there was a strong wind from the north. As soon as we lifted off, we got into a strong current of air flowing up the side of the mountain, lifting us up like we were riding an express elevator. So great was this natural lift, at the top of the hill we had to "split the needles" (disengage the engine) and go into autorotation mode to arrest our rate of ascent. Then we added just a bit of power to slide across the peak to the hole, dump the load, and jump off the mountain. We avoided the natural elevator on our way down, splitting the needles again for a quick descent, auto-rotating down to the truck for another load. This was great fun. We flew both helicopters hard all day long for two days

At first, it seemed to be an impossible job. The hole was as big as a small house, and we were carrying what seemed to be a tiny load each trip. We just kept at it...and at it...and at it...all day long for two days; eventually we filled the hole up.

October 4, 1984
Back to school

At the end of summer, I returned to school. I would work for CRANE Helicopters again a few years later.

Chapter 32
Fall, 1984
Marching with the SIKHS in Yuba City

During my summer stint with CRANE, the owners of ASTROCOPTERS Ltd, got to know my flying skills. Owner Duane Vandagriff and the chief pilot, Will Prater, hired me to fly weekends for KGO TV Channel 7, and KRON TV Channel 4. The little company owned two beautiful jet Rangers. As relief pilot, I would fill in for Prater so he could have some weekends at home with his family. I got called by one of the two TV news channels almost every weekend for some newsy reason or another, sometimes twice a weekend.

October 31

" Indian Prime Minister Indira Gandhi was assassinated at 9:29 a.m. on 31 October 1984 at her residence in Safdarjung Road, New Delhi. She was killed by her Sikh bodyguards[1] Satwant Singh and Beant Singh in the aftermath of Operation Blue Star. Operation Blue Star was an Indian military action carried out between 1 and 8 June 1984, ordered by Indira Gandhi to remove the Sikh Jarnail Singh Bhindranwale and his followers from the holy Golden temple of the Harmandir Sahib in Amritsar, Punjab. The collateral damage included the death of many pilgrims, as well as damage to the <u>Akal Takht</u>. The military action on the sacred temple was criticized by Sikhs both inside and outside India." Wikipedia.

Astrocopters launched my Jet Ranger 17W out to Yuba City, California, which has a large population of Sikhs. Again, I became part of the Channel 7 TV crew, carrying the battery pack into a parade of thousands of Sikhs, chanting, "KHALISTAN NOW! KHALISTAN NOW!" Invited into the local Sikh Temple, we removed our shoes and entered the peaceful place. Aaron Edwards interviewed the senior clerics of the temple for the evening's news broadcast. We never felt any danger because the enemies of the Sikhs had no presence in northern California.

I learned that the two other pilots working for Astro lived upstairs in the hangar. I asked if I could join them. The three of us made the place into a quite nice three-bedroom bachelor pad. The only thing we lacked was a stove, but we had a fridge and microwave. We installed an electric on-demand water heater for our shower, which we placed over a pre-existing toilet drain. What more do bachelors need? And we had five helicopters in our "garage."

I was still in school, and that worked very well for me. I didn't have to pay any rent, and management didn't seem to mind that I had a woman friend stay over on occasion. My daughters even were able to visit and stay with me when it was my weekend to have them visit.

October 31, 1984
Massive Oil Spill Cleanup

Just after midnight this Halloween day, the nearly 600-foot-long oil tanker *SS Puerto Rican* departed San Francisco Bay with a load of 91,984 barrels of fuel onboard plus 8,500 barrels of heavy fuel bunker oil for her engines. At 3:24 a.m., eight miles off the Golden gate, she exploded twice amidships. Of the three men who were blown overboard, two—the captain and a pilot—were rescued; one crewman was lost.

Heavy weather caused the ship to break up. Its stern sank into water 1,500 feet deep within the boundaries of the Gulf of the Farallons National Marine Sanctuary, spilling about 1.25 million gallons of refined petroleum products. It was estimated that 4,800 sea birds died. The sunken stern section continued to discharge oil for months. Fortunately, the oil didn't enter San Francisco Bay but spread northwards towards Bodega Bay, the coastal town of Stinson Beach, and the Pt. Reyes National Seashore with its miles of beautiful beaches. Perhaps more importantly, a large salmon fishing industry operates out of Bodega Bay. (Paraphrased from Wikipedia.)

Astrocopters to the rescue. Astrocopters leased CRANE's 500C for me to fly on this cleanup project while Chief Pilot Prater flew a company Jet Ranger. We spent days flying remediation crews around Bodega Bay and delivering cleanup supplies to these crews. It was challenging work. We started early each day and flew until nearly dark.

Prater was flying along Stinson Beach in a Jet ranger when his engine quit. He barely got the Jet Ranger onto the beach, right at the edge of the water...with an incoming tide. The cleanup crew brought a bulldozer to the stranded helicopter, hooked chains to the landing skids, and pulled it to safety before the Pacific Ocean waves could gobble it up.

One morning I departed Oakland Airport at zero-dark-thirty, headed for Bodega Bay to continue helping with the cleanup. I flew under the Bay Bridge, scooted low-level between Alcatraz and Fisherman's Wharf, and flew under the Golden Gate Bridge. At that point, I called Bay Area Control to let them know I was no longer a factor in Bay Area traffic. They rogered my call but told me that my radio was breaking up. I attributed that to the fact that I was low over the water, near the bluffs outside the Golden Gate, and perhaps all the metal in the bridge was interfering with my radio waves. I continued north.

When I landed at Bodega Bay's Westside Park and too-quickly shut down, I realized why my radios had become unintelligible. Eager to get to work when I started up at Oakland, I had neglected to switch my BATT/GEN switch up to GEN, for generator. I had flown the whole distance from Oakland to Westside Park on battery power only, so when I shut down, my battery was flat dead.

I was embarrassed to call the office for help, and besides, it was still early in the morning, no one would be at work yet. I called the local AAA service and explained my plight to the on-call tow-truck driver. He said, yes, he could help me. I explained that I had a 24-volt system, and I would need him to link up two 12-volt batteries in series to give me the necessary voltage. He seemed to understand and said he would come right away. I planned to pay him out of pocket to keep this quiet. I waited about forty-five minutes, and he didn't show. I phoned again, and he said he was coming. Still, he didn't show up.

I realized that I was sitting right next to a big rig that had huge batteries sitting behind the cab in plain sight. *Hmmm, maybe the truck driver could help me.* I tracked him down and told him my predicament. No problem; not only could he provide me with the 24 volts I needed, but he had extra-long jumper cables so he could reach my helicopter without the rotor blades being a problem. Problem solved. As soon as I got a good start, he disconnected the cables, and I made sure to flip the BATT/GEN switch up to GEN this time. My battery charged up right away. The AAA guy never did show up.

Later I was flying off the US Coast Guard helipad on Doran Park and my fuel filter warning light illuminated...one element of my engine fuel filters was clogged. I called the office, and they told me, "Well, just change the filter," and told me where to find a spare in the helicopter. I found it, but I didn't feel comfortable doing this mechanic's work myself. because I knew I had to break safety wire to remove the old filter, and I should replace the safety wire after installing the new filter. I called Lotspeich again, and he said, "Just do it." He didn't want to send a mechanic 100 miles just to change the filter. I took out the old filter but had trouble getting a good grip on the new one to get it firmly twisted into the port. I checked with the Coast Guard station. Surely, they would have some support tools for the CG helicopters that occasionally worked out of there. No such luck. However, they did have a plumber's tool called a basin wrench in their household tool kit. That little tool allowed me to reach up into the tight little area to get a good grip on the filter and seat it firmly into place. I flew around for the next two days with a not-safety-wired fuel filter.

A few weeks after the main oil spill, the stern of the *Puerto Rican* began to release large amounts of oil that bubbled to the surface and creating another oil slick. I was called out by Channel 7 News to go film it. I flew past where the slick was bubbling to the surface and then made a U-turn so that the cameraman in the back seat could get a good shot out the rear right window. In doing so, I made a terrible mistake. I failed to pay attention to the wind.

When I slowed down to allow the cameraman to get the shot, I inadvertently flew out of translational lift. I was now hovering at about fifty feet with full fuel, three passengers, and the camera batteries and equipment on board. Too heavy to hover out of ground effect, the Jet Ranger plummeted downwards towards the frigid Pacific Ocean. I thought for sure we were going for a swim...at best... maybe much worse. I pulled in all the collective I could and placed my left thumb on the switch to activate the floats, feeling certain that we soon would be in the water on an inverted helicopter with only the floats to cling to. Fortunately, the helicopter stopped descending just above the water as ground effect cushioned its fall. We kicked up a lot of spray, and water droplets covered the windows, but we weren't in the drink.

December 1, 1984

I had a simple mission to carry a big property developer around northern California to visit several projects he had in progress. I picked him up at Sacramento Metro Airport, and we flew around that area. As I plotted the path on my chart to our next stop at Bodega bay, I saw that we would pass directly over my ex-wife's house in Santa Rosa. I asked the developer if I could make a few turns around the house so I could wave to my kids. He was okay with that, and we circled around their house until they came out and waved back at their dad circling overhead.

To fly for Astro, I had to have yet another Part 135 check ride with an FAA examiner. I put it off as long as possible, but finally, Prater insisted I get it done. Now wise to these former army FAA inspectors/jerks, I was ready. When it came time to do my first autorotation, the examiner told me to autorotate to a spot that was just under my nose. The correct procedure would have been for me to make a spiraling 360-degree descent, but I wasn't going to accede to that pansy move. I was pissed off at these FAA jerks, and I wasn't going to pussyfoot around with them anymore. *I am in charge here.* I forcefully but gently lowered the collective lever and carefully pushed the cyclic forward, knowing full well that to press this maneuver too far into a negative 'G 'situation might cause the rotor head to separate from the machine. On the edge of zero Gs, I pointed the nose almost straight down and we dropped like a rock. I flared at the bottom, and planted the Jet Ranger on the spot. It wasn't by the book, but it was perfect and showed that I had absolute control of the machine. I observed that the examiner looked frightened as he wiped sweat off his brow. I looked him right in the eye and said firmly, "You want to see it again?" He shook his head "No." I completed the rest of the flight without a problem, yak-yak-yakking my way through every maneuver. "We are not happy until you are not happy!"

January 1, 1985

For New Year's morning, I took my girlfriend Rhonda and her daughter Maria to a nice restaurant in Concord for brunch. We sat down, and I ordered a pair of Bloody Marys. Just as our drinks arrived, my beeper alarmed. *Drat! Who would want to go flying at this time on this day?* I called dispatch, and they told me I had to be ready to take off in half an hour, the Channel 7 TV News people want to film the "Polar Bear Plunge" on Alcatraz island. Drat! I was half an hour from Oakland, and I would still have to take the ladies home to Walnut Creek first. Rushing, I threw a twenty on the table and told the waitress that we had an emergency and had to leave. At least we hadn't ordered food yet.

I dropped the girls off and drove like a maniac to get to the hangar before the TV crew. Fortunately, they were a bit late. We took off and flew over to Alcatraz Island to film the Polar Bear swimmers as they plunged into the frigid Bay water.

January 2, 1985

I was tagged to fly over the big annual CAL vs. Stanford football game in Palo Alto. Many news helicopters wanted to circle and shoot pictures of the big game, but the weather was foggy crap. Prior to the game, I learned the geography of the area and memorized several major landmarks. I had to report entering a checkpoint a mile out from the circular track around the field, enter the circuit and fly clockwise for only one circuit, then depart using a different pre-set path. Even with all this control, I still felt uneasy circling around the big stadium in foggy conditions where visibility was less than a quarter-mile. I was glad to be done with that. I have always had an aversion to mid-air collisions.

January 27, 1985

I flew Channel 7 TV News commentator Aaron Edwards out to view the whales passing by Point Reyes. It was a futile attempt because whenever the whales heard the noise of our machine, they sounded. We could see them with our eyes from a distance, but by the time we got close enough to catch the whales on film, they were gone.

February 17, 1985
Sewage Spill, Sonoma County

I was dispatched to carry the Channel 7 News crew to cover big news in Sonoma County. Because of heavy rains, the lagoons that usually contained the treated effluent from the local sewage plants were overflowing, and treated sewage was flowing into the Russian River. Although the water was nearly drinkably pure at the time of discharge, it was an illegal discharge and it got a lot of press.

After we cruised around the lagoons, filming acres and acres of water in ponds, the crew decided that they wanted to go north all the way to the source of the Russian River, at Coyote Dam north of Ukiah. We flew around the reservoir, and I landed on the dam so the reporter could do a stand-up report overlooking the lake. Taking off downhill from the dam, I dumped the nose to accelerate. Fortunately, one of my passengers saw a single strand of wire in our path that I hadn't seen. His yelling and pointing allowed me to swerve away from the wire and he may have saved our lives. From there, we followed the river all the way down to the town of Guerneville.

As we flew over the river near Guerneville, I had to fart badly. I didn't want to do it in the small confines of the helicopter with three other people in close proximity, but I could no longer control myself, so I released a rotten, noxious, vapor cloud. I heard the TV personality say, "Oh God, I can smell it!" He thought that stink of my rotten fart was caused by the sewage spill in the river, and I was too embarrassed to fess up. I missed the news that night, but I am sure he reported how badly the river stank.

* * *

One night, I was returning to base when I got a radio call for a rescue. Another pilot had dropped his passengers off at the wrong pier on one of San Francisco's wharves and took off without looking back. The passengers were stranded on the isolated pier behind a locked gate. All I had to do was pick up these people and hop them over to the next pier. When I arrived, I was delighted to encounter two most beautiful, lithe young models, that had been out on a photo shoot somewhere before they being dropped off on the wrong pier. I got my thrill for the day just seeing these two beauties and smelling their perfumes, feeling their silk clothing as I strapped them into my back seats for the ten-second hop over to the proper pier. I am sure that I saved their lives because they would have died of exposure if left there overnight in the cold, damp bay air in those skimpy dresses.

Chapter 33

All of 1990 and 1991
Kwajalein Atoll,
Marshall Islands, South Pacific

I graduated from Life Chiropractic College West in the spring of 1987, studied furiously for a few more weeks, took my state boards...and passed them. I was now a California certified, licensed Doctor of Chiropractic, and chiropractic radiologist. I was good at what I was doing but was a terrible businessman. I realized that I was frequently staring out the windows of my office, wondering what was happening outside, out there...up there. I missed flying. After two years of being bored and struggling financially, I was open to new opportunities. I figured by now my girls were old enough to survive my absence should I disappear from their lives for a period of time…or forever.

I received an Air America Association newsletter. In the back, I read a small advert placed by a former Air America pilot, Jim Brown, the chief pilot for DynCorp on Kwajalein Atoll (KWAJ) in the Marshall Islands. Brown was looking to hire a Huey pilot to fly on the US Army Corps of Engineers Missile Testing Program. I sent a resume, and, after some negotiations, Brown hired me. One of the items I negotiated was that I would be allowed to practice chiropractic during my time off. That was perfect because it is said that it took a population of about 3,000 people for a chiropractor to make a living, and KWAJ had 3,000 Americans. There would be no competition for literally millions of square miles. Late 1989, I sold my pitiful little practice and shipped off to the Marshall Islands, South Pacific.

Working through the hiring process, I was told that there would be no night flying and no instrument flying on KWAJ; all flying would be daytime, Visual Flight Rules. I liked that. Over my years of "bush" flying, my instrument flying skills had rusted. What I was not told was that I would have to maintain proficiency in those two realms of flight.

Prior to departure, I failed my FAA flight physical because my eyesight had deteriorated slightly. I said to the doctor, "If I go get glasses and come back, will I then be okay?" He said, "Oh, if you are going to get glasses, then you pass," and gave me my Class II medical certificate. I went to a local ophthalmologist and purchased glasses for the first time. I had no idea that my eyesight had been deteriorating until I put on the new glasses. What a difference! Distant things were no longer fuzzy. I made sure to buy the self-darkening kind that automatically tinted whenever I walked outside so I wouldn't have to carry separate sunglasses. This was to be a problem on KWAJ.

I knew KWAJ was going to be a lonely two years; I expected to be celibate for two years. There were many single men on the island and many married couples with children, but very few single women. To keep myself busy, I bought a Brother Word Processor 500 with the intention of writing down my flying stories. I thought it would be only one book, but it has, over the years, naturally morphed itself into three books, this one being the third. (As of January, 2022, this third book has been 32 years in the writing.)

When I arrived on KWAJ, I immediately started Huey pilot training, but I was not often on the flight schedule. In two months training, I flew few hours. It is hard to stay current and proficient if one does not fly regularly. It seemed to me, in retrospect, that the lack of scheduling was intentional.

The chief instructor, whom I shall call Y-Y, was a tiny former Marine who had jumped over to the Army after a single tour in the Marines. I never asked him why he changed services, but I guessed that he did so he could attend army flight school. His "Little-Man complex" was evident. That, and his dislike of anything Marine, portended trouble for this tall, former Marine.

Every other pilot on this DynCorp contract was a retired Army Warrant Officer. I asked around if any pilot other than Army had ever flown here. I was told that one former Navy pilot had come but didn't make it through training. I became aware of what the other pilots called the WOPA—the Warrant Officers Protective Association. I began to see a pattern here that too concerned me, but I thought that with my wit, charm, and flying skills, I could overcome such petty prejudices.

One of my very first flights was a night proficiency flight. I had only the self-tinting glasses to wear. I feel that they slightly affected my ability to see at night. Flying out over the Pacific Ocean on a moonless night was the darkest flying I ever experienced, but I did well anyway. Had I known there would be training on dark nights, I could have easily brought a second pair of non-self-tinting glasses.

I was pleased to learn that we were required to wear short-sleeved white shirts with epaulets on the shoulders, just like airline captains. I liked that. Unfortunately, supply didn't have shirts in my size in stock; they were on back-order. One of the first things Y-Y did was hassle me because I was out of uniform. I explained (and he knew this) that my shirts were on back-order and I would be in uniform as soon as I could. In the meantime, I flew in army-green flight suits. One day, a friend about my height, but much fatter, aware of the instructor's hassling me, offered to loan me one of his uniforms. I went to work dressed properly in an attempt to please Y-Y. He immediately gave me grief because the shirt was way too big for me and looked sloppy. I went back to army green flight suits.

Flying with another instructor, making conversation in order to befriend him, I mentioned that I had only about 1,000 hours in Hueys. By his reaction, I could tell he was incredulous that I did not have the thousands of hours of Huey time like all the other pilots. OOPS! I probably shouldn't have said that. I tried to counter by saying, "Even though I don't have lot of Huey time, I have thousands of hours in other machines, including the Bell Jet Ranger." Returning to the main airport, this same instructor asked me, "What would you do if you had an engine failure right now?" It seemed to me to be just a topic of conversation, and I explained in detail to him what I would have done: shoot an autorotation and land on the lagoon, tell my copilot to put out a MAYDAY call, and try to land near a certain marker buoy that we were just then passing. We could catch the rope on the buoy to keep us in one spot until help arrived.

Never in my life had I been given a simulated emergency that was not initiated with either the instructor rolling back the throttle and saying, "You have an engine failure," or at least saying, "You have a simulated engine failure." Later I found out that he wrote me up for failing to react properly to a simulated emergency. More concern.

I was slightly amused and also somewhat aghast that in US Army aircraft, in case of an in-flight emergency, the first item on the checklist was, "Maintain control of the aircraft." What? Who wouldn't? Does this really have to be on the checklist? I have to assume that somewhere in Army aviation history, some young pilot must have seen a Master Caution Light, thrown up his arms screaming in fear, and allowed his aircraft to crash. I am amazed that Army personnel are allowed to be married and have children. Surely, somewhere in the history of the Army, some soldier must have been injured while having sex.

Y-Y took me out time after time to the infield, and we practiced hovering autorotations by the dozens, several days...hundreds of hovering autorotations. I didn't feel like I should question the senior instructor why we were doing so many. I just went along time after time after time. A hovering auto is a simple thing to do. Should the engine quit in a hover, you just pull up on the collective and use the energy stored in the rotor system to cushion the landing and operate the rudder pedals to keep the nose straight so you don't land with any turning motion, which could be troublesome.

One day, after about the fortieth hovering auto, I made a small mistake, and the Huey landed a bit off level, it rocked back and forth once and settled to the ground on the floats. It seemed no big deal to me. Y-Y made a *great big deal* of it. He had me shut down the helicopter, called the tower to dispatch the crash crew, and called for maintenance folks to come out and inspect the helicopter for damage! This was totally uncalled for, and I knew this was done to embarrass me. I began to worry.

On instrument training flights, Y-Y kept telling me things like, "Watch your altimeter!" I was a certified flight instructor, and I knew that was incorrect procedure. To say something like that to a student is to invite him to fixate his attention on the altimeter and to stop scanning of all the other instruments. The proper thing to say would have been, "Keep your scan moving." Y-Y was sabotaging me.

Flying over the atoll was breathtaking at first. Sparkling blue-green Pacific Ocean as far the eye could see in every direction, with just a string of exotic, enticing tropical islands up either side of the lagoon. Beautiful coral heads peeked from under the water, telling us where the next island would form in a few hundred or few thousand years as the coral grew and raised the coral head nearer to the surface. Each coral head was a site that needed exploration by scuba, which I soon did.

It was incredibly beautiful…for the first week or so. Then it just became the "same old-same old" view every day. Nothing ever changed. We were located in the Intertropical Convergence Zone, the place weather starts to happen and then moves off to other latitudes. Almost every day, the weather forecast was the same: "A high of 87, and low of 83, with winds 5-10 knots out of the southeast. Chance of thunderstorms." Every other day or so we

253

would have a thunderstorm, but that would just wet everything down a bit and move on. The rain was so warm that, unless you wanted to stay dry, you could be out in the rain and not get cold. If you got wet, you would feel refreshed and dry off in a few minutes. The humidity was a little bit more than Hawaii, but nothing like Vietnam or the US East Coast.

The Huey flying job was simple. Up each side of the atoll were outposts festooned with telemetry and cameras that measured every missile that came into the lagoon. Every one of these small bases had personnel that worked forty-eight-hour shifts. Every day or so, each of these people had to be rotated out and replaced with a fresh person. We had two schedules, east atoll and west atoll. A crew of two pilots and a crew chief would take a full load of people northbound on either route, drop off the fresh people and pick up those being relieved. We carried twelve or thirteen people on almost every leg. Once in a while, if there was room, any person on the island could hitch a ride and see the atoll from the air. I was able to get my daughters a ride with me when they visited the summer of 1991.

I joined the yacht club, so I could go sailing. At one of the first functions I attended, I met and got involved with a sweet young nurse fourteen years my junior. Wonderful! I felt so lucky that I wouldn't have to be celibate for two years. We hit it off famously for several months until she started making strong hints that we should marry and make babies. I was brutally honest with her when I said, "I've been married before, already have two children, and have no desire to do it all again." She understood, and we parted. It was hard for both of us. A few months later, I attended her wedding to another fellow at the base chapel.

Finally, the day of my check ride to upgrade to captain came. I did well with the basic flying, the hovering autos, and the straight-in and 180-degree autos. Next, I had to shoot a standard radio instrument approach to the KWAJ airport, which included a procedure turn. For a few seconds, I got forty feet below the proscribed minimum altitude, a minor error, which I quickly corrected. Y-Y failed me because of that minor mistake. I didn't feel like that should have been a reason to fail me. After all, we were not even required to fly instruments on this job, ever. Heck, previous times in my life, I had small deficiencies in my flying on check rides, but most times, they were overlooked because I was a good pilot otherwise. Even on my final instrument check ride in US Navy flight school, I had omitted a small crosscheck on my final approach as I failed to report passing over the final marker beacon. The Navy instructor mildly admonished me for missing the beacon, but he didn't fail me, allowing me to complete Navy flight school. I always learned from my mistakes and rarely repeated them.

Chief Pilot Brown took me to lunch and asked me what happened. By this time, the flight side of the Fight or Flight reaction had taken control of my brain. I minimized the problem to Brown and just said, "Well, I failed the procedure turn." I knew that Brown and Y-Y had a serious mutual dislike for each other, and had I simply asked for another check ride with another instructor, I am sure that I could have passed it. But I just did not want to subject myself to further stress of impromptu line checks with Y-Y in the future. I felt sure there would be many more times that he would attempt to fail me...until he could get rid of me. I slipped into the 'flee' mode. (PTSD kicking in...again!)

I was now looking at being unemployed. I phoned a few helicopter operators in the USA., looking for another flying job, but it was late in the season. There seemed to be no pilot jobs available.

There was a need for an airport manager at the KWAJ airport. I had no experience and was not qualified to be an airport manager, but I was offered the job and hired anyway. The job sucked big time because it was not flying, and the pay was much less than what I'd been making as a trainee pilot, and a great deal less than what I would have earned had I passed the captain's check ride. But the living was easy in "Almost Paradise." I had managed to find myself another girlfriend, so I decided to hang out there for a while. In those many months, I did a lot of scuba diving and sailing.

Even though KWAJ is above the equator by a few degrees, it is considered part of the South Pacific. The Atoll is the largest in the world, about fifty miles from north to south, shaped much like the state of Florida, in reverse. Everyone on the island had a job. No one could come to that island unless they had a top-secret clearance or was married to someone who had one. I did, a remnant of my military service.

The US Army Corps of Engineers leased KWAJ from the Marshallese government for the US Army missile testing program. (The Marshall Islands were a protectorate of the US until about the year 2000 when they finally became independent.) Because KWAJ was part of the missile testing system, the international date line was juggled so that it was in the same day as the US. Otherwise, it would always have been in "tomorrow," and that would have caused confusion and difficulties getting work done. Missile Testing central is located in Huntsville, Alabama. Because of its roots in Huntsville, Kwajalein is very much like that small city in Alabama, southern accents and all.

All the test missiles launched from Vandenberg and Hawaii target KWAJ. None of them carried explosives, but were loaded with telemetry to continually calibrate the effectiveness and accuracy of missiles, making every effort to create better and better ways of killing everybody on the planet. But it was a job, a flying job. Somebody was going to do it; why not me?

Most of the island was taken up by the airport. We got two C-141 flights every week, bringing mail and supplies to keep the residents alive and happy. The government wanted to hire and retain top-level engineers and technicians, so they provided housing, medical, and good pay to all those involved, and a great K-12 school and teachers for the dependent children. Many of the high school graduates earned scholarships to major colleges.

We had a supermarket called "Surfway," a department store, a hardware store, an officer's club, and six other bars scattered over our little piece of "Almost Paradise." There was a big swimming complex that the high school used for sports, which was open to the public when not in use by the schools. We had a golf course, and even had military post office privileges. Our nominal address was an APO box in San Francisco, so I could mail stuff to and from home cheaply.

On Kwajalein, no one had a personal vehicle. Even the CO of the base, a full bird colonel, had to ride a bicycle to get around. The base hardware store did a booming business in bicycles, both for new hires and for replacements. Salt air corrosion on KWAJ was fierce. If you bought anything other than a one-speed Huffy bike, you could plan to buy another in six or seven months. I made the mistake of buying a three-speed bike with handlebar grip brakes that applied small rubber pads to the chrome rims of the wheels. Within seven months, the chrome on the rims was so corroded that rust bubbles acted like abrasive and ate away the rubber pads. At first, I tried sanding down the bumps, but that just exposed more raw steel to the open air. The problem quickly got worse. I threw that old bike away and bought a single speed Huffy. I took that new one all apart and added lots of extra grease to the bearings in hopes of keeping corrosion at bay. I never knew if my plan worked, as when I left I gave the bike to one of my Marshallese employees. But at least it had outlived my original three-speed at half the cost.

When I first arrived, I was housed in a three-bedroom trailer house with another pilot, Charlie. I had my own small room, and Charlie had the master bedroom. That was okay, but I didn't like having to sleep in a single bed. I'm a big guy, and I need room. I went to the clerk in charge of housing and requested a full or queen-sized bed. He told me that a single person only rated a single bed—no bigger bed for me. I tried to reason with the petty bureaucrat but got more resistance. Finally, I bluffed the clerk, "I am one of the helicopter pilots. It is imperative that I rest well. Should I not get enough sleep, I could fall asleep while flying, and a whole helicopter full of people will die!" A full-sized bed arrived at my trailer that afternoon.

A short ferry ride away was the Island of Ebeye, where almost all of the native population of the entire atoll lived. The people took an inter-island ferry to KWAJ Island to work for the Army but were not allowed to live on KWAJ proper.

At the north end of the atoll was an island called Roi-Namur. In the past, it had been two islands, but when the Japanese took it over in the years prior to WWII, they dredged coral from around the island and filled in the gap between the two. Much of the super-secret work was done on Roi, as we called it, and very few people stayed overnight on this small base. Because many people worked on Roi full time, it was necessary to create a small airline called the Roi Shuttle. Dozens of people queued up every morning for a ride to Roi and had to queue up again to get a ride home every evening. This work was done by DynCorp contract pilots who flew the SHORT Brothers 360, a small high-wing, 36 passenger twin-engine turbine airplane.

This had to be a very expensive operation. Near the end of my tour, the DynCorp contract for the Shorts Brothers. planes expired, and the Army didn't renew it. The government brought in Air Force C-130's to ferry the people. The C-130's didn't like the climate at KWAJ, and they seemed to break down a lot. Finally, the government contracted to bring in Bombardier four-engine transports, and things got back to some sense of normalcy.

Near the south end of the airport was a huge building somewhat resembling the Great Pyramid of Giza. Unlike the pyramid, it had two distinct features that jumped out as unusual. The first was that the building had a great big oval eye built into its high, slanted side. Rumor was that it had been built at a cost of $300 million to house some kind of secret radar, but it was obsolete before it was completed. Another feature, not quite so noticeable, was that on its east side, there was a door and no landing...ninety feet above the ground, with no way to access the door from the ground. Rumor, again, said that the building was an exact duplicate of one in Cheyenne, Wyoming, which was built into a hillside and needed the high door. The contractor building on KWAJ structure had simply erected the structure to the plans without asking whether this door was needed or not. While I was there, it was being utilized as a warehouse, a $300,000,000 warehouse.

I heard that the national anti-missile program described as trying to shoot a bullet from a rifle in California with the intent of intercepting another bullet shot towards California from New York. One of the problems is...how do you know if you have been successful or not? The missiles are pretty small compared to the vast expanses of space, and they are traveling at enormous speeds. The space engineers came up with a solution. They built a huge portable camera. It was not just any old Brownie box camera, but an entire Boing 737, which was modified to have an angular "dog house" on top of it, built with perfectly clear glass windows so that a high-speed camera could take pictures of the intercepts as the aircraft loitered as high as it could fly, somewhere near 40,000 feet above the sea.

Because the camera was most delicate and had to be absolutely precise, its components had to be chilled to sub-zero temperatures, which created the need to build a liquid nitrogen plant on KWAJ. Liquid nitrogen plants are not exactly cheap to build; this was yet another great expense of the missile testing system. To top it all off, because there was always the chance that the camera plane might be down for maintenance at any given test time, an entire second backup camera-plane was procured and fitted.

Security on this top-secret base was excellent. It was said that every seventh person on KWAJ was security of some sort. Some people we dropped off at the various island outposts were Army security. Some were Marshallese police officers, as per an agreement with their government to create some jobs for the locals. I know they were paid a lot less than the US personnel. My friend who worked at the airport unloading baggage from the Air Micronesia and Continental flight earned $2.14 per hour.

I can honestly say that I never saw anything that I would consider secret, and I never heard anyone say anything that I might consider secret. What was not secret was the missile tests themselves. We had a radio station, two TV stations, and a small newspaper on the island. Every time there was going to be a missile test, it was broadcast over all four channels of communications, like announcing the Fourth of July Fireworks. "Missiles will be visible coming into the lagoon at 5:30 this evening. Best place to view is on the north end of the island." People would gather and watch the missiles re-enter the atmosphere.

The missile re-entry was spooky. A bright speck would appear in the twilight sky and streak down from outer space with remarkable speed. In just a few seconds, it would disappear somewhere out in the lagoon. Several times I saw a missile that had multiple warheads on it. The single speck broke into maybe six bits; these bits moved around each other, each seeking its own target. If I had been out in the ocean in a sailboat and saw this happening and didn't know what it was about, I would have freaked out. *War of the Worlds!* For one missile test, engineers decided to use one of our helipads on one of the outlying islands for a target. I can't say if they hit it or not, but forever after, we had to land elsewhere.

One day we got a MAYDAY call from an aircraft in distress. The pilot of a small civilian airplane reported being caught up in a thunderstorm and needed a safe haven. By international law, no airport can refuse landing to an aircraft in distress, so we gave the pilot clearance to land his small airplane on KWAJ. The pilot was a young man ferrying a new airplane to its new owner somewhere beyond KWAJ, but the thunderstorm delayed his trip. I was assigned the task of being his "minder" to make sure he didn't wander around the island asking questions or taking pictures. He was young, tired, and hungry, so I took him to the officer's club and bought him lunch where we had a great conversation about flying. The leg he had been flying was an extremely long one, but he was trying to get the job done and return to the factory for another delivery, building up flight time to make himself valuable to the airlines. He told me that one of his ferry flights was sixteen hours from the bulge of West Africa direct to Johannesburg, South Africa…sixteen hours solo over water. I can understand wanting to do a good job, but I think he would have taken a more indirect route and stayed over land much of the way, plus he would have garnered more flight time. He carried survival gear, including a raft and an emergency radio, so he could have called for help if needed…if he survived a water landing.

KWAJ really was "Almost Paradise." One good thing was that, even though it was an Army base, when I first arrived, there were only about six Army men there. Everything was done by contractors. The old saying, "There is the right way, the wrong way, and the Army way," stood true. I saw things that made me shake my head and wonder, who the hell is managing this fiasco? One thing that comes immediately to mind is that, at some time after the first Gulf War, the Army decided it had to cut down on personnel or find jobs for them. Suddenly, a lot more soldiers began showing up on the base, taking over a lot of the jobs that had been contracted out. The expense for supporting a person in KWAJ was about two and a half times what it cost to fill a post stateside, yet the Army imported a soldier who had twelve children to be a mail clerk.

I had completed my first year at KWAJ and was home on Christmas leave when w. decided to attack Iraq. Returning, I was in Hawaii on a layover, and I watched the TV news all night to decide whether to return to KWAJ or go back and be near my daughters in case things went seriously bad. Saddam Hussein had, after all, the "Mother of all Armies." The next morning, I decided that there was nothing to fear, and there was no danger to my girls in northern California. I proceeded back to KWAJ. The situation there was ludicrous. Because it was a US Army base, the Army went on high alert, preparing to repel a beach assault by the entire Iraqi army which was ten thousand miles away and otherwise quite preoccupied. I don't believe the colonel in charge was afraid of a beach assault, but he had orders from the Pentagon, and he had to go through the motions.

The first thing they wanted to do was place a high cyclone fence all around the perimeter of the base. We had millions of square miles of ocean around us and a half-mile wide reef to slow down any landing party. But that was not enough. The fence would be built. The FAA-approved airstrip on KWAJ ran from one side of the island to the other. A fence at both ends would make the airport unusable, stopping all flights into KWAJ. That would be the end of our bi-weekly supply flights from Hickam, the stoppage of Continental Airlines service, and no more Air Micronesia flights. No one would be able to come or go from KWAJ. All activity on the island would screech to a halt in a week or less. Cooler heads prevailed and realized there was no risk. The perimeter fence was cancelled.

Most of the retired US Army Warrant Officers were excited about the war and began to inquire how they could go about getting back on active duty so they could be involved. Since the missile testing was considered critical to national defense, most were told they couldn't re-enlist.

The Worldwide Adventures of a Helicopter Pilot ... the rest of the story

* * *

I did an enormous amount of SCUBA diving during those two years at KWAJ. I probably used up two tanks of compressed air every week. Rumor had it that our dive club was the largest in the world with more than 700 members. Dues were $7.00 per year with unlimited tank refills. Both of my daughters got their scuba certifications when they visited in the summer of 1991—the younger turned twelve during training, the minimum age for certification.

Every month, the dive club sent out an old WWII landing craft with fifty divers on board. Soon I was on every one of those trips. Once we exited the west side of the reef and drove about twenty miles north. I am sure no one had ever dived in this spot before. I saw coral fans twenty feet in diameter and an abundance of giant clams. My dive buddy and I recovered a giant clamshell that was thirty-one inches long and weighed more than 150 pounds. I dove on the WWII German ship *Prince Eugen*. In the north of the lagoon, there was still a WWII Corsair with its propeller sticking up out of the water at low tide. We dove on several Japanese ships that were sunk in the lagoon. Almost every dive, we could see crates of mortars and stacks of torpedoes. We were strictly cautioned to not disturb any old ordnance. We complied.

Getting on a smaller dive boat was easy. Army Special Services provided two-engine runabouts for free to all divers. My dive buddy and I would go to the pier and wait for a boat to have open spaces and invite ourselves to go along. My female dive buddy and I called ourselves "Dive Sluts," because we would go down with anybody. I didn't have an army license to drive the boats, but she did. She would check out a boat, and I would drive it.

No digging was allowed anywhere, no gardening except in pots on the deck. EOD teams were at the ready to pounce on any explosive device left over from the WWII battles. While I was there, the Army dug a trench across a road to bury a steam line. They found several unexploded mortar rounds and hand grenades in those few feet of trench. Sometimes for recreation, we would go out and walk the reef at low tide, looking for seashells, sea stars, or anemones. Again, we were cautioned to be aware of explosives and not touch anything that might be ordnance. On Roi, the government spent a ton of money building a new gymnasium for the few workers who remained permanently on that island. One night just after construction was completed, a 2,000-pound bomb cooked off under it, destroying the brand-new structure.

I was visiting my buddy Mike at his apartment one day. When his phone rang, he answered it and handed it to me, "It's for you." I was amazed. How in the world did I get a phone call from the US at another guy's apartment where I had never been before? The telephone operator, Nita, was a young lady of mixed Marshallese and American Parents in her mid-twenties. We were acquaintances from the dining hall, and because the island was small and everybody knew everybody else, she had an inkling where I might be, so she tried my friend Mike's home and caught me there.

A few days later, as I rode my bicycle to work, I ran across the beautiful, tall, buxom and charming young Nita on the road, and we stopped to chat. Thanking her for finding me at Mike's place, I said what I thought was a compliment, "You are a princess!" Her face contorted a bit, soured, and she said: "How did you find out?" She really was Marshallese royalty and was working on the island to find an American husband. When I learned that, I kiddingly said, "Oh, Will you marry me?" She instantly accepted by holding up her left hand and said, "Just put a ring on this finger." I immediately back-pedaled because, as I said earlier, I had no intention of starting another family, and I did have a girlfriend at the time. Later she told me that she didn't want to have children. Drat! I could have become Marshallese Royalty – Prince William. Another big life opportunity blown!

Shortly before I departed KWAJ for good, a small tropical disturbance built up right over the island. On the local weather radar, it looked exactly like a giant, multi-colored eye hovering above us. My girlfriend and I decided to take a walk, making sure to stay on the upwind side of the island so that we wouldn't be in danger of being struck by flying debris. It was exciting to be walking around in fifty knots of wind and see the surf breaking over the reef a couple hundred yards away. The military police spotted us and demanded that we get inside to safety. Because we got all wet with salt spray, as soon as I returned to my room, I went into my shower wearing my raincoat to wash the salt off it. It is true what they say: wearing a raincoat in the shower is like wearing a condom.

Late December 1991, when my two-year contract with DynCorp was completed, I elected to return to California and be close to my daughters. I was home for Christmas.

Chapter 34
June, 1992
Flying Metal Meets Mountain Top

Sometime prior to June, 1992, two pilots, flying for the US Forest Service, accidentally drove A P-3 (Lockheed Electra) into an 8,700 foot-high cumulus granite at full speed and splattered the aircraft and two crew into mini-bits all over the mountaintop southwest of Missoula. The biggest remaining fragment of the aircraft, the remains of the empennage, was smaller than a VW bug.

The remains of the P-3 in a farmer's field below the mountain peak.
Author's pictures

Another Huey pilot, Skip Fisk, had been lifting the remains of the P-3 off the mountain and had already done all the hard work, but he had to return to his regular job, helicopter logging in Alaska. Ron called me in to finish the grisly job. Left for me was to haul nets full of potato sacks filled with small pieces and bits. The remains of the crewmen had already been removed months earlier, although the cleanup crew continued to be aware of anything that might be human remains so that it could be handled appropriately.

At first, I was a little spooked by the situation, this being the site where other pilots and crew had died. Another factor that made me a little nervous was the fact that I had never flown a Huey solo before. I had flown many hours of dual-pilot flying in the Huey. I had even flown as an aircraft commander in Laos, but I never actually flown a Huey alone. This Huey, the US Navy N-version, had some minor differences from the average Huey I had flown, but nothing serious. I never told Ron that I had never flown solo. Had I, he would have loved it, true maverick that he was.

It took about five days to do this job. Early each morning, I hauled two crews of six or seven workers to the top of the mountain. They wandered around gathering bits and putting them into sacks. When they had enough sacks full to fill a few cargo nets, they'd call me on the radio. I flew up to the top and hauled the nets full of sacks to a farmer's pasture below, where all the wreckage was staged. The nets full of aluminum and other plane bits were quite light. I never used anywhere close to my full torque available.

When the crash was all cleaned up, Garlick asked me if I would like to hang around and fly a Bell 206 Ranger for him on a USFS contract. *Sure, why not?* The particular Ranger that he owned had been cobbled together by his rebuild crew from several crashes of different models of the Jet ranger, so they couldn't call it a Jet Ranger, nor could they call it a Long Ranger, nor could they call it a Long Ranger II. They decided to call it the "Jet Stranger." I flew the Jet Stranger up to the Missoula Forestry base for a check ride with the USFS check pilot.

Right away, he called me on something that I had always done while flying Jet Rangers. I am tall, and I have a long back. I had trouble getting my head out the window and back in easily while wearing a helmet, so whenever I flew a Jet Ranger, I always removed the seat cushion and sat on the hard metal seat base. When the USFS check pilot saw that, he said, "You can't do that." I replied, "Well, I've been doing it for years."

That debate was settled by a phone call to the Bell factory for a final decision. The factory tech reps said that the seat cushion was considered an essential crash-worthiness part of the helicopter and must be in place. I didn't feel I could safely fly external loads with the Jet Stranger while having to duck my head way down two times on every maneuver, so I declined that job and returned to California.

Late 1992, while living in my motor home in a friend's driveway, I saw an advertisement in the *Santa Rosa Press* by North American Van Lines for long-haul drivers. I could operate a heavy machine for long hours, navigate my way across the country and manage fuel. Easy-peasy. I figured it would entail lots of time on the road, that I would see lots of the country and probably make good money. I went through training for three weeks in Fort Wayne, Indiana, and hit the road mid-winter. This was truly the worse job I ever had. I was on the road constantly, moving heavy objects in and out of the truck at each stop, subsisting on truck-stop food, and sleeping in the "coffin" in the back of the cab every night. The money was awful. Not only did I not earn money, but over my four-month career, I lost $3,000.

I started using the truck as a platform to search for a helicopter flying job. At an airport somewhere, I bought a *TRADE-A-PLANE*.

In it, I saw an advert for helicopters pilots—heli-logging in Alaska. Hence my fourth and final tour in the "Last Frontier."

Chapter 35
July 4, 1993
Helicopter Logging Insanity

I arrived in Ketchikan at the start of the Fourth of July three-day weekend. I was told someone would meet me at the airport. No one did. I phoned the local chief pilot and his irritated response was, "Who are you? No one told us you were coming." He crossed the Inside Passage on the ferry (later the most expensive "bridge to nowhere"—made famous during the 2008 presidential campaign) to the Ketchikan Airport and delivered me to the company hostel at the extreme north end of Ketchikan's twelve miles of isolated waterfront road. I had the three days to hang out and get to know the other pilots for CRI Helicopter Company. One of the other pilots had been fishing and offered me a piece of the small shark he had skinned and cooked. I declined, saying: "Professional courtesy. I feel if I don't eat shark, perhaps they will return the favor and not eat me should I ever crash into shark-infested waters."

When I told the other pilots that I had flown for Air America, someone asked, "Do you know Ted Cash?" Heck yes I knew Ted Cash! We flew many hours together in Laos. During a three-week period in late 1972, we nearly died together three times on perilous missions. I sought out Ted and we lifted a few drinks. A few days later, another old Air America hand, Dick Elder passed through.

Captain Bill with two other former Air America pilots in Ketchikan July, 1993. Ted Cash-left, Captain Bill-middle, and Dick Elder-right. Unknown pilot in right seat of BELL 214. Author's picture.

I made every effort to avoid helicopter logging for years, but a few bad investments and a divorce, compounded by a few dumb career decisions in the middle of a rough economy, and I found myself doing work I never thought I would do. Helicopter logging is perhaps the most hazardous occupation that exists, but is also very rewarding—for the survivors.

I wander out back of the hangar and see a pile of three wrecked helicopters…a Bell 205 and two ruined Bell 214s representing three dead pilots *just* this year.

Crashed helicopters behind the CRI hangar in Ketchikan. Author's picture.

I ask the other pilots about the wrecks and pick the brains of the mechanics to find answers for myself. Knowledge is power...power to avoid repeating the mistakes of others...power to stay alive.

The First Crash

From what I was able to piece together, the first accident had several possible scenarios. Two pilots were flying logs into a landing. The two huge logs composing their load landed with one balancing vertically atop another for a few seconds. The pilot in command felt the slack in the line and thought the logs were on the ground, but the top log slipped off the lower one and plummeted towards the ground, reaching the limit of the choker cable before it reached the ground. Such a heavy weight falling twenty feet jolted the aircraft enough to give the helicopter a giant "hit." It jerked the helicopter hard enough to fling the copilot up through the overhead window and broke both his legs at the hip joints. The pilot's head bounced around inside the bubble window hard enough to disorient him, if not knock him unconscious. The helicopter, now un-piloted and still attached to the 8,000-pound load, began to drift until it reached the end of its steel tether with the logs. It pulled that line taut until it teetered itself into oblivion, destroying itself and the two unconscious men on board.

Another possible scenario for this accident was that when the logs stacked, the pilot hit the release switch at that time, but the logs didn't release because there was no weight on the hook to trigger the release. The pilots, thinking the logs were released, pulled power, and before they could release, the load pulled them down into the stack of logs. Evidence supporting this scenario is that just before impact, the hook did release. Was one of the injured pilots trying to recover, but too late?

It had been the chief pilot's policy that the electric release for the cargo hook on the bottom of the helicopter always be in the OFF position. A load or two had been dropped inadvertently, along with the entire long-line and lower hook assembly, an expensive bit of hardware to lose in the woods or the bay. To prevent such losses, the policy became: upper hook disarmed, disabling the emergency backup release the pilot needed to jettison the entire load. Ironically, the chief pilot was the aircraft commander this day, and his own policy possibly contributed to his own demise.

Post-crash investigation revealed that one of the major flight control linkages was broken. Could it have broken before the crash, and indeed, could that be what caused it? Most likely it was broken by the "hit" or the crash.

Second Crash: A Lone Pilot In A 204

Someone working underneath a pilot told him that a puff of smoke emanated from his tail rotor. Instead of landing quickly, the pilot elected to return to the service landing even though there was a place to land closer. Upon arriving at service, he could have punched the long-line, but instead chose to coil it slowly onto the ground. While hovering down, the tail rotor assembly departed the aircraft, throwing his center of gravity off, causing him to pitch over and go in straight down…fatally. The mechanic on the ground dove under the service truck but was still hit by enough flying debris to put him out of action for six weeks. The machine was smashed flat like a bug after the main rotor and transmission system departed the inverted aircraft. Was the cause of this crash pilot error or mechanical? Both, of course.

Third Crash

Another pilot flying solo in a Bell 214 had an engine failure. He managed to pull collective pitch and use the stored energy in the rotor system to slow his sinking into the woods with a bit of control. He was able to land in small trees and didn't roll over. The lucky pilot walked away from this one. Shithouse luck; except to hear the pilot tell it, it was all his skill. His Bell 214 was destroyed. Subsequent investigation of the engine showed it had come apart internally from over-stress.

These logging machines are used very hard. A good logging pilot can make a turn every 90-120 seconds. A turn is flying out to the forest, handing the hook to the hooker, pulling the log out of the forest, flying it to the landing and returning to the hooker…ready for another turn. Two complete surges of the engine from minimum power to maximum power twice every two minutes. One every minute.

Once every minute. These things weren't designed for such abuse. It's no wonder they break. Throw in extra power changes for pilot's erratic maneuvers, trying to "yard" a log out from under the brush or another log, or dragging a log down the hill to mate it up with another to complete a turn, mistakes in landings or approaches..

On top of all that, there is always the pilot with a big ego who must outperform all the other pilots, regardless of the abuse on the machine. Some pilots have discovered that if they rear back on the cable and give the machine a little forward speed before they put the full weight of the log on the machine, they can yard a much heavier load off a hillside. Sometimes 20-25% or more than normally allowed. Usually, though, it only works to kill them, or one of their more conservative buddies who fly the same machine later after it has been mortally wounded. Not too many of these pilots remain, for obvious reasons.

The pilot who had crashed the 214 was lucky to survive. He was what we called a "cowboy." When they broke down the engine of his crash to determine why it had quit, many of the bearings and races were badly damaged from his abuse. Later, I watched him fly another 214, pulling out logs obviously heavier than he should have. When one of the other pilots asked him on the radio how much that log weighed (we had onboard strain gauges that told us the weight of each load), he said, "You really don't want to know." He was fired shortly thereafter. Inspection of the second 214 he had been flying showed a lot of damage to the engine—an engine failure in the making—his making. Good riddance to him. Cowboy pilots do the rest of us a disservice. We know who they are, and no one wants to fly a machine after one of these guys had his hands on it.

Of course, with any accident, the pilot always gets the blame. Even in cases of catastrophic failure, the pilot should have anticipated this event, or should have reacted quicker or better, or should have caught the fatal flaw on pre-flight before taking off. There is only one chance, no experience to draw upon, no references, within personal or collective memory, and he is expected to be the instant expert on something that may never have happened before in history and may never happen again. Or he may be just a little less swift than he was when he was a twenty-one-year-old combat pilot in Nam. Then he dies.

You don't get to be fifty years old in this business and not have a few "Late" friends. It's mostly about timing and "shithouse" luck. Some of the best pilots I have known are dead; some of the most awful pilots, flying for the airlines. I'm new with the company and I don't expect to garner much seniority.

Shakan Bay, Thorne Bay, Hoonah

We usually worked off barges anchored in various bays around the Inside Passage. It struck me just now that living aboard an anchored barge must be like living on an intergalactic space freighter. Lots of workers aboard, long halls of room after room. Several decks; one deck for utility, one deck for storage, one deck for living. Life is confined to the walls around you. A separate section for food service, a holo-deck (tv room/library), toilets down the halls. The constant droning of the generators creates a constant hum and vibration that you notice by its absence when by chance, it ceases operation for a while. This is certainly the slow boat to nowhere.

* * *

I toddle across the room and shut off the alarm, struggle into my shorts, bounce off the walls of the hallway to the urinal and drain my bladder, struggle up the stairs to the kitchen, and pour myself a cup of hot, black coffee. I walk over to the window to evaluate the day's weather. Then back in my room, I sit on the edge of the bed to sip my coffee, and contemplate the day ahead while coming slowly to consciousness.

One morning I took my coffee and staggered out to the rear platform of the barge. A group of us watched as a young man riding a log-pusher Bronco-boat like one would ride a wild mustang. The little Bronco is hardly more than a tiny boat built around a huge engine, with big teeth vertically on the front of it. It is used to push logs around in the raft to line them up. This morning the young driver was having a ball riding his steed and showing off to his audience. He hit a log hard, and instead of digging into the log, the teeth slipped, and the little boat slid up onto the log, and slid back down into the water tail first and kept descending until it was out of sight. As the young driver came sputtering up to the surface, a few of the fellows retrieved him from the cold water. The workers threw in a circle of oil-absorbing barriers to contain the fuel bubbling up from the Bronco. A few hours later, it was raised from the deep and was soon back in service.

Since I have been here, the 204 has gone down twice for tail rotor failures. Both times the pilots were able to slide it down without damage, and there have been several tail rotor gearbox warning lights. There are always bits of carbon, metal powder, and fine metal shavings from a replacement being broken in. But you never know.

The money here is good to outstanding; where else can a small-town boy make ten to twelve thousand dollars a month. Seniority gets guys promoted into the safer twin-engine Sky Cranes, where the money is bigger yet. This is comparable to airline pilot's pay, with similar schedules.

I've looked into death's steely eyes; stood nose to nose with the grim reaper several times. So far I have not flinched. I've had no crashes, but numerous close calls. Some too close, and at least three near mid-air collisions, too.

What close calls did I have and don't even know about?

I contemplate death; quick, violent, sudden death. Death by slicing, dicing, burning, drowning, decapitation, squashing, dismemberment. In this country, I seem to be in the right profession at the right time.

The big IT.
The end.
Eternity.
Passing on,
The Big One,
Being deceased,
The great beyond,
The final solution,
The great adventure,
The big ready-room in the sky,
Meeting Jesus, God, Bhudda, Mohamed, Yowhe, the Great Spirit.
Going to heaven, the hereafter, The Happy Hunting Grounds…
Every culture, every religion, every language has many euphemisms for IT.
It seems no one wants to talk about IT directly because
IT is such a big mystery, full of wonder, awe and fear.
To talk about IT directly may bring IT on.
One on one, even the bravest of us fears IT.
What if we are wrong? What if our religions are wrong?
What if there is no God and heaven is a lot of bunk?
What if this existence is all there is?
What if after life there is no life, we draw a blank, an empty hand?
Will we know it?
We all fear the unknown, yet we still press on in life,
Taking chances with our precious lives.

I face my fears.
I see potential death in every tree top,
In every tree branch,
Every pressure and temperature gauge,
Every turn of the blades, every beat of the rotor.

> I am careful doing the world's most dangerous job.
> I keep fear locked in a steel cage in the back of my mind.
> Death is no stranger.
> He has taken many of my friends over the years.
> Yet I continue to fly.

I wrote this piece in my journal during a break from logging (my first and only attempt at poetry until years later) as I sat on a stump in the wilds of Alaska, not logging because, "The winds are too gusty for logging." We are grounded.

Safe. For now.

One of the senior pilots, who was making the big bucks, returned from a break with several large stickers that said, "NO FEAR!" the logo of some sporting equipment maker. He placed them on the nose of a Bell 205. Somehow this struck me as a bit too much of tweaking the devil's nose and asking for trouble. I felt uneasy flying that machine.

A group of us were standing around discussing operations. It seems that the company was suddenly short a Bell 214 copilot; someone quit abruptly. Originally built for the Shaw of Iran as a combat and heavy lifter, the huge beast had come onto the US market as a heavy lift machine. It carried with it a reputation that the tail rotor often failed, causing it to crash, usually killing the crew.

The talk was about who was going to get to fly copilot for Ben Sizemore in the big beast. I was reluctant to volunteer, and no one else in the group spoke up. Finally, it was determined by our chief pilot that the most junior guy with the company would go. That meant me. Even in helicopter logging in Alaska, seniority counted. I had just signed on with the company. I wouldn't last long either.

We climbed into the 214 and flew a few turns, lifting the 8,000 pound maximum load maximum weight each lift. This was a bit spooky for me as my sole job was to watch the torque meter and warn Ben if he was coming close to exceeding maximum allowable torque. I couldn't see what was happening below the right side of the machine.

Ben was hovering right at the top of tall trees, leaning out into the bubble window to watch his hook as he dangled his long-line between the trees to get it down to a hooker. On our third load, Ben started pulling a large section of cedar logs out of the trees. As I monitored the strain gauge on the instrument panel, Ben suddenly and violently slammed the collective down, causing us to plummet towards the treetops! It seemed to me that we were going to crash into the tall trees. I was going to die right here, right now.

I didn't know Ben made that abrupt maneuver on purpose. On his side, he could see what I couldn't see, that the log was about to slip out of its cable and plummet to the ground. This could cause the log to split, making it worthless at the market, but also it would cause us to take a serious "hit" on the aircraft as the heavy load fell abruptly away, which would cause the 214 to jump up violently.

He arrested our violent descent right at the treetops, then explained to me what had happened and why he had to take such drastic action. I was not impressed. In my mind, I had just escaped death by a few centimeters. I said, "Take this sumbitch back to the landing and let me out RIGHT NOW!" That was the end of the logging for that day because he was not allowed to fly the 214 solo. I knew I was going to be fired right away, but I didn't care.

The hookers knew about how much each log weighed and cut the logs into appropriate lengths. Approximate is the word here; sometimes logs were heavier. Most of the hookers were young, athletic fellows right out of high school or high school dropouts. They were, for the most part, under-educated but hard workers. Most of them chewed tobacco. I find that disgusting, so I educated them a bit. I asked them if they knew that tobacco chewers had a high risk of lip cancer. They said, no, they didn't know that. I told them, "You know, there is only one place on your body that has skin similar to your lips. After surgery to repair your lips of chew-induced cancer, the doctors use skin from your penis to repair your lips. That means you will be able to go around for the rest of your life giving yourself oral sex." I think half of them quit chewing on the instant.

I wasn't fired as I expected to be but was assigned to fly a 206 to support the hookers. As the logs were lifted out of the forest, each log had a thirty-five-pound cable around it. Over time, the cables accumulated in the landing. The log-landing crews collected them in bundles weighing 1,450 pounds, and my job was to return them to the woods where they could be reused. I was still doing long-line work over the forest, but in most cases was flying over where the trees had already been cut down, and there was a much better chance that, in case of engine failure, I would be able to land without a thrashing trip down through tall trees. Also, in the Jet Ranger, I was a single pilot. I was in command. I was not placing my life and wellbeing in the hands of another pilot, regardless of how good he might be or how much experience he had...or didn't have.

I could very easily smoothly and gently place a 1,450-pound bundle of slings on a large tree stump. This came from the experience I had in unloading ships in Saudi Arabia. At one point, I had picked out a large stump to place a load. The hooker below was directing me, and I thought he would get out of my way as my load approached the stump. He didn't read my mind and was signaling me to place the bundle beside the log. Continuing to maneuver the load to the stump, I gently brushed him off the stump with the load. He was not hurt, but I apologized over the radio. I was surprised there were no repercussions from that, as I could have hurt him.

Ben Sizemore planted a 204B into the tundra near Thorne Bay after his tail rotor control link failed. He was able to slide it down onto the tundra without it digging in enough to cause the aircraft to flip over. The mechanics flew out and repaired the broken linkage. I was sent out to retrieve the machine which had sunk into the tundra until it was about fifteen degrees nose up, the tail rotor within inches of the surface. I started it up and carefully and gingerly brought it up to full speed, then wiggled the tail while I lifted it to make sure I was breaking free of the morass equally on both skids and flew it home.

Other duties included ferrying loggers and hookers to the field so they could start at first light. I then would wait around all day and go fetch them in the evening. I landed in creek beds and other convenient clearings. One day, I went out with a slightly senior pilot to be checked out in the company 500. I flew a good ride in the left seat until he told me to land on a tree stump with the right skid of the 500. I couldn't see the stump, and I thought this was utterly stupid and refused to do it. If someone was dying and in need of an immediate ride, I might try something so daring, but no one was dying. During this exercise in futility, the former army pilot yelled and screamed at me.

Our quite attractive and buxom boss lady lived on her huge powerboat at a marina near the company hanger area. On the evening after I wrote the poem above, she invited me over for drinks. There were two other couples, and it seemed obvious to me that I was in for a treat...if I wanted her. We had a few drinks and a nice dinner and adjourned to a nightclub in Ketchikan for more drinks and dancing. I realized that this helicopter company was not for me, and I knew that if I got involved with her, I would be making a commitment to staying with the company. I made excuses and made my escape, one of the few times that my big brain overruled my little brain. The next day I was laid off for, "Not being aggressive enough."

Author's photo.

I hitched a ride back to Ketchikan in an old de Havilland Beaver flown by an Aussie fellow. The pilot let me fly the aircraft straight and level for about fifteen minutes. That was a thrill for me to drive such a classic old airplane.

Chapter 36
Rocky Mountain Helicopter Company

During my working for CRI Helicopter Company, I had met Gene Tolls, former Marine Corps H-53 pilot and the chief pilot for Rocky Mountain Helicopter Company (RMH). He said to me one day, "I won't steal you away from CRI, but if you ever find yourself in need of a job, come see me." I looked him up, and he hired me to fly support for the RMH logging operation in the same area. Gene flew with me on a check ride in a 206 to make sure I could do the logging support he needed. I found it amazing that not once did he yell, scream, or belittle me or my skills. The difference between an army instructor and a Marine instructor was remarkable.

RMH flew me out to the company barge where my 206 lived on the roof.

My 206 on the roof of the company barge in Shakan Bay, Inside Passage, Alaska.

At least on the RMH barge, there were women. Two. Stella Jones the cook, and sweet Cherri P., the cook's helper. I got quite close to Cherri in the ten days or so that our life tracks coincided. She was college-educated and well-read. We spent hours each night talking in the mess hall and sometimes later in her room. I treated her with my magical chiropractic hands for sinus and sniffles that had been bothering her for some time. Before I left, she said she was getting some relief and was no longer taking antihistamines. I hoped to hear that her menstrual problems cleared up, too. I made no great effort to seduce her. She let it be known right up front that she wasn't interested in getting sexual, and I wasn't too hot on it either. Too scary these days. I believe she was suffering from PTSD too. I believe she might had been sexually assaulted early in her life.

There was a little rare bit of beach where the walkway from the barge reached the shore. It had been a trading post sometime in the far past. Traders and natives had lost hundreds of tiny trade beads on the beach. In our spare time, Cherri and I went to the rocky beach and searched for these historical beads. We called it "beading off." I still have a small vial of the beads.

From my journal:

"Things have been interesting around Shakan Bay the last few days. Three evenings ago, just at shutdown time, the 61 developed trouble in No 2 engine, it couldn't generate enough power. Investigation showed a problem with the fuel control, caused by clogged fuel filters. Water in the fuel! Water had bypassed the filters and gotten into the fuel control...it requires a new $125,000 fuel control (carburetor). A day later, a new one was sent out to us, followed immediately by a phone message to NOT use it. It seems the whole engine was a leased item from another company, so it would be better to replace the whole engine instead of just the fuel control. Fog held the seaplane in Ketchikan almost all day yesterday, and the new engine finally arrived. I used the 206 to lift it over to the service pad. Of course, about the time I delivered the engine to them, it began to rain, and mechanics Scotty and Levi had to work all night in the cold rain. On start up this a.m., the new engine puked a big puddle of oil! Some seal somewhere was wrong; we are again awaiting more parts from Ketchikan to replace the seals."

"In the meantime, another little saga is going on. Gene assured me that I would be paid when I was in town, but that RMH was on shaky financial ground. Of course, all we get out here in the field is a bunch of 2nd hand rumors, but it sounds as if RMH will either go bankrupt this week or will be bought out by the Canadian helicopter company, Okanagan. I hope the latter, and I hope that somewhere in all this, there may be a permanent position for me. I sure would like to have a full-time, permanent job, instead of going back to STS for the winter, unemployed. I called the CRI office to inquire about why my paycheck was so small, and about the per diem, which I have never received, and there was no answer. More than $1000 at stake here. Fifty days at $21 per diem, plus half a month's pay. The wonderful world of helicopter flying."

"We had another engine go belly up, so we ordered a new fuel control. At first, they sent one, then a whole engine. Rumors flew. The company said to look out for any strange person in an H500 or an airplane who might try to attach the H-61. Then they said, 'Never mind things are alright now." Then someone DID show up and put chains on the H-61 controls and rotor head. We called the home office and management was completely surprised. The fellow who put the chains on said it was a mere formality, and the chains could come off Monday. The office said cut them. The office changed its mind and said don't cut them. Then they talked to the man who had said he would be out Monday to take them off, but he was at the airport leaving town. But he said we could cut the chains, home office said. Paranoia...is the office lying. 'Trust me," Curt said. Sure, but who goes to jail? Skip Fisk balked at the offer to cut the chains and stalled, saying we had not the tools to do it. The office sent out the Beaver with bolt cutter, a special trip. We cut the chains and went back to work yesterday, Saturday. Normal work schedule today, Sunday. Just waiting until Monday to see what happens next. If the Canadian company does buy RMH and keeps everything together and offers me a full-time job, I'll probably take it. The money isn't great, but it could be steady, and I really do enjoy all this time getting paid to write my memoirs."

One day I wrote eighteen pages with my little Brother WP 500.

Talking to the S-61 pilots, I heard some great stories. One fellow said he had been in seven major accidents, "...every one of which should have been fatal." Yet he kept logging. Another told the story of how, one day when he arrived back home, he found a brand new Ford Falcon in his driveway, and he knew his wife didn't have enough money to buy one. Entering his bedroom, he found his wife in bed with another man. Not one to be violent, and knowing his marriage was over, he sat down and negotiated with the couple. He traded his wife for the brand new Falcon, then ripped out the passenger seat and made himself a bed on that side, so he would always have a place to sleep while working out in the woods.

Just before I left, one of the loggers asked me to take him up to the top of a hill above Shakan Bay. He said he was on company business, and I believe he had clearance from the company. He directed me to land in a clearing area near the top of the mountain. He said, "Come back for me in two hours." When I returned he had the head and skin of a mountain goat draped over his shoulder. He company "business" was a hunting expedition.

October, 1993

Nothing ever materialized to keep RMH alive, and I was laid off. I returned to Santa Rosa in late September without my last paychecks. I went to work for the local North American Van Lines affiliate, driving truck. I retrieved my Jamboree Motor Home from storage and installed it into a mobile home park south of downtown. I knew it was hard on the big engine of the machine to start it up just to drive it a few miles twice a day, so I decided I would ride my bicycle to work and back, five miles each way, and get some exercise too.

Fall, 1993
Disaster!

On the first Friday payday, I decided I would drive my motor home to work so I could go to the market with my paycheck and buy food. I followed the same backroads path I had used while riding my bike to work to avoid traffic on the busy city streets. I didn't realize how low the entry to the parking lot was behind the big downtown mall and I smacked the top front of my motorhome into the overhead. In one fell swoop I destroyed my wheels and my place to live! I was now broke, homeless and had no transportation. My last paycheck from RMH wouldn't arrive for a year. I was in a serious pickle.

My ex-wife, Michele, was kind enough to let me stay at her place for a while until I could get my act together. I had a few bucks left, but I wanted to rent from someone who was willing to rent me a room in their house, as I knew it wouldn't't be long until I would pick up another flying contract. I responded to an advert in the local press for a condo to share. The advert said that the person was willing to give up his master bedroom if he could have the garage for his motorcycles. I liked that, because I didn't have a car anyway, and the condo was close enough for me to ride my bicycle to work.

We met and evaluated each other. I liked Matt because he didn't smoke, didn't drink, didn't use drugs, didn't party, he was active in the local army guard unit and was attending the community college nearby. He liked me because I was a helicopter pilot between jobs and...I could pay rent. I wanted the master bedroom because I had my king-size bed and my desk and bookshelves and books in storage and wanted my things around me. We agreed that I could share the condo he was renting, no deposit required.

After a few weeks, he said to me, "You gotta meet my mother." I was not interested in dating. I felt so low, that I didn't want to date anybody who would go out with me. It was the old Groucho Marx joke, "I don't want to join any club that would have me as a member." When he said to mom that she should meet his roomie, she was puzzled why her twenty-five-year-old son was living with a fifty-year-old man.

Finally, one day, roomie Matt told me that his mother was moving, and I should give her a bid. Good; perhaps I could make some extra money. I called his mother and made an appointment to bid on her moving job. I was lucky in that the only other company who agreed to make a bid failed to show up. Her escrow had closed, and she had to move the next day, so I got the job. I rented a box van, hired a helper, and we did a great job of moving Matt's mother, Carla, to her new home.

Near the end of the move, I was carrying Carla's desk into her new bedroom. I got this feeling of déjà vu...in reverse... a vision of her and me lying together in her bed, reading. Carla could tell that I was tired, and she suggested that I return the next day to complete a couple of small details of the move. Good idea. The next day I took extra care to spruce myself up a bit and to try and make a good impression on Carla. After the small details were completed, she asked me if I would like a glass of wine. Would I! As they say, the rest is history. Three weeks later we were in her bed together, reading.

Chapter 37
Early 1994
CRANE Again

CRANE Helicopter Company owner Steve Lotspeich phoned me and asked me if I would be interested in being his relief pilot on a short US Forest Service contract in Tennessee. The contract required that the main pilot (Steve) could work twelve days sequentially, but then he had to take two days off. I was hired to be the relief pilot for those two days out of every fourteen. Steve and I flew his 205 from Stockton, California, to the forestry base at Copper Hill, Tennessee, north of Atlanta, Georgia. This was my fifth long-distance, multi-day ferry trip. We departed Stockton, California, on February 25, 1994, with stopovers in Kingman, Arizona; Amarillo, Texas; Elk City, Oklahoma; and Jonesboro, Arkansas. During this ferry flight that I had my first introduction to GPS. I learned to dial up the distance to my destination airport, view my ground speed, and how far to the nearest airport in case of emergency. I never got beyond those simple tasks. I flew home commercially. After that, every eleventh day, I would go to San Francisco, get on a plane and fly to Atlanta. There I would pick up a rental car and drive to the company-rented cabin in the woods somewhere near the base. I remember that the cabin was in North Carolina, so we had to go into another state to go to work every day. I made the trip round trip from San Francisco three times in this short term contract.

I had another FAA Part 135 check ride in McMinnville, Tennessee. High winds and almost violent turbulence made it impossible for me to show the FAA Inspector a good flight, but because he was a Vietnam veteran comrade, a former Marine Corps H-46 crew chief, I think I could have all-but crashed, and he still would have passed me.

During the check ride with the forest service check pilot, I believe he was impressed that I could do long-line work from the right seat of the 205, but I never flew on a fire. There just weren't any fires during my time there. I was dispatched only once, and canceled before I got off the ground.

At the end of the contract, Steve and his wife, Linda, assured me that they had another contract coming up right away. They would call. I went home and waited, sure that they would call me within a short time. It never occurred to me that I should ask for pay during that interim. After three weeks, I received the following message on my answering machine, which I quote verbatim: "Bill, this is Steve. We have hired someone else who has a mechanics license, and we won't be needing you anymore." No "Hello." No "Goodbye," no "thank you for your help until now," not even a, "Fuck you very much." Nothing except that terse message. I was incensed. I had waited three weeks for a call back to work, and I felt very shit on. I wrote Steve and Linda a strong letter demanding that they pay me for the time I had been waiting. They did send me a check for the pittance that I demanded.

Chapter 38
June 4, 1994
Evergreen Helicopter Company
Orange County Fire Department, Southern California

Getting dumped by CRANE turned out for the better. During my time with CRANE, I heard that the Orange County Fire Department (OCFD) in Southern California was hiring Huey pilots. In 1993, a huge wildfire swept the hills of Laguna Beach, destroying hundreds of expensive homes on the coastal bluffs. If there had been a helicopter on duty, it could have extinguished that fire while it was in its infancy. Orange County had an inter-agency agreement with Los Angeles County and Riverside County that they would come to the aid of Orange County. However, that particular day, all the helicopters of both counties were involved fighting fires in their own counties and couldn't help Orange.

The political pressure was on. Orange County had to create a fire-fighting helicopter unit, and they had to create it NOW! There is no way they could do that quickly in-house, so they advertised a contract for a helicopter company to fill the void. Evergreen Helicopter of McMinnville, Oregon, won the contract.

It had been weeks since I had heard of the OCFD program, and I assumed that the positions had been filled, but I phoned Evergreen Chief Pilot George Converse anyway. I learned they had not filled both the pilot positions. They paid my way to John Wayne Airport so I could have a check ride with George. I flew well. He hired me. Sad to say, only a few weeks later, George Converse died when the Sikorsky Skycrane he was ferrying home from Florida came apart in the sky, killing him and the entire crew. George was another of the few pilots that I ever met who worked his way up the food chain and became a senior civilian pilot without the benefit of military experience.

I reported to the Evergreen HQ in McMinnville, Oregon, for new-hire processing and a physical, including an EKG, since I was older than fifty. While at McMinnville, Oregon, I learned that that town had been named after its founder, Mr. McMinn, the very same Mr. McMinn who had founded McMinnville, Tennessee, where I had had the check ride just a few weeks prior.

During the same time frame, I had been jumping through the hoops to get hired by the California Department of Forestry (CDF). I drove six hours to a CDF base near Red Bluff and interviewed with Cecil Gil, the chief pilot of CDF. A couple weeks later, I drove down to Paso Robles to fly a check ride with Cecil. I went to Mather Air Base near Sacramento and got checked out in the CDF Super Huey. I passed and was hired to fly the summer season at Kneeland Firebase, atop the coastal hills east of Eureka, California.

Now I had a conundrum. Should I go with Evergreen/OCFD on a full-time job, but with only a one-year contract, or should I take the summer contract with CDF? My CDF pilot friend told me that there were times a CDF pilot would be on "Golden Overtime," during which a pilot received triple pay, even though he might be asleep in a motel room bed. That was very tempting. I knew that eventually, I might be hired on full-time with CDF, but I wanted the security of a full-time job. My hope was that I would eventually be hired on full time by OCFD and be a real fireman.

It was a hard decision. The deciding factor was that OCFD schedule was six days on, six days off. I could commute from

Northern California and not have to give up the love of my life, who was willing to live the six-on/six-off schedule. Otherwise, I would have been commuting six hours each way to and from Kneeland once every twelve days. Twelve hours of each two-day break would be spent commuting—not enough time for my sweetie. This relationship had developed into my best one ever, and I wanted to hold on to this wonderful lady. Reluctantly, and knowing full well that I was burning a bridge, I called CDF Chief Pilot Cecil Gill and turned down the Kneeland summer contract.

* * *

About this time, I discovered a brochure describing the symptoms of PTSD. After I read it, I threw myself onto my bed and bawled myself unto exhaustion. I had discovered why, for twenty-seven years I had had so much trouble holding onto jobs and girlfriends and staying in one place very long.

Carla was a giant factor in my doing this. I began to finally allow myself to get close to a woman. She was beautiful and charming and smart and the most caring person I have ever met. She was a few years younger than me, a highly paid executive with Hewlett Packard, and had no desire to create any more children. She was—and still is after 28 years—perfect for me.

Several times, when I told one of my flying stories, and she would ask, "How did that feel?" *Feel? Feel! I don't got to show you no stinkin' feelins!* Usually, a question like that would have me in the next county by sunrise, but she did it in such a loving, caring way that I actually began to question myself: how did it feel to feel?

Carla had a degree in psychology and worked in Human Resources for Hewlett Packard in Santa Rosa. She was a people person and saw something in me that warranted rescuing. She helped me find my way out of the abyss of confusion and anger that had clouded my thoughts and directed my actions, usually in negative, self-sabotaging ways. Sometimes she had to use a little hard love, but mostly she carefully, lovingly, and tenderly manipulated my dumb ass until I was able to look at my shit without being afraid and trying to run away from myself again! Like the song says: "I sold my soul, you bought it back for me."

She eventually convinced me to try and get some psychological counseling. That led me to the VA Office in Rohnert Park, California, and group counseling. I was in with a great bunch of other Vietnam Vets who also had suffered severe trauma. This counseling eventually made a huge difference in my life.

* * *

I reported to John Wayne International Airport, formerly known as Orange County Airport, for OCFD duty. I had never fought fires with an LA tank before, but it was simple to learn. The LA tank is a flat tank that tucks up to the belly of the helicopter between the skids, and holds 3,000 pounds of water, a maximum load for the 205A-1.

Author learning to drop water from an LA Tank for Orange County Fire Department. Author's picture

OCFD had acquired two surplus UH1-Hs and was having them converted to "Super Hueys" at San Joaquin Helicopter Company, Delano, California, at the cost of hundreds of thousands of dollars each. They were scheduled to be finished by the end of the Evergreen contract. They were not.

Once the Evergreen 205 contract was up and running, OCFD decided to have a press conference. They invited reporters and dignitaries to watch as I demonstrated the water-dropping function of the machine. Just before the demonstration flight, my LA bucket malfunctioned; the doors wouldn't close after a drop. DRAT! We had a demonstration to do...now! Rather than cancel the press conference, my mechanic came up with a clever solution. After every demo drop, I would hover over the tall rushes next to the pond, and our mechanic would stand up under the 205 and manually close the drop doors so that I could make another drop. No one caught on.

Initially, we were stationed at John Wayne International Airport, very near the Marine Corps Air Facility at Tustin, where I had spent my last eighteen months in the Marines. The OCFD airport crash-rescue fire detachment on that airport was our home for a while.

In January, 1995, we had a tremendous heat spell. Temperatures reached over 100 degrees with torrential rain, causing local streams to overflow their banks. We flew low and slow around the Santa Ana neighborhoods after midnight, looking for anyone who might have fallen into the rushing streams. It seemed stupid to me because there was no way to rescue someone who was being rushed away in a stream surrounded by trees and with lots of wires overhead, with frequent bridges crossing the streams...at night. Fortunately, we didn't see anyone in distress.

OCFD decided that John Wayne airport was unsuitable, for what reason I never learned, and began to look for a new home. For me, it made ultimate sense for us to base at the former USMC jet-fighter base, El Toro. Most of the wildland fires were in the east and southern portions of the county, so El Toro would put us much closer to most fires. No, they decided to move to Fullerton Municipal Airport (FUL) near Knott's Berry farm, a good fifteen minutes of flying time north of John Wayne and that much further from the average fire. "Mine is not to question why..."

The crew at OCFD from left to right: Pilots Bill Collier and Andy Campbell, "Big Bird" Eric Wood, Chief Drake, firemen Edwards, Brian Stevens and Captain David Lopez. In front of Evergeen's 205A-1 at Fullerton Municipal Airport, 1995

I rented a room from a nice older couple within walking distance of the hangar and was able to walk to and from work at Fullerton Municipal Airport. I commuted by Southwest Airlines and accumulated a pile of frequent flier miles. Whenever I flew to/from work, I wore my Evergreen Airlines Captain's uniform with epaulets. Once or twice, when the plane was full, I got to ride up in the cockpit on the jump seat with the pilots. That was a real thrill for me.

Most of the time, we simply stood by. During the summers, there were a few "campaign fires," which meant that sometimes we had to bring in helicopters from LA County Sheriff, LA City, and Riverside County. In my two years with OCFD, I flew on only three or four campaign fires. Most of our time was simply waiting around for the beeper to chime. We fought a lot of small fires, but few required assistance from other agencies. Several months I didn't get what I considered to be the minimum flying hours to stay proficient, four hours. I occasionally said that this was a "novel job" because I read a novel every day. I should have spent more time writing.

We could drop water in one big splash, or, by varying speed and altitude, we could spread the water over a larger area. It was up to the pilot's judgment to decide what was best. At one time, I was dispatched to a tiny fire on a small hill called Turtle Rock. I filled with water and homed in on the fire. As I approached, I forgot to toggle to single tank, and I dropped both sides of the LA tank on my first pass. Then I had to return to the local fire hydrant to refill. Soon the firemen from the local fire station were on the hill, and it was too dangerous for me to drop near them. Had I made two passes, I could have extinguished the fire entirely by myself. I lost my big chance for fame and glory.

We often flew to remote areas of Orange County and trained other fire departments on how to use the helicopter. We would give them a lecture and then demonstrate how we could drop water. We demonstrated at the former Marine Corps Bases El Toro, MCAF Santa Ana (aka Tustin Lighter than Air facility), and Mile Square, which is now a regional park. I feel that I am the last Marine Corps pilot to land at these three former Marine Corps bases, as all the OCFD pilots who followed me are former army.

Many times, at the outlying bases, we would invite ourselves for lunch, called a "buy in." At each fire department, the firemen chip in and buy their own food and prepare it in their station kitchen. We would pay a fair share for our lunch or dinner and relax for a while and get to know the local crews. Every station had a TV lounge where the firefighters could sit back and relax after meals in their Barcaloungers and sleep if they wanted to. I liked that. At the outlying stations, I often had a nap after lunch.

Unfortunately, at Fullerton, we were not allowed to take a nap after lunch. Chief Drake, always political, worried that his boss might stop by and find us sleeping and think he was not running a tight ship. How that differed from the other stations where the firefighters were encouraged to sleep in their Barcaloungers, I never understood.

One day, breaking the Chief's rules, I sneaked upstairs from the office. It had been a general aviation transient pilot's lounge at some time in the past, and there was an old shuffleboard game table along one wall. Perfect! I slid under it and had a nap. I always carried a beeper; it wasn't like I was disappearing from the earth. One of the fire captains spied me sleeping on the job. He said, like a grammar school kid would, "UHHHMM!" and then tattled to the

Chief. I expected to be chewed out, but nobody said anything to me directly.

That night about 11:30 p.m., I got a call from my immediate boss. His boss had heard from his boss that I was sleeping on the job. The fireman who had caught me sleeping told chief Drake, who called his boss, who called the CEO of Evergreen, who called my bosses' boss who called my immediate boss to tell me no more sleeping on the job. How incredibly petty! All anyone had to do was talk to me personally, directly. This pattern would prevail. I soon found another, more secret place to nap atop the parts room, where I was never discovered. There was even an old army cot there, so it was much more comfortable.

I found it interesting that elsewhere in the OCFD, two active firemen, brothers, flew Hueys for the local army air guard unit. Somehow the OCFD was not interested in hiring these experienced army Huey pilots and training them for airborne firefighting.

There were a few memorable moments of flying with the OCFD. One day I went out to the hinterlands of the county and rescued a mountain biker who had tumbled over his handlebars, smashing his face on a rock. I transported him to the rooftop pad of a local hospital. Another time I showed an airspeed of thirty-five knots while hovering in the strong Santana winds, loitering downwind from a structure fire. I carried a full load of water in my tanks, ready to pounce on any embers that might blow away in the wind and start a secondary fire. None did.

On night, we got called out to try to rescue a teenage boy. He and his father had been camping with a group somewhere in the Silverado Canyon. Trying to get back to their vehicle to escape flash flooding, they had to cross a raging steam. The father made the mistake of tying electrical cords together to fashion a rope. The son was crossing mid-stream when the wires parted, and the boy was swept away, never to be recovered.

Captain Lopez and I were returning to the airport from the east foothills. I saw an isolated little hill poking up from the farmlands. I decided to let Lopez have a little stick time and had him make an approach to the pinnacle. He flew the helicopter nicely down a gradual flight path, using the stick and collective only, without his feet on the rudder pedals. As we approached a hover, I told him to bring in some power by gently lifting up on the collective. The reaction of the helicopter surprised even me, as we did three quick 360s around the top of the peak. I was amazed at the effect of not having input in any anti-torque, which caused us to spin out almost violently of control. I quickly assumed control of the Huey and got us straightened out. That was our cheap thrill for the day.

Another time, my friend Mike Taylor, the army Huey mechanic, and I made up an excuse to do a post-maintenance check ride. We took the 205 out for what was basically a joy ride. I have met up with him again later in life after I retired.

Several times we flew to the top of Santiago Peak at 5,687 feet MSL so that a techie could replace batteries in a repeater radio. One of the knowledgeable crew on board pointed out the remains of a Marine Corps H-53 that had crashed there years ago. The hulk was too heavy and too large to remove. Looking back over the Los Angeles basin was like looking into a swimming pool. Above the surface of the pool, the air was clear and cool. Beneath it was a septic tank of stinky, putrid air. As we descended to Fullerton and passed through the 'surface' of the pool, I could smell various pollutants in the air. Most significantly, the smell of diesel fuel filled my nostrils. Probably the exhaust of thousands of trucks on the highways and jet engine exhaust from LAX.

The next morning my beeper awakened me quite early. I jumped out of bed and rushed to the airport. A very confusing and convoluted group of messages indicated that a helicopter might have crashed somewhere in the eastern foothills. Someone was out in the foothills searching for a missing helicopter and calling for assistance, but his driving around in the hills made cell phone reception most difficult and garbled. No one knew for sure what was going on.

We launched and flew out to the foothills to take a first-hand look-about. It was early morning, and the coastal fog shrouded the foothills. As we dodged around and under the fog, we couldn't see much. Finally, we spotted a pickup on a dirt road and a man walking on the road talking on his cell phone; the caller.

Then we saw the accident. I am not a trained accident investigator, but I have seen enough accidents that it was simple for me to figure out what had happened. The pilot of the only twin-engine Bell 206 Jet Ranger ever built, known as the 'Gemini', was scud running trying to get through to the El Toro area. I surmised that he saw a gap under the clouds over the road and made a dive for it, knowing once he got through the gap, he would be home free. His misjudgment cost him his life.

Where the road dipped between two hills, I saw the impact marks of the landing skids of the Gemini. Irregular dig marks between the skid's marks told me that the tail rotor blades had dug their way across the road, too. The skids separated from the helicopter as it rebounded from the violent impact, and they lay on the hillside, about 200 feet down the steep, grassy slope. The rest of the helicopter was about 500 yards down the slope, a crumpled pile of wreckage partially hidden by brush. The rotor system of the small craft had departed the airframe on impact and was nowhere to be seen. Whatever was left of the pilot was probably still in the fuselage. There was no fire, which told me that the pilot was low on fuel, which increased his anxiety about getting through.

There was nothing more we could do, so we returned to base. Here is the Los Angeles Times article about that crash:

1995
LOS ANGELES TIMES

Mystery Shrouds Crash Site: Accident: Helicopter pilot dies in steep canyon, 8 miles off course. An unidentified man who said he was a friend vanishes after leading authorities to the location.

By GEOFF BOUCHER
SEP. 21, 1995, 12 A.M.
TIMES STAFF WRITER

The search for a missing Newport Beach helicopter pilot ended Wednesday when rescue workers retrieved his body from a steep canyon east of Orange, where his craft had slammed into a ridge line in Tuesday night's heavy fog.

Hanspeter Karl Guggisberg, was flying a Bell 206 helicopter, a charter craft operated by HeliStream Inc. of Costa Mesa, and was en route from San Diego to John Wayne Airport when he crashed, officials said. The wreckage was found in a remote area about one mile southeast of Lake Irvine and about eight miles north of the airport.

The pilot made his last contact with air traffic controllers about 10:45 p.m. but gave no indication that he needed help, according to a spokeswoman for the Federal Aviation

Administration. An alert went out about 1:15 a.m. when the craft was overdue. Rescue teams did not discover Guggisberg's body until eight hours later, as the morning haze burned off to reveal the trail of silvery wreckage a few miles off Santiago Canyon Road.

A broken barbed wire fence and a gash in the crest of the ridge, along with another impact mark about 100 yards down into the steep ravine, led authorities at the scene to speculate that the helicopter might have somersaulted after ramming at high speed into the 1,200-foot-high ridge.

"He was coming in too fast in the dark and the fog," said Bill Collier, the helicopter pilot for the Orange County Fire Authority, who ferried the pilot's body out of the canyon. "There's a landing skid that broke off [the helicopter] at the top of the ridge. They don't come off easy. He must have hit pretty hard for that to happen."

Investigators from the National Transportation and Safety Board on Wednesday began a probe into the cause of the crash. A spokeswoman for the Orange County Fire Authority said the pilot was an employee of HeliStream, but HeliStream officials did not return phone calls on Wednesday.

The dense fog cover early Wednesday morning hampered the airborne search for the 31-foot helicopter, an effort that was further delayed by early eyewitness accounts that placed the downed craft some 15 miles away from its true crash site. The first person to locate the helicopter was a friend and apparent co-worker of the pilot who was searching the area on foot, a firefighter said.

"He waved us down as we came up," said city of Orange firefighter Robert Stefano, who, arriving about 9:20 a.m., was the first emergency worker on the scene. "He was in tears. He said he was the guy's best buddy. He said he had already been down there, so he told us the best way to get down. He kept saying 'He was the best pilot I've ever known.'"

The unidentified man, believed to be the person who phoned in the location of the crash, left the scene before he could provide more information, Stefano said. By some reports, the friend also told rescue team members that the pilot was alive when the friend first arrived and had even called him via a cellular phone. But Orange County Sheriff's spokesman Lt. Ron Wilkerson said he was skeptical of those accounts.

"I'd be very surprised if anyone could have survived that kind of crash," Wilkerson said. "It is possible, I suppose, but without verification I would tend to doubt that."

Orange County Fire Battalion Chief Mike Burnett said he was puzzled by how the unidentified friend could find such a remote crash site on foot, and he hoped for more answers when authorities reach the man. "There's too many unanswered questions, starting with the initial report," he said.

Just for the record: I did not carry the pilot's body out.

Chapter 39
1995
San Joaquin Helicopter Company

After the one-year contract with Evergreen was up, the OCFD-owned Super Hueys were not yet completed at San Joaquin, so the contract was rebid. At first, it was announced that Evergreen had again won the contract, but petty politics got involved, and the contract was re-awarded to San Joaquin Helicopter Company (SJH) of Delano, California. I was considered a valuable pilot and retained by SJH to stay on board with their new contract.

* * *

Senior Pilot Andy Campbell was not retained, making me the senior pilot. When I asked the OCFD officers why Andy was not kept around, they said that Andy had broken the OCFD rules about staying out of the fixed-wing traffic patterns while flying around Fullerton. What nobody ever bothered to ask Andy was why he had occasionally made airplane-type approaches into the airport instead of our proscribed helicopter patterns. Andy had a helicopter Air Transport license (ATP), the highest possible license a pilot can hold. (I never bothered to get one, never seeing the need.) To maintain his proficiency and confidence as an ATP pilot, Andy was required to make a certain number of instrument approaches every quarter. When Andy was "breaking the rules," he was actually keeping himself proficient at maintaining this highest professional license; but he never told anybody that, and they never asked. They just assumed he was breaking company policy, being rebellious or contrary, and decided to not retain him. Andy was replaced by another former army pilot, Jerry Casman, who I found to be standoffish, even though I made every effort to be friendly.

As time progressed, it looked very good for me to be hired on with OCFD when the time came. The pay would be excellent and the benefits superior. The only catch was that it looked like the pilots might have to change from the six days on/six days off regimen to a regular fireman's schedule, which is normally a most irregular schedule. This was not going to work for me if I was going to stay with my sweetie. I seriously loved this woman, and I intended to keep her in my life. I began to wonder about future with OCFD.

While flying for the OCFD, the powers that be were concerned about how they might be able to help should an aircraft taking off from John Wayne International Airport or LAX splash down the Pacific Ocean. We practiced a lot of what we called "short haul" rescues (see picture on cover), where a fireman would be hardwired to the helicopter and I would dip him into the water so he could grasp a survivor of a water crash. I called it "Dope on a Rope," because should there ever be a problem with the helicopter and it crashed, the "dope" on the rope would have only a few seconds — at most — to unlatch himself from the line before he would be wound up into the rotor system. Not a pretty thought.

Over open water, it is most challenging for a pilot to hold a steady position over a point and to hold a constant altitude, even more so at night. Even though we practiced over a small reservoir close to shore, I sometimes had trouble holding stable hover during the day while simultaneously looking straight down at the dope on the rope.

I began to contemplate about what we might toss into the water that would create a plane of reference to combat those two challenges. My first I thought was Ping-Pong balls. They are lightweight, cheap, would float, and show up nicely on the surface. The negatives were that Ping-Pong balls would take up too much room in the helicopter, and throwing hundreds of them out of the Huey would start to become expensive after a few trainings. Also, because they are very light, they would disperse quickly. These small, indiscriminate points would be hard to see from any altitude at all, and they are not at all biodegradable. Scratch Ping-Pong balls.

I came up with the idea of using sections of the Sunday newspaper. It's cheap, readily available, light in weight, and small enough to store in a specially created box right under the pilot's seat. We flew out to our favorite training reservoir and gave my idea a try. It worked wonderfully. My primary concern was that the newspaper pages might fly up into the rotor system and create a blizzard of paper bits as the rotors chopped the pages up. That worry was instantly dispelled with our first trial. The rotor downwash violently slammed the papers into the water. As the pages hit the water, they peeled away and dispersed, creating a perfect plane of reference on the surface with pieces of known size and shape. It was biodegradable, too. Cheap, easy to use, light in weight, effective...this was the perfect solution on how to hold a stable hover over water, even at night.

I wrote the idea up for a trade magazine, *AIR BEAT, JOURNAL OF THE AIRBORNE LAW ENFORCEMENT ASSOCIATION* of Tampa, Florida, which published it in their Vol. 24 No. 3, May/June 1995 issue, p. 14-15. That got the attention of the Los Angeles Times, which ran a short article about the magazine article. Then the July 17, 1995, issue of *AVIATION WEEK & SPACE TECHNOLOGY* picked up on my idea and wrote this under "INDUSTRY OUTLOOK" p. 17.

Instant Horizon

"Helicopter Pilots for the Orange County (Calif.) Fire Dept. are experimenting with a simple and inexpensive technique to make tricky open-water rescues easier, quicker and safer. Once hovering over the victim, the Bell 205A-1's back-cabin observer throws a 1 in. thick stack of white newspaper, arranged much like you buy it off the newsstand, horizontally out of the helicopter. The papers are blown straight down by the rotor wash, then peel apart and spread themselves out on the water surface. They create a series of reference points of known size to aid the pilot position-holding and hover. Until use, the papers are stored in a narrow box, open only at one end."

Shortly thereafter, GPS, radio altimeters, and other technologies made my idea obsolete. A pilot can now simply push a button and hold his position and altitude over water.

Since retirement, I have made friends with Thomas Beard, a retired US Navy and US Coast Guard helicopter pilot living in Port Angeles, Washington. He has written extensively about the history of US Coast Guard Helicopter Aviation. In the Summer and Fall 2012 reprint edition of the *American Aviation Historical Journal*, page 17, he writes about how the number two (at the time) Coast Guard pilot, Ross Graham, came up with the same idea of using newspapers in 1945.

"Graham explained their first problem was one of positioning the helicopter above the water in a stationary spot "keeping the suspended sonar cables vertical while dipping the sonar head. [We needed] a reference on the water to hover over. [We tried] float lights and dye markers but the helicopter's downwash from the main rotor blades swept away the float lights, and scattered the dyes over a wide area, thus making precision hovering impossible. Finally, *recalling the simplicity in which they solved the problem—bursting forth with a gusty laugh*—Graham said, "(we) found that a sheet of the Sunday newspaper comics worked best as a reference. The brightly colored paper soaked up enough water to keep it from blowing away, and could be easily seen at a flight altitude of 20-25 feet."

Late one afternoon, we were way out in the Silverado Canyon, educating the local fire station troops on how to use our machine when someone heard screaming nearby. Two young men had climbed up a steep rocky cliffside and got stuck there, frozen with fear. They couldn't climb any higher, and they were too petrified of falling to climb down. We rigged up a short-haul rope, flew up there, and plucked the two Huck Finn wannabees off the cliff. When we returned to our station at Fullerton, Chief Drake chewed us out for doing something for which we hadn't trained. What were we supposed to do, just leave those two young men on the hillside overnight to perish? Besides, we had done lots of short-haul practice over water; this was just short-haul work over land. This was the only time I rescued someone using the short-haul technique, and this was also the only time Drake actually spoke up about something

I was dropping water on a grass fire on the north side of Highway 91 that was burning its way up a cliff. There were no homes in danger, no urgency here. I found a large McMansion nearby that looked unoccupied with a huge swimming pool in the back yard. While I hovered over the pool and sucked my tanks full from it, my rotor wash blew all the pool furniture into a pile at the end of the patio. As I dropped several salvos onto the fire, I found that if I flew directly at the fire, the instant I dropped my load, the release of the weight, combined with the updraft of the fire, would balloon me up and over the top of the cliff like an elevator, where I would make a quick U-turn and return to the swimming pool. My elation and exuberance got the best of me.

About my third pass, I realized I was making a colossally stupid, amateur mistake, and I should have known better. I was flying directly at the cliff, depending on the fire updraft and releasing my load to balloon me up and away from the fire. What if my tank system malfunctioned and I was unable to drop my load? I did not have room or time or power to turn, and I would have smashed smartly into the cliff! I immediately changed my tactics and started running my drops parallel to the cliff face.

As a result of this, I came up with my own bit of aviation wisdom:

> "Never let your exuberance—or your arrogance—outfly your experience."

Another fire in the same area was in a neighborhood that was developed with streets, power sewer, and a water system, but the McMansions hadn't yet been built. The fire was burning up the ravine right toward the building lots at the top of the draw. There was a most convenient large lot with a fire hydrant right beside it. This was a perfect setup. I landed on the vacant lot, and the firemen ran a fire hose to the hydrant. As soon as I had my tanks full of water, I lifted off. Almost instantly after clearing the edge of the lot I dropped both tanks, I made a quick circle back to the lot and refilled. I did this again, and again, never flying more than ten seconds before I dropping my load. I spent more time on the ground refilling my tanks than I did flying. This was great fun, too.

The petty politics got worse.

With Evergreen out of the picture, I had to go to Delano for a check ride with SJH Chief Pilot Chuck Damerow, then drive a company Huey to Fullerton to replace Evergreen's 205. Here I ran into the same Army problem I had run into several times before. Flying around Delano, Damerow could not stop hollering and yelling and belittling me and my flying. There was no way I could satisfy him, no matter how good my autorotations were. I was a good pilot, and I knew it, but because his constant harassment rattled me. Under his harassment, I didn't fly my best, but he did sign me off.

I was given a crusty old Bell 205 to fly back to Fullerton. Because it had been painted to match the color scheme needed for some movie, it still had patches of blue paint scattered all around its drab green/brown exterior. I didn't like it very much, but it seemed powerful.

Chapter 40
June 21, 1996
My Last Engine Failure

Flying south, abeam Bakersfield airport, just as I triggered the mike to call the tower to request clearance to pass through the westernmost edge of their control area, the engine chip warning light illuminated on the instrument panel. Instead of requesting clearance, I notified the tower that I was making a precautionary landing in a farmer's field about five miles west of Bakersfield.

The engine ran well as I landed beside a paved country road and watched the rest of my instruments for any other indications of trouble. None. When I rolled back the throttle to start the engine cool-down period, the engine began to make loud grinding-grumbling noises. Something was coming apart, so I executed an emergency shutdown to minimize internal damage to the engine, bypassing the usual two-minute cool down.

There I sat, rotors winding down, a quarter-mile from the nearest farmhouse. This was before I had a cell phone so I was in a quandary. Should I leave the helicopter unattended while I walked to a phone or wait for someone to come to my aid? The question was answered for me right away when a perky young blonde stopped and asked me if I needed help. She had a cell phone. I used it to call the SJH office and reported my problem to the office message machine and—with her help—where I sat. The pretty young woman said it was getting late, could she go fetch me some food? I said sure, and I handed her $20 and said, "Please go buy me a big combination pizza." I didn't know how long it might take for someone to hear the message on the office machine; I was preparing to spend the night. When Bill, the SJH Chief of Operations, finally did arrive, I was obviously not in dire straits; the cutie and I were sitting on the grass in front of the Huey having a pizza picnic. The first thing Bill did was climb into the Huey and try to start it. As soon as the engine began to turn, it made the grinding-grumbling noises I had heard. "Toast," Bill said.

A while later, Chief Pilot Damerow showed up, and he, too, made a start attempt. Again the same awful sounds emanated from the engine.

Later I learned that both jokers tried to blame me for the unusual amount of metal debris that got spread throughout the engine, ruining it. It was their repeated attempts to start the engine that exacerbated the damage. I also learned that the chief pilot and the DO Bill hated each other. From my recent check ride with Damerow, I understood why. It would get worse.

Damerow took me to a motel where I spent the night, and the next day I flew another drab, grubby Huey to Fullerton, a 204. I had been spoiled by Evergreen's spotless 205A-1, and was not real happy flying these helicopters that I considered to be refugees from a scrapyard. Always the politician, Captain Lopez changed my attitude when, instead of agreeing with me that this 204 was a piece of shit, he called it an "Honest little helicopter." Sometimes a simple attitude change can make a huge difference.

One morning shortly thereafter, I was in the OCFD office when Chief Drake came into the main office. He glared directly at me, then slipped into his office, closing the door behind him. Intrigued, I wondered what was up, so I went into the adjacent parts storage room and put my ear to the wall. What I heard enraged me.

Through the wall, I heard the Chief say, "Well, if he is not a safe pilot, I don't want him here." Damerow had told the Chief that I was not a safe pilot! Nobody ever talked to me or suggested that perhaps I had a bad day or anything else supportive. I felt stabbed in the back. That was another time when I should have demanded another check ride with a different pilot and punched Damerow in the nose, but my modus operandi has always been, with that one small exception of self-defense in Saudi, one of nonviolence. I reached the decision that there was no future for me with the OCFD, nor within the helicopter industry anymore. I was not going to continue to put up with all this petty political crap, and I for sure was not going to give up my sweetie to work with this bunch of jerks.

An hour later, I was dispatched on some minor flight. When I returned to Fullerton, I only had an hour left in my six-day shift. I shot a perfect autorotation right to the ground, right in front of the office. It was against OCFD rules for me to shoot an auto with a fireman aboard. I didn't care. It was also illegal for me to shoot an autorotation at the airport without informing the tower. I didn't care.

I had finally reached my limit of what I considered abuse by the helicopter industry. After the full autorotation, I saw chief Drake outside the door talking with the FAA chief tower operator. They were talking about my illegal autorotation. Again, no one bothered to call me into the office and ask me my side of the story, or just chew my ass off—like would have been done in the military service—or even cite me for my illegal trick. Soon off duty, I went into the locker room and gathered all my gear. I drove my car to Delano and had a meeting with SJH D O Bill. If I had wanted to save my job, I could have told him my sad story and demanded a re-check ride with a different check pilot. I knew he and Damerow were at odds with each other, and he probably would have been sympathetic to my having a re-check. I no longer cared. I asked him to lay me off. He seemed glad to do so.

I had my fill of helicopter flying. The super-petty politics at the fire department and the fact that I would have to give up the love of my life in a few weeks to retain this job, pushed me over the limit. I'd had it! I was done! Done with helicopter flying forever.

Ten few years after I retired, I visited the OCFD hangar to say hello to anyone I might know—and to market my two books. Their fleet had grown to four Hueys, and they had moved across the runway to a much bigger, nicer hangar. The pilots worked a six-days-on six-days-off schedule! Could, woulda, shoulda... I wonder if they are allowed to nap after lunch.

Just before publishing this book in 2022, I made friends with former US Army helicopter pilot, Byron Edgington. In his two or three books about his life as a helicopter pilot (see bibliography), he verifies my observation that Army instructors did indeed yell, scream, and belittle flight students. This is completely contrary to what I experienced in Navy flight school, where the instructors explained in detail what they were trying to impart, and were much more patient, understanding and supportive. I don't recall *ever* being yelled at or belittled by a Navy instructor. Maybe the Army flight instructors were trying to instill into their student to be calm and persist under pressure, but I felt I got just as good training as any army pilot without the constant petty harassment.

Chapter 41
Post-Flying
Disaster II: I Lose My Sweetheart!

I bumbled around in Santa Rosa for a few weeks but was unable to get my act together. I was fifty-three years old, broke, unemployed, and had no assets to speak of. I was driving a broken-down older Rambler American, and saw little prospect of improving my lot. My sweetie, who was a highly paid executive for Hewlett Packard, finally got tired of my inability to hold a job and generate a decent income, so she threw me out of the house. I was devastated! All I could do was sit at the dinner table and bawl. I Eventually, there was a huge silver lining in this darkest of clouds.

A basket case, I phoned Randy, my VA counselor, and when he answered, all I could do was bawl into the phone. Randy told me to be at the local VA clinic at 8 a.m. the next morning, and he would arrange for me to be transported to the VA hospital in San Francisco. Randy was a former Marine, a Vietnam veteran of my vintage. He was badly wounded in a battle in the areas where I had flown. There is a small chance that I was the pilot that carried him to the field hospital, saving his life. The next morning, I arrived at Letterman Army Hospital in San Francisco and resided in the psych ward for three weeks while Randy arranged for me to be accepted into the National Center for PTSD in Menlo Park, California.

I spent six months in that hospital getting my act together. Because I was in the hospital for six months with almost no income, it seemed a good time to file bankruptcy and dump $202,000 of debt. I started life anew with no debt weighing me down. (I eventually paid all my personal debts.)

For a few months after I "graduated" from Menlo Park, I lived and worked as a clerk in a newly built apartment building in Palo Alto, across the street from Stanford University. I remember well the first task the apartment manager assigned me. He handed me a box of applicant files and said, "Here, organize these." My first impulse was to thrust the box back at him and walk out. I controlled myself. *No, Bill, it is this kind of thinking that has gotten you into this deep hole you have been in. Try another approach.* I settled into the menial job, excelling at it. I processed hundreds of applications for the low-income subsidized apartments, doing all the correspondence and calculations required to verify that applicants qualified for the subsidized apartments. Before I left, I made it a point to write down in exact detail a procedure manual for my eventual replacement on how to do all the processing. I was offered another job with the Palo Alto Housing Authority but passed on it. Had I stayed, I would have soon been the manager of the 106 units where I had been residing.

Chapter 42
Golden Gate Transit

My sweetie could tell I was getting my act together, and we reconciled, taking turns to visit back and forth between Palo Alto and Santa Rosa. Rather than drive through the city, I found it easier to take the train into San Francisco and hop on the Golden Gate Transit (GGT) bus to Santa Rosa. One Sunday night, while returning to Palo Alto, I talked with the bus driver. He said he was having a great day and expected to make $350 that day. The only reason I didn't say, "You're lyin'!" was that he was a huge black man, and I thought he might stop the bus and pummel me into a puddle of pulsating purple protoplasm. Instead, I asked him if GGT was hiring. Yes, they were. I applied and was hired to drive transit buses for Golden Gate Transit, a subsidiary of the Golden Gate Bridge Highway and Transportation District. Not adjusted for inflation, this job was the best paying job I ever held...and a whole lot safer. I made more money while flying for Air America, but I earned more dollars with GGT. For eight and a half years, I regularly drove a forty-five-foot-long transit bus into San Francisco and back out again, fighting rush hour traffic both ways. We had a strong union; some rare days, I earned more than $600.

In many ways, transit bus driving was much like helicopter flying. I would show up early in the morning, pick up my assignment, go out on the tarmac, do the "Captain's walk-around" of my big machine, depart on a route, and pick up passengers and deliver them into San Francisco. Because we had to be available both early and late in the day, we often had long breaks in the city.

I could do anything I wanted on my breaks. I often took long walks, frequented various ethnic restaurants, *slept in the driver's lounge in the Barcaloungers*(!) and read a lot. I bought a laptop computer and taught myself stock investing. I did well once I had my act together.

Because of the heavy rush-hour traffic conditions, we were expected to have an occasional small accident. I probably had more than my share. Part of it was my attitude. I didn't care if I had an accident. What the heck, I was on the ground, encased in 45,000 pounds of hardened steel. If someone wants to run into me, either by accident or on purpose, let him. I wouldn't die, and I got paid extra for filling out the accident reports. I never had an accident on purpose, but I must admit being a little lackadaisical. I liked GGT a lot, and I worked with a great bunch of fellows and gals.

I also retired with full medical bennies. Because I earned great money during those eight-and-a-half years, my potential Social Security doubled, and I started receiving a small VA pension for PTSD. That and my small GGT pension allowed me to retire on my sixty-fifth birthday. I was done with working forever at noon that mid-August day in 2008 in Marin County, and I was in Sandpoint, Idaho, before sundown.

My sweetie and I married in November of 2003. She retired before I did, and she was waiting for me in Sandpoint. We live in a small waterfront condo right downtown in the small friendly, liberal, artsy city...a small blue dot in a giant sea of red. I belong to the local chapter of Idaho Writers League and almost every veterans organization that exists. My second book, *Air America: A CIA Super Pilot Spills the Beans, Flying Helicopter in Laos for Air America,* won first place in 2016 in our annual state-wide contest. I was awarded "Idaho Writer of the Year" in 2018.

I reconnected with Mike Taylor, the volunteer Huey crew chief at OCFD. When I abruptly quit, I never said goodbye to him. He retired and moved to Priest Lake, Idaho, about forty-five miles from me. One day he was reading a local magazine for seniors, the *WISE GUIDE*, in which I'd published an article about flying helicopters in Vietnam. He recognized me from the article and gave me a call. We have reconnected like old friends that we are. He now lives about two hours away, and we don't get together often enough.

* * *

Captain Bill is a life member of almost every veterans organization. Sandpoint, Idaho Chapter 890 of the Vietnam Veterans of America recently rescued a derelict H-34 from the scrapyard. They have refurbished it enough to make it towable for Fourth of July parades, fly-ins and other veterans' activities. They named the old H-34 "Charlie.

See Captain Bill's blog about H-34 Charlie at:
http://dawgdriverforever.blogspot.com

Chapter 43
2011
I Fly An H-43 "Husky" Synchropter

I got bored and felt like my retirement pay was not quite enough, so I decided to see if I could return to flying. A local company, Timberline Helicopters, had just lost their senior logging pilot to retirement. He was about my age, and with my logging experience, I figured I had a shot at replacing him. I called the chief pilot, went to their shop, and flew two short hops in their turbine powered H-43 Synchropter for a total of 1.4 hours of flying. I could still do it!

The H-43 is the weirdest helicopter I ever flew. Because of the intertwining blades, it has a two-per hard lateral knock-knock-knocking beat in its rotor system, which I found most disconcerting. The intertwining blades negate the need for a tail rotor as they cancel out torque. To affect rudder control, the machine has a trim system in the main rotor blades that interacts with the rotor pedals. The catch is that the trim system doesn't engage between 15 and 40 knots (or between 40 and 15 on landing). At those speeds, I could work the pedals like I was riding a bicycle and get zero response. I suppose I could have gotten used to these characteristics. The two short flights took place on a Friday, the start of a three-day holiday weekend. Over those three days, I came to my senses. Tuesday, I called the chief pilot and said I wouldn't the pursuing a job with Timberline. The chief pilot was okay with my decision. (You can find videos of the H-43 starting up on YouTube.)

That was last my attempt at helicopter flying.

After writing all three of my memoirs, I realize how many times I have come within a royal whisker of death. I have used up all my luck for several lifetimes. (I'll never make it to twenty-five!) I have broken my vow to never fly again except commercially three times. In addition to the H-43 flights above, my good friend Roger King (R.I.P.) owned an impeccable 1946 Aeronca Chief and took me flying for my seventieth birthday. I returned safely. Later, another neighbor bought a brand-new Maule, and he talked me into taking a short flight around our neighborhood. I survived that too. Now I leave all the flying to the captain of whatever airliner I am traveling in.

Captain Bill Collier
Port Townsend, WA
Early 2022

If you enjoyed this book,
please be so kind to go to
amazon.com and write a review.
Thank you,
        Captain Bill

Companies/Entities I Flew For

1. US Navy Naval Air Training Command, student.
2. USMC, New River NC, Vietnam, Santa Ana, CA NAS Alameda, CA
3. Rotor Aids Ventura, CA. a quick check ride.
4. ERA Helicopter, AK. North Slope and Amchitka.
5. USMC Reserves, Alameda, three times.
6. Air America, Taiwan, Thailand, Laos.
7. Calicopters, Stockton, CA. Local crop dusting, spraying, frost control US Forest Service, Peppermint Helitack Base; Markleyville, CA.
8. Carson Helicopters, Perkasie, PA, Saudi Arabia
9. "WAYco." Santa Rosa, CA, Utility work; C D F; barnstorming fairs.
10. Sonoma County Sheriff, local, relief pilot
11. Garlick Helicopter, Concord, CA, Bay Area. MT. Industrial lift work.
12. California Helicopter, Oakland, CA. Industrial Lift work.
13. CRANE Helicopter, Fremont, CA Local utility work, Lift work. USFS, Relief Pilot Copper Hill TN. CDF work.
14. Astrocopters Ltd., Oakland Airport, Channels 4 and 7 TV News.
15. Bristol Bay Helicopter, Bristol Bay and Talkeetna, AK. Fisheries, power line intertie.
16. CRI Helicopter, Ketchikan, AK; logging inside passage.
17. Rocky Mountain Helicopter, MT. Logging support Inside Passage.
19. California Division of Forestry, Kneeland, CA
20. Evergreen Helicopter Co., McMinnville, OR
    Orange County Fire Department
21. San Joaquin Helicopters Ltd., Delano, CA
    Orange County Fire Department.
22. Timberline Helicopters Ltd., Laclede, ID.
    Logging...training only.

Breakdown of Aircraft flown and locations.

Year	Machine	Company	Location
1964	T-34C	USN Flt School	Pensacola, FL
1965	T-28B&C	USN Flt School	Whiting Field
1965	H-13/Bell 47	USN/USMC	Ellyson Fld, FL
1965	H-34	"	"
1966	H-34s	USMC	New River, NC
1966-67	H-34s	"	Vietnam
1967-68	H-34s	"	Tustin, CA
1967	H-53A	USMC	"
1967	H-46	"	"
1968	Bell Cobra	BELL	El Toro MCAS
1968	Blimp	GOODYEAR	Tustin, CA
1968	Cessna 150	El Toro	SoCal
1969	H-19	ERA	Ventura, CA
1969	H-19	ERA	AK
1969	Hiller 1100	with Jowers	AK
1969	Bell 206	ERA	AK
1969	H-19	ERA	Amchitka, AK
1969	H-34	USMCR	Alameda
1970	Piper Arrow	Training	Sacramento
1970	Piper Twin Apache	Training	"
1970	T-29	USAFR	Gulf of Mexico
1970-72	H-34	Air America	Laos, Thailand
1972	Bell 204/5	"	"
1974-75	Al-III	Calicopters	Stockton
1974	Piper Arrow		Stockton
1974	Cherokee 6	"	"
1974	Cessna 182	"	California
1975	H-34Cs 2 ea.	Moshe	Mohave, CA
1974-75	Bell 47	Calicopters	Stockton, CA
1973-76	H-53A	USMCR	Alameda, CA
1976	S-58T	Carson	PA, Saudi, CA
	Hughes-500C	WAYco.	Santa Rosa, CA
	Hughes-269	"	Santa Rosa, CA

Year	Machine	Company	Location
	H-34s	Garlick	Concord, CA
1983	UH-1N	Garlick	MT
	Jet Stranger	Garlick	MT
1983-84	H-34	Mahrt	AK
1984	H-500C	Crane	Fremont, CA
1984	H34C	Crane	Fremont, CA
1985	Bell 205A-1	Crane	Tennessee
1986-87	Bell 206s	Astrocopters	Oakland, CA
1991-92	UH1H	Dyncorp	Kwajalein, M I
1993	UH-1	CRI	AK
1993	214	CRI	AK
	Bell 206	CRI	AK
1993	Bell 206	RMH	AK
1994	Bell 205 A-1	Crane	CA, TN
1994-6	Bell 205 A-1	Evergreen	OCFD
1994	Super Huey	CDF, Cal Fire	CA
1996	Super Huey	San Joaquin	OCFD
2013	H-43 Husky	Timberline	Idaho
2013	1946 Aronca Chief	Sandpoint	Idaho
2014	Maule	Sandpoint,	Idaho

Long Ferry Trips Flown

ANC AK to Ventura, CA	5 days
Hamilton, MT to Dillingham, AK	5 days
Stockton, CA to Dallas, TX area	4 days
Stockton, CA to Tennessee.	4 days

Professional Certifications:

Certified school bus driver.
Certified Red Cross First Aid.
Officer of Marines; 2nd Lt, 1st Lt., and Captain.
Naval Aviator with instrument rating, airplanes and helicopters.
NBC Warfare Defense expert.
SCUBA diver, open water, instrument repairman.
FAA Commercial Pilot, airplanes and helicopters.
Air America, Air Charter Captain.
CA Real Estate agent.
CA Certified and licensed crop duster apprentice.
Certified US Forest service Pilot several times
Certified trained international tour manager, ITMI.
Licensed Doctor of Chiropractic, Chiropractic Radiologist.
Certified CPR .
School trained Private Detective, West Coast detective School.
Captain for Cal Fire.
Captain for OCFD.
Commercial Truck driver 3x, with tanks, double, triples and hazmat certs.
GGT Transit Bus driver.
Award-winning author.

Bibliography

Beard, Tom, "Number Two; Helicopter Pioneer Stewart Ross Graham," Reprint Edition from *American Aviation Historical Society Journal*, Summer & Fall 2012.

Boyington, Gregory "Pappy," "Baa Baa Black Sheep."

Charles River Editors, "The Aleutian Islands Campaign: The History of Japan's Invasion Alaska during World War II"

Collier, Captain Bill, "The Adventures of a Helicopter Pilot, Flying the H-34 in Vietnam for the United States Marine Corps."

Collier, Captain Bill, "Air America: A CIA Super Pilot Spills the beans, Flying…in Laos for Air America."

Collier, Bill. author's logbooks, journals, personal photos and…memory.

Collier, Bill author's web site http://captainbillfliesagain.com/

Gentry, Curt, "The Last Days of the Late, Great State of California."

Goodwin, Jim Psy.D. READJUSTMENT PROBLEMS AMONG VIETNAM VETERANS. The etiology of Combat Related Post-Traumatic Stress Disorders, Published by Disabled American Veterans National Headquarters, Cincinnati, OH. December 1971. (Brochure).

H-34 Charlie blog, dawgdriversforever.blogspot.com

H-34 NATOPS, (Naval Air Training and Operating Procedures Standardization Program), Flight Manual Navy Models UH-34D, G, & J helicopters.

Lundh, Lennart, "H-34 Choctaw in Action." Squadron/Signal Publications

Michener, James, ALASKA

Nickerson, William, "How to Make a Million Dollars in Your Spare Time in Real Estate."

Videos:
"About Amchitka, historical WWII photos."
https://members.tripod.com/airfields_freeman/AK/Airfields_AK.htm#amchitka
"About the Alouette III helicopter," youtube:
https://helicopter.youtube.com/watch?v=QIpud3igxvc
dawgdriverforever.blogspot.com about H-34 helicopter Charlie

"The History of the Coast Guard in World War II," youtube:
https://helicopter.youtube.com/watch?v=snwSCugd-W8

"The Rescue of Raven 1-1" (Captain Bill makes a spectacular rescue) youtube.com)
"Winnebago H-34 Heli-Camper," youtube:
https://helicopter.youtube.com/watch?v=MJRlQrN8RAY

The helicopter equivalent of Captain John Gillespie McGee's "High Flight." author unknown.

LOW FLIGHT

Oh, I have slipped the surly bounds of earth
And hovered out of ground effect on semi-rigid blades:
Earthward I've auto'ed
And met the rising brush
Of non-paved terrain - and done a thousand things
You would never care to -
Skidded and drooped and flared
Low in the heat-soaked roar.
Confined there,
I've chased the Earthbound traffic, and lost
The race to insignificant headwinds.
Forward, and a little up, in ground effect
I've topped the General's hedge with drooping turns,
Where never Skyhawk or even Phantom flew.
And, shaking and pulling collective, I've lumbered
The low trespassed halls of Victor Airways
Put out my hand and touched a tree.

Other Books by Captain Bill Collier:

"The Adventures of a Helicopter Pilot, Flying the H-34 in Vietnam for the United States Marine Corps"

"AIR AMERICA: A CIA Super Pilot Spills the Beans, Flying Helicopters in Laos for AIR AMERICA"

All three books are available on Amazon. For books SIGNED by the author: $20 each, $35 for any two, or $50 for all three. Add $5 for S&H for any purchase to: Wandering Star Press, PO Box 105, Port Hadlock, WA 983390-9800.

Thank you.

Made in United States
Orlando, FL
23 December 2023